F H
CHAPMAN

FRONTISPIECE: *A contemporary engraving of Chapman* (author).

F H
CHAPMAN

THE FIRST NAVAL ARCHITECT
AND HIS WORK

by
Daniel G Harris

Naval
Institute
Press

IN MEMORY OF MICHAEL

First published in Great Britain in 1989 by
Conway Maritime Press Ltd, 24 Bride Lane, Fleet Street,
London EC4Y 8DR

Published and distributed in the United States of America by
The Naval Institute Press, Annapolis, Maryland 21402

Library of Congress Card No. 88-63418

ISBN 0-87021-052-1

Manufactured in Great Britain.

Half-title page: *Chapman's Coat of Arms*

HERALDIC DESCRIPTION

*Arms. Azure a chevron or between three crescents argent, the shield ensigned
with a barred helm of three bars affrontee.*
Crest. *On a wreath of the colours or, azure and argent a demi lion or
supporting a ship's rudder azure with a sinister forepaw, the dexter grasping
the tiller which rest on the dexter shoulder.*
Mantling. *Or. argent and azure.*

Note. *The arms differ from English heraldry in one particular, the wreath
(the twist of colour between the helm crest) and the mantling are in three
colours not two. The inscription below means enobled 13 September 1772
installed in the House of Nobility 30 April 1778.*

The author is indebted to Philip Chaplin of the Heraldry Society
of Canada for the above description

CONTENTS

ACKNOWLEDGEMENTS

This book is based on material collected over a period of twenty-five years, together with visits to Sweden, conversations and correspondence with many individuals over the same period. My interest in af Chapman began on my initial visits to Sweden in 1936 and 1937 when I was privileged to stay with a very charming and kind family in Karlskrona and had the opportunity of visiting af Chapman's house at Skärva. When I was in the British Government's service in Stockholm from 1940 to 1946 and in residence thereafter for some years, I became better acquainted with Chapman's work. References to Chapman in the literature on the development of the ship are many, but no account of his life and work has yet been published in English. Conversations at the United States Naval Institute's history symposia have suggested that this gap ought to be filled. This book is an attempt to fill that gap.

Very special thanks are due to Commodore (E) Gunnar Schoerner RSwN (Ret.) who has not only assisted me in research over many years, but has also very kindly scrutinized each chapter from the technical standpoint, also to Dr P Lundström and the staff of the Swedish National Maritime Museum and the *Wasa* yard Stockholm, and especially to Mrs Åsa Arnö, the Chief Archivist, B Lemoine, head of the photographic unit, the Naval Museum, Karlskrona, Peter V Busch, the Director, Mrs Ylva Lindström, Archivist, Mrs Marie Louise Lundin and S Warfvinge, Curator, Dr L Rosell of the Royal Swedish Military Records Office, Dr F Ludwigs of the Swedish National Archives, the Director of the Maritime Museum, Göteborg, and Captain Celsing of the Royal Society of Naval Sciences, Karlskrona, Dr John Harland, author of *Seamanship in the Age of Sail*, Dr R Grenier and A Wilson of the Marine Archaeology branch of the Department of the Environment, Ottawa, L Öhman MSc,P.Eng. of the National Research Council, Ottawa, and Professor Alf Åberg, Stockholm. Special thanks are also due to Lieutenant Commander (E) E Bramwell MSc,P.Eng. RCN, who examined Chapman's calculations of displacement and metacentric height for a 50-gun ship and wrote the report given in Appendix 5; also to L Romert, Press Counsellor, the Swedish Embassy, Washington, USA, without whose interest and kindness the completion of the research would not have been possible, and Cai Mengsun of the Chinese Embassy, Ottawa, who kindly arranged for me to see the ancient Chinese scrolls illustrating various pleasure craft.

I wish to recognize the assistance of the following institutions: the Royal Library, Stockholm, and the libraries of the Universities of Göteborg, Uppsala, and the City of Stockholm; the National Museum, Stockholm, the National Board of Antiquities, Helsinki, Finland, and the Danish National Archives, also Dr M Callway and Ms C Chaplin BA, Ottawa, who have revised part of the text to provide greater fluidity.

Finally, my thanks to Mrs G Litchinsky and Mrs M Jones who typed the many drafts of the manuscript.

May I urge all interested in the history of the ship to visit the fine collections of the Swedish National Maritime Museum, Stockholm, the Naval Museum, Karlskrona, the Maritime Museum, Göteborg, and Chapman's house at Skärva.

Dan G Harris
Ottawa, August 1987

DEFINITIONS

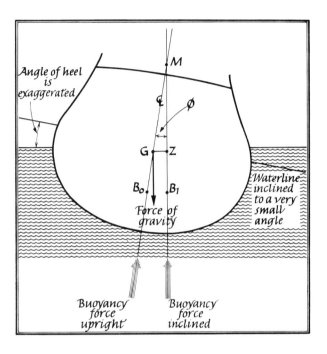

Centre of buoyancy (B)—The geometric centroid of the submerged volume of a body or ship through which the total buoyancy may be assumed to act. Its position, measured from the baseline or keel $(\overline{KB})$ is called the vertical centre of buoyancy.

Centre of gravity (G)—The centre through which all the weights constituting the ship and its contents may be assumed to act. The distance measured from the baseline or keel $(\overline{KG})$ is called the vertical centre of gravity.

Metacentre, transverse (M) and longitudinal (M_L)—The intersection of the vertical through the centre of buoyancy of an inclined body or ship with the upright vertical when the angle of inclination approaches zero as a limit, for transverse or longitudinal inclinations respectively.

Metacentre, transverse and longitudinal; height above the baseplane $(\overline{KM}$ and $\overline{KM_L})$—The height, measured vertically, of the transverse or longitudinal metacentre above the baseplane of a ship in the upright position.

Metacentric height, transverse $(\overline{GM})$ and longitudinal $(\overline{GM_L})$—The distance between the centre of gravity and the transverse or longitudinal metacentre, measured vertically in the equilibrium position. It is positive when M is above G when the ship is said to have *positive metacentric stability;* ie; on inclination to a small angle a restoring moment arises that acts to return the ship to the vertical.

Metacentric radius, transverse $(\overline{BM})$ and longitudinal $(\overline{BM_L})$—The height, measured vertically, of the transverse or longitudinal metacentre above the centre of buoyancy of a ship in the upright position. Geometrically, $\overline{BM}$ is the radius of curvature of the locus of the centre of buoyancy related to transverse inclinations, and $\overline{BM_L}$ the radius of curvature of the locus of the centre of buoyancy related to longitudinal inclinations.

TRANSLATION
NOTES

1. As I hold a Royal Canadian Navy first class interpreter's certificate and was qualified by the Secretary of State's Department as a technical translator, I am responsible for the translations. Nevertheless, Commodore (E) G Schoerner RSwN (Ret.), L. Öhman MSc,P.Eng., head of the High-Speed Aerodynamics Laboratories, Ottawa, and Dr John Harland of Kelowna, BC, have all given me valuable assistance.

2. The Swedish-English technical dictionaries of I Gullberg and E Engström rarely provide translations of eighteenth and nineteenth century nautical terms. Dr John Harland's famous book, *Seamanship in the Days of Sail*, Conway Maritime Press, does provide some translations of Swedish nautical terms. Sohlman's *Sjölexicon* contains explanations of Swedish nautical terms with the occasional English translation, but it is hard to find secondhand book stores.

3. In the text:
  National Archives means the Swedish National Archives, Stockholm
  National Maritime Museum means the Swedish National Maritime Museum, Stockholm
  Royal Navy means the Royal Swedish Navy
  Royal Academy of Sciences means the Swedish Royal Academy of Science
  Royal Society of Naval Sciences means the Swedish Royal Society of Naval Sciences
  Royal Academy of Military Sciences means the Swedish Royal Academy of Military Sciences
  Royal Academy of Painters and Sculptors means the Swedish Royal Academy of Painters and Sculptors

THE SWEDISH LANGUAGE

These short notes may be of use to the reader:
  Swedish like Norwegian is a lip language, whereas Danish is one of the throat, but all three have their origins in Icelandic. All have three additional letters 'å' pronounced like 'aw', except in the most southern part of Sweden where pronunciation is similar to the English 'o', 'ö' which has the same sound as 'er' in English, and 'ä' which has the sound of 'air', the letter 'o' is pronounced like double 'o' in English, and the letter 'u' has the same sound as the French 'u', 'e' is pronounced like the English letter 'a', 'i' like a double 'e'. The language has two genders, common and neuter. The nouns do not decline, and the definite article is formed by attaching the indefinite to the end of the noun — thus a book = en bok — the book = boken, a ship = ett skepp — the ship = skeppett. The conjugation of verbs is simple, the future is formed with either 'skall' or 'vill' in the same way as 'shall' or 'will' in English, and the perfect tense is formed with the verb 'hava', employed in the same way as the English 'have'.
  Here are some rules of pronunciation, 'sj' or 'sk' followed by 'e', 'i', 'ä' or 'ö' and very occasionally 'u', are pronounced like the English 'sh', thus Sjö meaning sea is pronounced 'sher', 'Skär' meaning skerry is pronounced 'shair', 'Sjuk' meaning 'sick' is pronounced 'shuk', 'skön' meaning beautiful is pronounced 'shern', 'själv' meaning 'self' is pronounced 'shelv', 'skiöld' meaning 'shield' is pronounced 'sherld', 'skepp' meaning ship is pronounced 'shepp'.

The order of words in Swedish is similar to English. When spoken, each word must be pronounced clearly, distinctly, and separately — there is no liason as in French. Although some words may be run together in the written language, each would be spoken separately. It is the easiest of the three Scandinavian languages to learn.
  The Swedish spoken in Skåne, the most southern province, is influenced by the close connections with Denmark — Copenhagen is only 66km away, whereas Stockholm is 620km and Luleå is 1438km.

OLD SWEDISH HANDWRITING

The Swedish Genealogical Society has published Professor Alf Åberg's study of Old Swedish handwriting which covers the years 1615–1788, and includes a large number of rare abbreviations and some unusual expressions mostly found in church records. The publication shows examples of handwriting from documents of the periods together with their transliteration into modern script on the opposite page.
  Professor Åberg's study is an essential to all researchers examining holographic documents of the period. Its price is very modest. It may be obtained from Genealogiska Föreningen, Box 2029–10311, Stockholm 2.

SWEDISH EIGHTEENTH CENTURY WEIGHTS AND MEASURES

The Genealogical Society of Sweden has had a table drawn up to provide details of eighteenth century weights and measures and their metric equivalents. Particulars of weights and measures pertinent to ships are set out below:

(a) *Linear*

1 Swedish mil	=	10,688 metres
1 famn	=	1.78 metres
1 aln	=	59 cm
1 fot	=	29.7 cm

(b) *Weights*

1 skeppspund	=	170 kilos
1 center	=	42.4 kilos
1 lispund	=	8.5 kilos
1 skålpund	=	0.45 kilos

(c) *Liquid*

1 ankare	=	39.26 litres
1 kanna	=	2.67 litres

SWEDISH CURRENCY

The Swedish eighteenth century budgets for the two fleets showed expenditure estimates in terms of 'tunna guld' — barrels or kegs of gold which was a money of account term. The keg of gold was originally equal to 100,000 daler but by 1776 it had become the equivalent of 16,666 2/8 riksdaler. The value of the riksdaler in terms of British currency in the years 1780–1800 is difficult to determine; according to Professor Michael Robert's book, *British diplomacy and Swedish politics*, in 1771 50 riksdaler were equal to £1 sterling (ref page 483 note 18), but the rate of exchange could change rapidly at any sign of political instability.

INTRODUCTION

No historian of naval architecture can avoid mention of the eighteenth century Swedish shipbuilder Fredrik Henrik af Chapman, an Enlightenment figure otherwise almost unheard-of outside Scandinavia. The foremost ship designer of his time, he owed his dominance to his extensive scientific training. He was the first to build ships on scientific principles, and his books, far superior to the work of his contemporaries, became the basic texts of his profession.

Fredrik af Chapman was born in 1721, the son of a British naval officer who had joined the Royal Swedish Navy in 1716. He died at eighty-seven in 1808, and he was a scientist, naval architect, and shipbuilder all his life. His largest commissions were the building of two distinct and separate fleets, the Inshore Fleet for use among the skerries of Finland and Sweden, and the High Seas Fleet. A skilled organizer, one of his lasting achievements was the reorganization of the Royal Dockyard at Karlskrona, for which he designed not only the shipbuilding equipment, but also the buildings, many of which are still in use.

Chapman was interested in the arts, and possessed that natural curiosity about the nature of things around him which is a trait of Swedish people. That curiosity, aroused in his apprenticeship as a shipwright, produced his life-long obsession with ship design, and a determination to learn how to solve the sailing ship's mysteries. Ultimately, Chapman was responsible for changing ship construction from a traditional craft to an industry based on the application of scientific principles to the solution of design and construction problems.

One

1760: THE STATE
OF THE ART

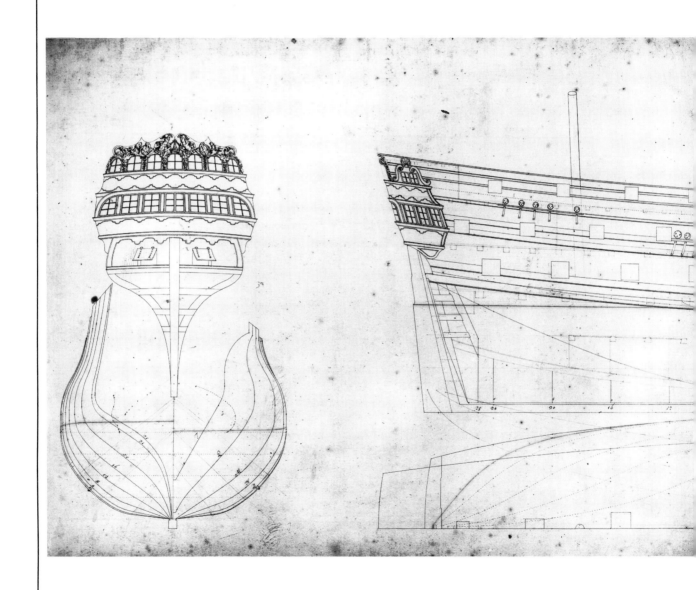

redrik Chapman began his first major assignment in 1760, on his return to Sweden from studies in Britain, France, and the Netherlands. Let us then consider the state of shipbuilding as practised at that time in the northern European countries visited by Chapman.

BRITAIN

In 1706, believing that the art of shipbuilding had reached its peak and no changes should be made in design, the British Navy Board established a set of rules to fix the dimensions of vessels of all except the very largest and smallest class to be built in the foreseeable future. These rules essentially required that builders imitate the most successful ship of each class, but individual master shipwrights continued to be responsible for drafting the detailed design. These rules were unaltered until 1719, when the Royal Navy added 20- and 100-gun ships to the Establishment. Minor alterations were proposed in 1733 but before war broke out in 1739, the British were generally satisfied with the size of their ships — for example the length of 60-gun ships remained the same from 1690 to 1740, although the beam was steadily increased.

From 1739 to 1748, Britain was continuously at war, and its demands forced a review of naval shipbuilding. A long drawn-out action between one 70-gun Spanish vessel, the *Princesa* and three British 70s revealed the

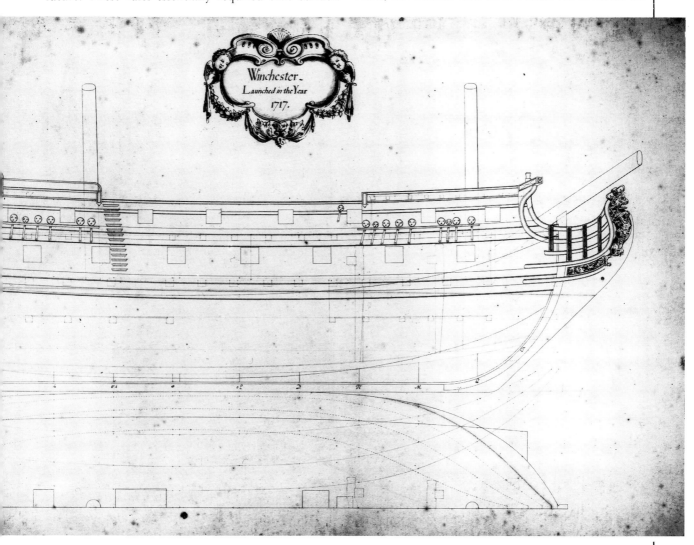

Fig I/1.
Winchester, *a British 50-gun ship,*
built to the Establishment of
1706 dimensions
(National Maritime Museum).

11

weaknesses of British design, but the Navy Board made only minor changes in its Establishment dimensions. The French 74-gun ship — one had been captured as early as 1712 — had made a great impression on the Admiralty which ordered similarly-armed vessels built, but the traditional Navy Board's preference for larger numbers of smaller simple ships meant that the British 74 was only introduced slowly and was smaller than the French pattern. The Navy Board's lack of enthusiasm for innovation was compounded by the introduction in 1745 of a complicated and rigid system for letting contracts for new ships, requiring Orders-in-Council to fix their dimensions, and to cover any amendment to the Navy Board's rules. The Order-in-Council requirement made it impossible for constructors to profit from experience at sea; it was so complicated that in theory no contract incorporating advanced design changes could be filled without breaking the law. Despite these drawbacks, the Admiralty continued to press for the French-style two-decker 74, and in the 1750s was able to break free from the legal shackles. In the 1750s there was a tendency to lengthen ship of the line, whereas in the 1730s the fashion had been to increase their breadth and draught.

No new principles were promulgated in this period. The major work on shipbuilding seems to have been Sutherland's *The Shipbuilder's Assistant*, published in 1711. In Sutherland's opinion, nature is the best guide to the form of vessels; ducks, dolphins, and mackerel, amongst others, are good models. He stated that it is necessary to know the longitudinal centre of gravity to determine correct placement of masts, suggesting some appreciation for the technical theory of ship design, but also bemoaned the current public view that 'the proper business of a shipwright is counted a very vulgar employ . . . . a man of indifferent qualifications may be master of.' Mungo Murray's treatise of 1756 was a later work of some influence, but it concentrated on practical aspects of shipbuilding rather than the principles of ship design.

The British Government encouraged very little research into the theory of design; such intervention would have run against the prevailing laissez-faire philosophy of the eighteenth century. Consequently, although British shipbuilders were fine craftsmen and their workmanship was first class, because they lacked knowledge of the scientific principles of design, the ships they built were often slower and less handy than those built elsewhere. The rigidity of the Order-in-Council system indicates what little pressure the government felt to build a better fleet to meet a variety of commitments, and because the Navy was not interested in technological development, British industry did not adapt its traditional wares. British shipwrights relied on experiment and intuition rather than the application of scientific theory — which they usually lacked the education to assimilate — and craftsmen jealously guarded their knowledge and experience so there was little exchange of ideas. Their attitude is neatly summed up in the words of the seventeenth century shipwright Sir William Petty, 'The perfection of sailing lies in my principle, find it out who can'.

FRANCE

French shipbuilders of the same period were as loath to apply scientific theory as their British contemporaries. In spite of their indifference, by the late seventeenth century, members of the French Royal Academy of Sciences were attempting to solve the problems of naval architecture.

In 1690, the French Jesuit Paul Hoste (1652–1700), who had served with the fleet, published an analysis of the forces acting on sails. He pointed out that the same constructor building two ships after the same model, working by eye, could not make them identical. At a conference on naval architecture held at Paris in 1681, in the discussion of the shape of hulls, Renaud suggested that these be considered as geometric bodies. In 1702, Aubin published his *Dictionaire de la Marine*, wherein he tried to explain the closely guarded secrets of the shipwright and to coordinate current shipbuilding knowledge.

In 1730, the Comte de Maurepas, then Minister of Marine, directed Duhamel du Mouceau to enquire into the use of steam to curve wood for frames, dry rot, and preservation of ships' masts. Duhamel's investigation revealed that the chief builders kept everything in their heads. In 1741 he recommended the foundation of an elementary school where shipwrights' apprentices would be taught mathematics, physics, and design. (By the end of the 1750s all the chief constructors of France has passed through this school, but in 1759 it was closed for lack of money.) In 1748, Duhamel published the training manual *Elemens de l'Architecture Navale*, which contained no mathematical principles, but organized basic concepts and replaced mere tradition with the best practice. In spite of the trend established in his published work, Duhamel rejected the notion that shipbuilding could be improved and developed by applied science.

In 1746, Pierre Bouguer (1698–1758) published *Traité de Navire*. In it he developed the concept of the metacentre rule, and made studies of masts and hogging of hulls. He believed that only the forward parts of a ship's hull offers resistance to water. The Royal Academy of Sciences encouraged this sort of research and the publication of scientific papers by awarding annual prizes. In 1749, the Royal Academy's winner was the Swiss mathematician Leonard Euler, for his *Scientia Navalis Tractatus de Construendis et Dirigendis Navibus*. This work on the theory of construction and handling of ships was a significant extension of the world of mathematics, and is particularly notable for Euler's techniques for calculating displacement and the metacentre of ships. In 1755, the prize went to Charcot for a paper on a method for reducing pitch and roll. Earlier in the century, Bourdé de Villeheut and de Missiessy Quies published papers about weight and buoyancy of ships, and the placement of cargo. Unfortunately, shipwrights, as mere craftsmen, had little access to — and less understanding of — this kind of work, so the effect of scientific research on the French shipbuilding industry was marginal. But in spite of the French Government's lack of need for a large fleet, French ships were generally regarded as better than the British product.

THE NETHERLANDS

In the Netherlands ship design stagnated after 1630, and the Dutch shipping industry lost its dominance by 1700. In the middle of the eighteenth century, Lieutenant Admiral C Schrijvers wrote, 'Dutch shipyards adhere obstinately to old-fashioned methods of construction'. The standard Dutch ship design principles of the seventeenth century were still in use a hundred years later, although they were restricted by unchanging geographical conditions. The silting of the Zuider Zee and river mouths caused problems for large vessels, which had to lie offshore, off the Marsdiep for example, and discharge part of their cargo into lighters before being high enough in the water to enter

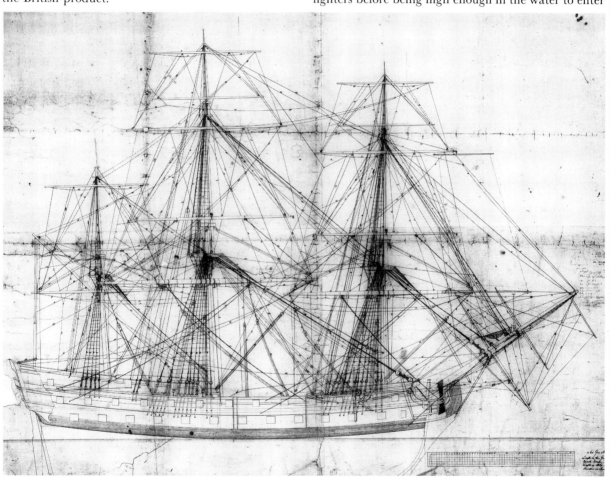

Fig 1/2.
The rigging plans of a British
60-gun ship of the 1745 Establishment.
This is one of the drawings collected
by Chapman during his visit to
England
(Sjöhistoriska Museum, Stockholm).

harbour. Because of the shallow waters in the main ports, no Dutch ship had a draught greater than 4 or 5 metres.

The Dutch East Indiaman's transom stern was not modified until 1725. By the mid-eighteenth century, the Dutch had finally adopted the British rounded stern, possibly because many of their shipwrights were imported Britons. This rounded stern was a distinct improvement; the new-pattern Indiamen were more seaworthy and answered the helm much better and when fitted with an improved rudder, has as much aft cargo space as older types. The strict Dutch guild system, which controlled the training of shipyard carpenters, probably prevented the introduction of new techniques, and had no interest in research for improvement of ship design.

DENMARK

Danish shipbuilders were hampered in their efforts to compete with the major European navies, because every Danish ship had to be able to make the shallow Drogden and narrow Sound passages fully loaded. Therefore Danish warships were usually two-deckers carrying 50 to 84 guns. Discussion about the size and sailing qualities of ships caused many disagreements about design. Danish apprentices routinely went abroad to study ship design, so their guilds were aware of changes taking place in France and Britain. In the

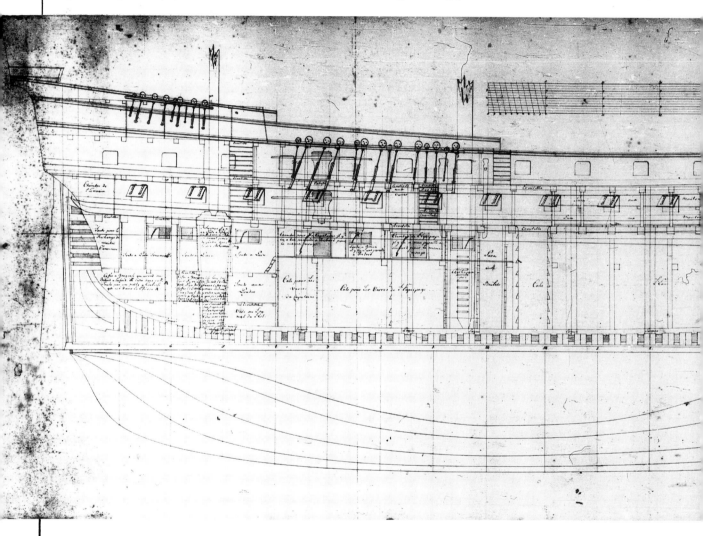

middle of the century the French builder Barbé was engaged to take over Danish naval design and construction, but the ships he built were not successful, though he was able to build slightly larger vessels than his predecessors had. As a result, Denmark reverted to the British style of shipbuilding.

The principal bone of contention in Denmark was the size of vessels suitable for the fleet. From 1746 to 1788, in spite of a lack of convicts, slaves, or even freemen to man such craft, the Danes concentrated on galleys and small boats. Henrik Gerner, appointed Chief Shipwright in 1772, changed that policy slightly; he was not only the leading Danish theoretician, but also a highly practical man. His designs were in use

long after his death in 1784.

SWEDEN

Swedish shipbuilding was dominated by Dutch methods until 1659. In 1620, Gustaf II Adolph ordered the establishment of well-equipped yards to build a new fleet of large vessels. The Dutch builders Van Horn and Wilshausen took over a yard at Västervik, and the king contracted with them for several ships. Similar contracts were made with Dutch builders at Göteborg and Stockholm; it was the Stockholm yard that produced the now famous *Wasa*, lost in 1628 and raised in 1961. In 1659, King Carl X Gustaf was highly impressed with the English ships which operated in the

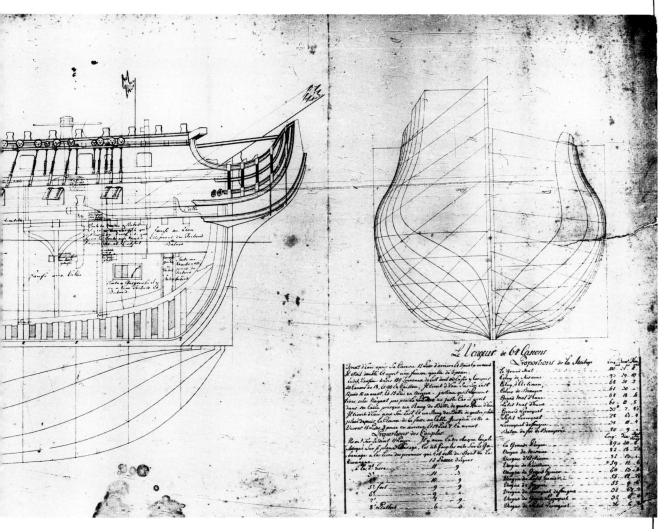

Fig I/3.
An internal profile drawing of the
64-gun ship Vengeur, *typical of*
French design in the mid-
eighteenth century
(Rigsarkivet, Copenhagen).

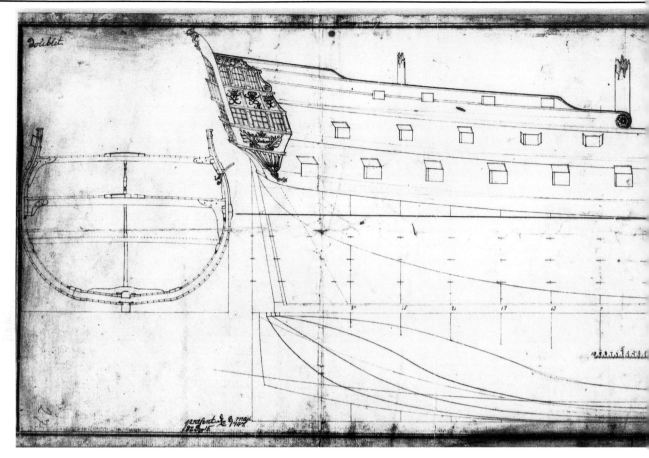

Fig I/5.
Gilbert Sheldon's 50-gun ship
(length 140 feet, beam 37 feet, maximum
draught 17¾ feet), plan dated 1748
(Krigsarkivet, Stockholm).

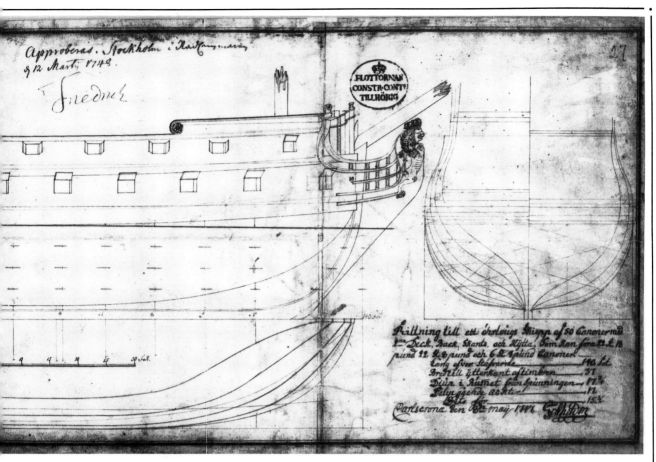

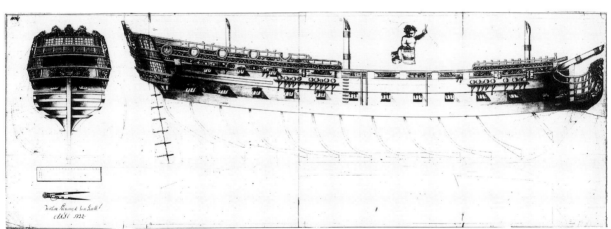

Fig 1/4.
The Dutch Boekenrode, *58 guns,*
was built by the Englishman
Thomas Davis in 1729. It is a rather
conservative design and, not
surprisingly, reminiscent of English
vessels of the period
(Scheepvaart Museum, Amsterdam).

Sound during the war with Denmark. The English ships had sharper bottoms, greater draught, and were better sailers than the Dutch-designed Swedish-built navy. Carl X Gustaf asked Oliver Cromwell to obtain two English master builders, and that same year Francis Sheldon and Thomas Day arrived in Sweden.

Francis Sheldon, who had trained under the famous Phineas Pett at the naval dockyard at Chatham, founded a 110-year dynasty of shipbuilders which dominated the Swedish trade. His son Charles and grandson Gilbert followed him as chief shipwrights to the Swedish crown. Francis was very able; Colonel Rålamb, author of a book on Swedish ship construction published in 1691, averred, 'Sheldon is one of the great masters, as great as any in England.' In 1686, he went to work in Denmark, but the Danes did not like him at all, so his employment there came to an early end.

In 1722, the Swedish Admiralty tried to standardize the navy by having new ships built to regulation patterns, but builders — the Sheldons among them — did not comply. Ships of the same class differed in length, beam, and draught. Admiral Sparre of the Swedish Navy compared British and Swedish ships, and found the British stiff in heavy weather. Charles Sheldon's ships were considered only partly successful.

Gilbert Sheldon, Charles' son, succeeded his father as Chief Shipwright at the age of twenty-nine, in 1739. Gilbert, born in 1710, was thoroughly educated, both in the Karlskrona shipyard and at Lund's University. In 1732, Gilbert was successfully examined in his art by Admirals Wachtmeister, Thomas von Rajalin, head of the fitting-out department, and shipwright W Smith. Gilbert's drawing of a 50-gun ship, prepared for the examination, is still held in the Stockholm National Maritime Museum. (Fig 1/5)

He presented two papers to the Swedish Royal Academy of Sciences; the first, in 1741, was entitled *Thoughts on Ships' Speed and Sea Tonnage and Capacity;* the second, which appeared in 1742, was *Ships' Centre of Gravity and Its Most Advantageous Place in Regard to Ships' Speed.* In his research, Sheldon used models to determine a vessel's displacement and centre of gravity. He attempted to calculate the displacement by lowering the models to the actual waterline, and measuring the volume of displaced water. On the basis of these experiments, he found certain coefficients, which he used to calculate displacement. It was a rough and none-too-accurate method. To obtain the centre of buoyancy, Sheldon placed the model in a sort of weighing device, so that the waterline took the same horizontal position as when the model was in the water. He examined the importance of the position of the centre of gravity and the midship frame in building a fast ship with good sailing qualities. From these experiments, Sheldon developed coefficients for determining the best position for the midship frame and the centre of gravity, but his knowledge of mathematics and design theory was very scanty.

In accordance with the 1746 directive, all newly-built ships were to be suitable for shallow harbours and for covering landings; they also had to be cheap. The result of this order was that new designs were broad in beam, were shallow in draught, and were consequently poor sailers. Gilbert Sheldon prepared new rules to comply with the directive, and completed, in 1747, one 50-gun ship, the *Sparre*, and a few frigates, in the new style.

The Swedish Admiralty's construction committee surveyed a generation of ships and found that all four ships built between 1722 and 1732 failed, one good vessel was completed in 1732 and two in 1746, but three built in 1747 were failures. By 1751, the Admiralty had decided that Sweden needed ships which could carry heavier armament; they were interested in French designs, ships with fine lines, greater draught, and better sailing qualities. So in 1762, a commission was established to decide on new ship designs for the navy. In a letter to the shipwright Solberg, Lieutenant-Colonel Ehrenbill of the Commission states, after a conversation with Fredrik Chapman, 'that a change ought to be made in our ship construction.' Swedish ships were too deep in draught, and lay so low in the water that the lower gun deck lay too close to the water to allow the gun ports to be opened. 'When other ships can carry top gallants', wrote Ehrenbill, 'ours must take two to three reefs in the mainsail.'

The scene was set for great changes. However, Fredrik Chapman's appearance in Sweden's ship-building circles created tremendous opposition.

Two
YOUTH AND EDUCATION

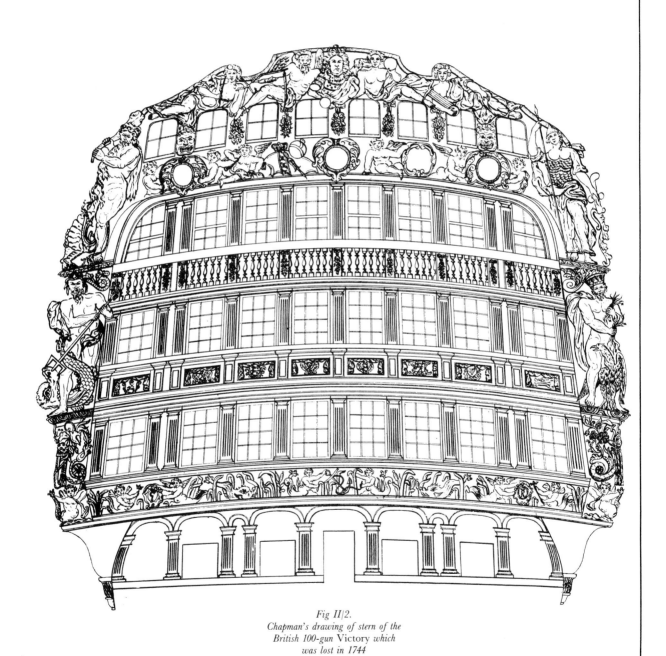

Fig II/2.
*Chapman's drawing of stern of the
British 100-gun* Victory *which
was lost in 1744
(Sjöhistoriska Museum, Stockholm).*

Fredrik Henrik af Chapman was born within the walls of the Royal Dockyard (Nya Varvet) at Göteborg in 1721. His father, Thomas Chapman, the son of a Yorkshire tenant farmer, was a British naval officer who had joined the Royal Swedish Navy in 1716; in 1720 he was captain of the dockyard. Fredrik's mother, Susanna Colson, was the daughter of William Colson, a shipwright in London. Fredrik, born in a royal dockyard, of parents born to seafaring and shipbuilding, was predestined to do both.

His formative years were spent in Sweden. In 1731, at the age of ten, young Fredrik's interest in ship construction was whetted by a Flemish shipwright's gift of a drawing of the Ostende privateer *Neptunus*. The boy made a body plan from the drawing (fig II/1). His father was so pleased with it that he ordered 'the shipwright to space out the frames in their actual size at the Billings battery at Nya Varvet Göteborg, so that I should see how such a spacing was done.' At fifteen, Fredrik was sent to sea, and in his late teens he worked in both private and state-owned yards. At nineteen, he helped build a vessel for the Spanish trade, and the profits from that venture enabled him to spend almost three years (1741–1744) working as a ship's carpenter in London. It was during this period that he completed the drawing of the *Victory*'s stern (fig II/2). (This ship was not Nelson's flagship but the previous vessel of that name, lost in 1744.)

On his return to Göteborg, Chapman established a yard in partnership with a Swedish merchant called Bagge, in which he built a few small vessels and did repair work for the Swedish East India Company. The business prospered, but Chapman was not satisfied with the progress being made in ship design. He was convinced that he needed an advanced education to be able to solve the design problems he saw, and he realized that practical experience in shipyards and at sea was not sufficient. He was therefore determined to acquire the knowledge of higher mathematics and physics which he believed would give him the skills to determine the draught and stability of vessels in the design stage.

He sold his interest in the Göteborg yard about 1748, moved to Stockholm, and studied mathematics under Baron Palmqvist for two years. He discovered that he could acquire an even more extensive education outside Scandinavia, so he moved to London in 1750. There he attended classes held by the famous Professor Thomas Simpson, the promulgator of the famous rule for finding the area or volume of irregular surfaces and bodies. Simpson had been elected a member of the Swedish Academy of Sciences and Letters in 1743, and that fact probably determined Chapman's decision to study under him. Chapman worked under Simpson for only one year, but at the end of that period he toured the royal dockyards at Woolwich, Chatham, and Deptford, to study British shipbuilding techniques.

In an eight-page document entitled *Directions for Building of a Ship of 50 Guns*, he describes not only the various construction methods but also British launching procedures (Appendix 2). Chapman also noted that certain British shipwrights maintained that the bowsprit length should be 9/16ths of the height of the foremast, but he never discussed the rationale for this particular proportion.

Chapman's thorough research and thirst for knowledge attracted the attention of the British authorities. The very day that he left Deptford, he and two British shipwrights were arrested, and Chapman was charged with trying to persuade dockyard workers to enter French service. Chapman's drawings and notes were confiscated and sent to the Admiralty, and he was questioned by a Foreign Office official called Wallis. For a month he was kept under house arrest, paid a half-guinea a day, and allowed to visit the parks and theatres of London with an escort. Eventually, Chapman was freed, and his papers, with the exception of a rigging diagram, were returned when he explained that he could reproduce them from memory. Neither the Swedish Legation nor the commercial representative would help Chapman, or even admit to knowing him, after his arrest. As it happened, at that time both the Danish and Swedish governments were trying to discover British manufacturing secrets, and to persuade artisans to emigrate to Scandinavia; Wynantz, the Swedish chargé d'affaires at London, received written instructions about the plan to recruit emigrants in 1758.

On his release, Chapman attended Professor King's lectures on experimental physics for some months, and took lessons in engraving. In 1754, a little later, he went to Holland; but he left no notes about his stay in the Netherlands, probably because Dutch shipbuilders had little of interst for him to learn.

In 1755, Chapman arrived in France, and through the representations of the Swedish minister, Baron Ulrik Scheffer, obtained permission to visit Brest. Louis XV, in a letter dated November 1755, commanded that the intendant of the navy, Gilles Hogesart, 'obtain all the facilities available'. The intendant replied that he had arranged for Chapman to acquire the latest knowledge of the art, and that learning he wished to follow the construction of the ship *Célèbre* under Sieur Geoffrey the Elder, 'I have been able to give him that satisfaction'. Chapman stayed in Brest for six months, and observed the construction of the 60-gun *Célèbre* from keel-laying to launch, and to the completion of the rigging in 1756. It was probably during this sojourn in Brest that Chapman became convinced that a 60–gun vessel would meet Sweden's needs.

As well as following the building of the *Célèbre*, which was sunk at Louisbourg, Nova Scotia, in 1758, and of which, unfortunately, no drawings survive, Chapman also made line drawings of the *St-Michel* and the *Superbe*, construction drawings of the *Soleil*, profiles and plans of the 118-gun *Ville de Paris* and the *Belle Poule*, and body plans of the *La Bienfaissant* (64) and the *Palmie* (74). He made pen and ink drawings of the rich ornaments of the French ships (figs II/3 and 4) and his artistic side was undoubtedly stimulated by association with the French artists and carvers employed in the Brest dockyard. Chapman's work shows that influence very strongly, especially in overall appearance and decorative work.

In France, Chapman's abilities and thirst for knowledge were soon recognized, and the French authorities tried to persuade him to stay. On his return to London in 1756, the British Admiralty's First Sea Lord, the Earl of Winchelsea, also recognized Chapman's abili-

ties, and appealed to his British heritage in an attempt to encourage him to stay in England. Chapman was attracted by Winchelsea's offer; in his memoirs he wrote, 'The Earl, who I met several times, offered me good conditions, and had he not lost office very soon after our meeting, I would have stayed in England and joined the British service.' But the Swedish minister in Paris, Ulrik Scheffer, later Gustaf III's Minister of External Affairs, learned of both the French and British offers to Chapman. He informed his brother, Carl Fredrik Scheffer, Counsellor of the Realm, who was able to have Chapman appointed assistant shipwright to the Royal Swedish Navy at the Karlskrona Dockyard, in 1757.

After seven years of study in Britain, France, and

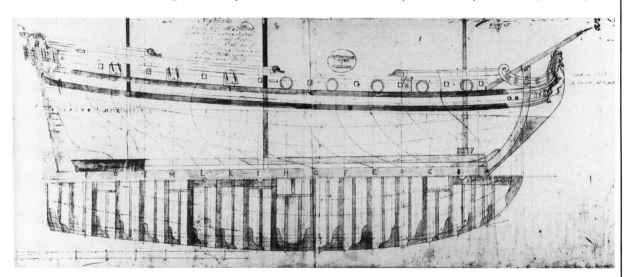

Fig II/1.
Draught of privateer Neptunus
made by Chapman at the
age of ten
(Sjöhistoriska Museum, Stockholm).

Figs II/3 and 4.
Chapman's drawings of the sterns
of two French ships of the
line completed during his visit to
Brest 1755/6
(Sjöhistoriska Museum, Stockholm).

the Netherlands, Chapman returned to Sweden, which profited for the next fifty years from his thorough, comprehensive, and consistent training. He was to put all his carefully-acquired knowledge to good use, but he encountered considerable opposition to his new ideas from the old-school shipwrights.

Fig II/5. Scandinavia in 1771 (Map by Denys Baker).

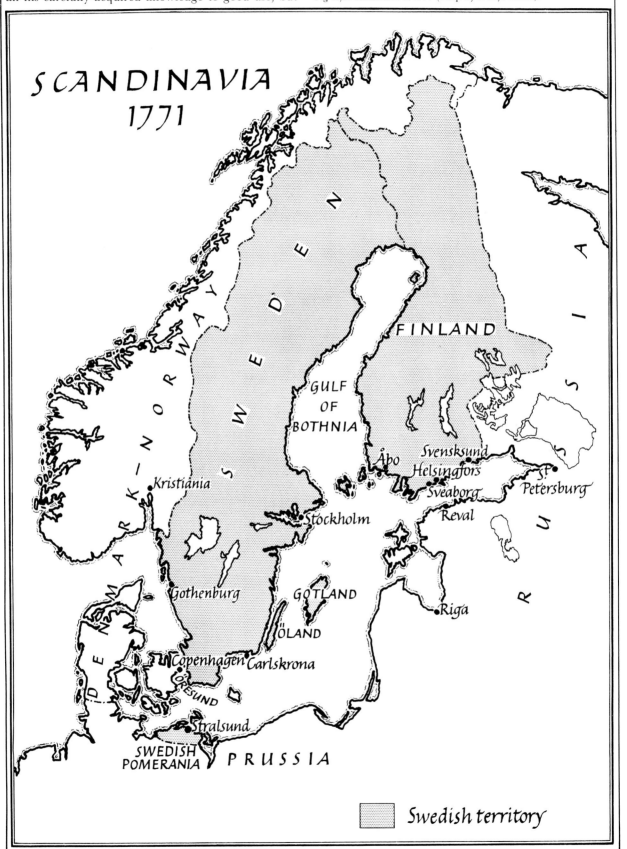

SCANDINAVIA 1771

NORWAY

SWEDEN

FINLAND

GULF OF BOTHNIA

RUSSIA

DENMARK

Kristiania

Åbo

Svensksund
Helsingfors
Sveaborg
St. Petersburg
Reval

Stockholm

Gothenburg

GOTLAND

Riga

ÖLAND

Copenhagen *Carlskrona*

ÖRESUND

Stralsund

SWEDISH POMERANIA   PRUSSIA

Swedish territory

Three
THE INSHORE FLEET

Chapman returned to Sweden from France in 1757 to take up the Crown appointment of assistant shipwright at Karlskrona, the principal naval base. On 24 April 1758, he completed a paper on the ideal naval arsenal for the Admiralty, in which he wrote that 'it should be able to repair and preserve all ships and equipment, and, moreover, keep the ships free from dry rot and other damage.' Store houses and workshops should be close to the dock, he wrote, so that work on ships could be easily carried out, and the storage space for sails ought to be well ventilated to prevent rot. In addition, he recommended that horse and man-power be used as well as wind-power, to pump out the dry-docks. When he was finally put in charge of the Karlskrona dockyard some twenty years later, Chapman was able to carry out some of these basic reforms.

Between November 1758 and April 1759, Chapman made a timber cruise from Åbo, Finland, along the Finnish and Swedish Bothnian coasts. He reported stands of timber suitable for two and four inch wales, masts, and planking, and described two places where ships could be built from the timber available in the area. He meticulously noted the particulars of each day's activities and how much distance he covered.

THE SKERRY FRIGATES

In 1760, Chapman began his first major task. He was sent to Stralsund in Swedish Pomerania to take up the office of shipwright to General Augustin Ehrensvärd, the military commander of Sweden's continental province. At this time, Sweden was at war with Prussia, and Ehrensvärd was responsible for the construction of the Sveaborg fortress, which lies on the seaward side of Helsingfors (Helsinki), and for the creation of the new Inshore Fleet. This new force, distinct from the navy, was intended to operate under army command in the Finnish and Swedish skerries, the rocky islands in the Baltic Sea which form natural defences for the principal settled areas of the Finnish and Swedish coasts. Helsingfors and Åbo in Finland (then a part of Sweden), and Stockholm, Karlskrona, and Göteborg in

Sweden all lie behind this natural barricade. Chapman was to design special vessels for this new defence arm. He was well-qualified for the task, since he had acquired considerable knowledge of the new force's principal area of operation from his timber-cruising season in the Finnish Archipelago to supplement his skills and experience in shipbuilding.

Sweden's need for a special inshore fleet for the defence of Finland arose from the creation of a fleet of galleys in 1702 by Tsar Peter I, with the aid of Ivan Botzis, a Greek who had served for many years in the Venetian galley fleet. The Russian galleys enabled the Tsar's forces to avoid action against the Royal Swedish Navy in open waters. The galleys could outflank Swedish strong points in Finland, and not only were they cheap to build, but they required no skilled seamen, only oarsmen, who could be recruited from river-boat crews.

In 1720, Sweden had few galleys and no separate Inshore Fleet. In the war with Russia, a Swedish squadron consisting of one ship of the line, five frigates, and six galleys under the command of Vice Admiral K G Siöblad entered the Åland skerries at Ledsund and fought with a large Russian galley force. At first, the Swedish force was successful but the wind died away and the large Russian galley force overwhelmed four Swedish frigates. The Russian losses as a result of the action, a storm, and heavy seas were 43 galleys. The battle ended Russian coastal raids but Admiral Siöblad was court-martialled for the loss of the four frigates and sentenced to forfeit one year's pay.

Following this battle, on the advice of the British Admiral Norris, Sweden drew up an ambitious plan for a considerable inshore galley fleet, but she was suffering an economic depression which made it impossible to build so lavishly. In 1723, Major-General Loewen reported to the Swedish Admiralty that Russia had been able to overcome the natural defences of Finland because she possessed a special galley fleet for operations in confined waters, and the whole of Finland would be lost if Russia gained control of the coast. Loewen's ideas were to become the basis for all subsequent defence plans for Finland.

Sweden fought another disastrous war with Russia in 1741, and finally in 1747, the Admiralty sent a commission to the Mediterranean to study the French, Genoese, and Maltese galley fleets. Lieutenants Rajalin and Kullenberg of this commission reported in 1750 that these nations all possessed human resources which Sweden lacked, namely large numbers of galley oarsmen. In order to protect her most eastern province from the ravages of Imperial Russia, Sweden had therefore to create a force suitable for operations in the confined waters of the skerries, but which would not require large or highly-trained crews, or any other resource which Sweden did not have in abundance. General Ehrensvärd was searching for a new type of vessel which could replace galleys, and he gave Chapman the responsibility of designing these vessels.

In 1760, Chapman and Ehrensvärd received information that Russia had added a new type of vessel to its inshore fleet. This ship was a variant of the Mediterranean chebeck (or xebec), rigged for sail, capable of carrying some stores, and possessed of better sea-keeping qualities than galleys. Chapman and Ehrensvärd agreed that because the chebeck gave little protection to its crew, it was unsuitable for Baltic waters. Chapman chose to design three types of heavily-armed ships, manoeuvrable under both sail or oars, which he later called 'skerry frigates'. Ehrensvärd was enthusiastic about Chapman's plans, writing:

Fig III/1.
A drawing by E Martin
of Chapman resting on a rock
during a timber cruise in the
Finnish skerries, 1763
(Statens Konstmuseer, Stockholm).

My builder is as keen about new developments as I am — if we agree, and are allowed to, we shall remodel the whole fleet. He has brought with him a drawing of a chebeck — we talk about it as we talk about the Kingdom of Heaven — we are not able to argue about that before we get there — such is the case with the new construction — Lord, let us get started.

Chapman stayed in Stralsund for two years. He then accompanied Ehrensvärd to Sveaborg, Finland, where he stayed until 1764. (A drawing by E Martin from this period showing Chapman resting on a rock, is dated 1763; fig III/1.) During the Stralsund period, Chapman designed two classes of inshore Udenmää (fig III/2) and the Pohjanmää (fig III/3). Their dimensions varied, but when built at Sveaborg and in Sweden they generally were as follows:

	UDENMÄÄ	POHJANMÄÄ
Length	118 feet (35.05 m)	90 feet (26.73 m)
Max beam	25 feet (7.43 m)	26 feet (7.72 m)
Draught	5 feet (1.49 m)	7 feet (2.08 m)
Oars	14 pairs	4 pairs
Rig	3-masted polacco bark, no topgallants	ketch
Complement	220 men	100 men
Armament		
24-pounder	—	4
12-pounder	10	—
6-pounder	—	1
3-pounder	2	10

In the Udenmää class, the guns were mounted on traversing carriages on the centreline, to allow them to bear on either side. The four 24-pounders of the Pohjanmää class could be brought to bear on either side, ahead, or astern. Ehrensvärd sailed the Pohjanmää *Fröja* two hours after her launch at Sveaborg, and she proved satisfactory in every way. These ships were designed as dispatch vessels.

Chapman designed two other classes of inshore frigates, the Turunmää (fig III/5) and the Hemeenmää (fig III/6), also named after Finnish counties. Their characteristics are given below.

Both of these classes were built with oak frames and pine planking.

The Turunmääs built after 1770 were increased in length to 123 feet and in beam to 31 feet, and their 12-pounders were replaced with 18-pounders. Because of the length of this vessel, Chapman used cross-bracing to strengthen the hull. Chapman designed figureheads for four of the Turunmääs himself; three represented Nordic heroes and the fourth was a dragon. The famous Swedish artist Sergel made wax models of animal

	TURUNMÄÄ	HEMEENMÄÄ
Length	117 feet (34.75 m)	142 feet (42.17 m)
Max beam	31 feet (9.21 m)	10 feet (10.09 m)
Draught		10 feet (2.97 m)
Oars	16 pairs	20 pairs
Rig	3-masted ship rig, no top-gallants	3-masted ship with separate topmasts and topgallants
Complement	220 men	
Armament		
36-pounder	—	22
12-pounder	22	2
3-pounder	10	4

figureheads for the six Turunmääs built at Sveaborg. Sterns of the Turunmää class were not elaborately carved, but were trimmed only with simple moulding, with the name of the ship painted in gilded letters. Figs III/7–10 show Chapman's stern designs for the Udenmää, Turunmää and Hemeenmää vessels.

Oars of the Hemeenmää class were worked through ports arranged in pairs between the guns. (Two ships of this class built in 1808 had only ten pairs of oars, and ten 24-pounders supplemented their armament.) Chapman's design for these ships may have been influenced by the sweep-port arrangements of British Sixth-Rates, with which he probably became acquainted during his stay in Britain.

Fourteen Turunmää frigates were built before 1788. These vessels were the main strength of the Inshore Fleet. They proved to sail well, but rowed badly; the records show that the sweeps could scarcely move them when they faced contrary winds, and even in a flat calm their speed was only about half a mile an hour. The sweeps were probably used only for manoeuvring.

Chapman designed a fifth special type, a 48-foot schooner-rigged gun-boat with eight pairs of oars. It carried one 12-pounder, one 24-pounder, and sixteen swivel guns. Ten vessels of this type were in service by 1788.

The five new classes of inshore craft were more seaworthy than galleys; they could operate in the inner skerries in all weathers, and in the outer skerries in most conditions, which galleys could not. The crews had better accommodation in which they could sleep in hammocks, and the new ships could carry more than three times the quantities of stores and fresh water than galleys could. With these improvements came the flaws of greater draught and less manoeuvrability. When it became clear that line-ahead tactics could not be used in the skerries, the frigates worked from predetermined positions from which their broadsides could be most effective.

Ehrensvärd and Chapman did not accomplish all this without opposition. The Board of the Admiralty —

particularly Rear-Admiral Falkengren and Captain Tersmeden — fought the new designs with great vigour, fearing the development of a maritime force outside their control. At a conference in 1763, Tersmeden criticized Chapman's ideas severely, maintaining that Chapman was no seaman, but he was finally forced to admit the shipwright's greater knowledge of advanced mathematics and science.

In defence of his new fleet, Chapman drew up a table in 1771, comparing the Turunmää frigate with a Swedish galley. In addition to the qualities described above, the table indicates that galleys required ninety more men than the Turunmääs, and had only one-third of the frigate's stowage for water and stores. The advantages were so obvious that eventually Ehrensvärd's and Chapman's designs were approved.

AMPHIBIOUS WARFARE VESSELS

By 1762, Chapman was already burdened with other responsibilities. The Privy Council decreed that the Inshore Fleet should be able to move troops and their gear about the confined waters of the skerries, and ordered Chapman to design special vessels for this purpose, which were to be built of pine instead of oak for economic reasons. The additional tasks assigned to the Inshore Fleet required highly specialized ships, like the 36-oared gun-sloops whose crews were to lodge ashore, and Chapman had to design and build the various new types.

King Gustaf III approved Admiral af Trolle's pro-

Fig III/2.
Inshore Fleet: a model of the
Udenmää Thorborg
(Sjöhistoriska Museum, Stockholm).

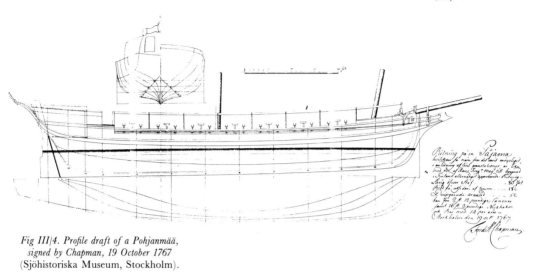

*Fig III/4. Profile draft of a Pohjanmää,
signed by Chapman, 19 October 1767
(Sjöhistoriska Museum, Stockholm).*

*Fig III/3.
Inshore Fleet: a model of the
Pohjanmää Brynhilda
(Sjöhistoriska Museum, Stockholm).*

posal of 26 October 1776, that each division of the new force should consist of:

2 Turunmääs
1 Udenmää or Hemeenmää
1 Pohjanmää
1 vessel to combine dispatch and stores duties
1 ammunition barge
1 freshwater-carrier
1 hospital ship

The four dispatch and stores ships were the *Colding*, the *Snapp-Opp*, the *Atis*, and the *Camila*. Their dimensions were:

Length	64 feet (19.01 metres)
Maximum beam	12½ feet (3.71 metres)
Draught	8 feet (2.38 metres)

These cutter-rigged vessels were designed to carry 45 lasts, approximately 110 tons. The *Snapp-Opp* (fig III/13) and her sister, the *Jehu*, were laid down in 1764; the *Atis* and the *Camila* were slightly smaller than the *Snapp-Opp*, and were built earlier, in Stralsund.

The gun-lighter barge is illustrated in a drawing signed by Frederik Henrik af Chapman, dated 26 August 1774 (fig III/14). This craft was intended to be towed by another ship; the drawing shows no oars or ports. Its dimensions were:

Fig III/5
Profile draft of a Turunmää,
signed by Chapman, 19 October 1767
(Sjöhistoriska Museum, Stockholm).

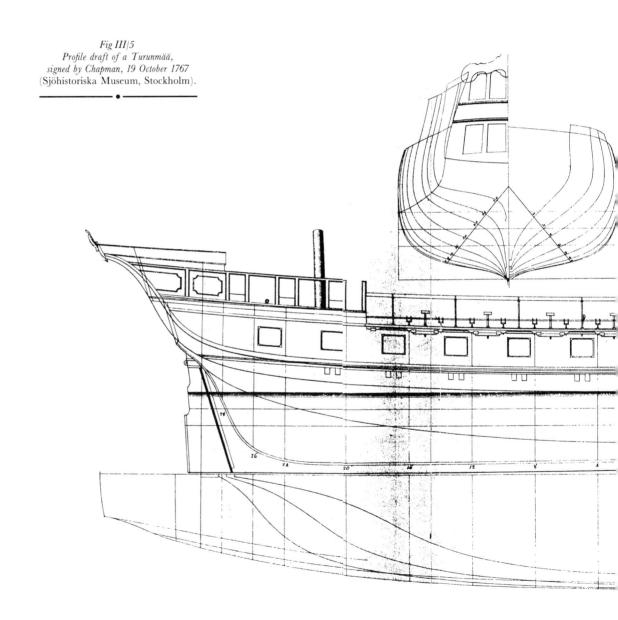

Length	72 feet (21.38 metres)
Maximum beam	11¼ feet (3.34 metres)
Draught	3 feet (0.89 metres)

The barge was designed to carry twenty-six iron guns, sufficient for a Turunmää frigate. The guns were two 18-pounders and twenty-four 12-pounders, which were stowed alternately on deck, as shown in the drawing. The barge was fitted with a 20 foot crane of 7 tons capacity in the bow, supported by four sheer-legs secured to the floor timbers by knees. The crane's cable was rove through the hollow mast, on which the crane pivoted, below decks to the eight-bar capstan at the stern. The counter-weight could have been iron weights

or stone blocks. The barge carried a crew of one lieutenant, one warrant officer, one carpenter, and twenty-four seamen. As the maximum headroom aboard was only about three feet, they probably lived ashore or in other ships. One of these barges was built at the Stockholm Djurgård yard, of which Chapman was part-owner.

Two freshwater-carriers (fig III/15) were built at the Djurgård yard in 1776, and six in the Royal Dockyard at Karlskrona in 1786. The dimensions of these special craft were:

Length	70½ feet (20.94 metres)
Maximum beam	15¼ feet (4.98 metres)
Draught (fully loaded)	4½ feet (1.21 metres)

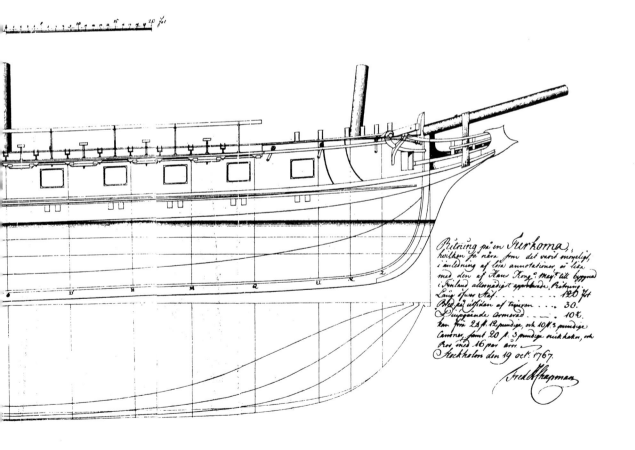

They could carry 12,000 cans of water, a can holding about 2.67 litres. Fresh water was only for the use of the fleet's crews, as the brackish water of the skerries was considered adequate for horses.

Chapman introduced an innovation in this design, a longitudinal bulkhead to prevent hogging in these long shallow-draught vessels, with their wide waists and sharp sterns and bows. The bulkhead ran the whole length of the hull, and extended vertically to the deck beams. Chapman held that this new feature would stiffen the water-carrier, increase her stability, and make her sail better when fully loaded. Fig III/15 shows the bulkhead, the position of the pump, and that the vessel could be rowed with twelve pairs of oars, one man at each. The sail plan (fig III/16), dated

24 November 1775, shows that the water-carrier was rigged like a ketch. The main mast carried two spars for a square sail or a big topsail, probably for use when running before the wind, and a staysail, a jib, and a sprit-rigged main sail. The mizzen carried the ordinary gaff sail. Chapman may have copied the water-carrier's rig from the Dutch tjalk, shown in Plate LXXII No 13 of the *Architectura Navah's Mercatoria*. It is also similar to the rig of a Thames sailing-barge and rigs used in the Baltic at that time. The water-carrier probably proceeded under sail only when fully-loaded or when running before the wind in ballast. The six of this class built at Karlskrona were named after the large Swedish lakes: the *Mälaren*, the *Hjalmären*, the *Roxen*, the *Göta Älv*, the *Vänern* and the *Vättern*.

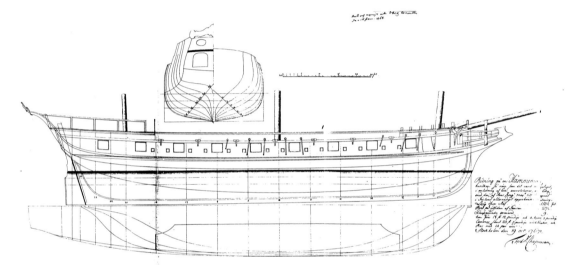

Fig III/6.
Profile draft of an Hemeenmää,
signed by Chapman, 19 October 1767
(Sjöhistoriska Museum, Stockholm).

To support the land forces in accordance with the Privy Council's decree, the Inshore Fleet needed special vessels to move horses from one point to another. The Tsar's fleet was known to have ships specially built to carry twenty horses. Chapman had the responsibility for designing these vessels, and his problem was to build ships to meet the army's requirements which also had good seakeeping qualities and needed only a small crew. His first design was a ship which would take only twelve horses, an armed cutter-rigged vessel whose drawing is dated 1791 (fig III/17). The horse-carrier's dimensions were:

Length	75 feet 10 inches (22.52 metres)
Maximum beam	18 feet (5.35 metres)
Draught (fully loaded)	4 feet 3 inches (1.26 metres)

The armament proposed was an 18-pounder mounted on the forecastle, and two swivel guns on the cabin roof to provide covering fire during loading and disembarkation of the horses. A crew of twenty was needed to work the ten pairs of oars. The horses were to be stabled in twelve stalls facing fore and aft, and an entry port (A in fig III/17) was provided in the stern, with a portable ramp. A cabin (B in fig III/17) for the officers was located aft, fitted with movable

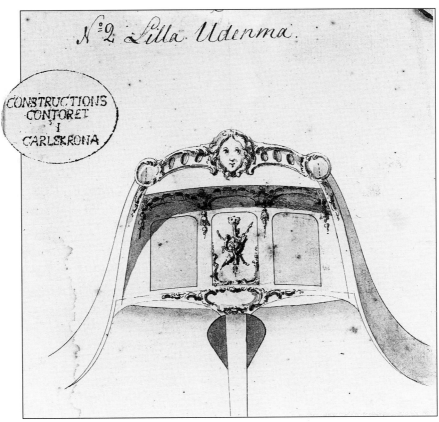

Fig III/7.
Chapman's design for the small
Udenmää stern
(Sjöhistoriska Museum, Stockholm).

partitions to clear the gangway during loading. The main deck was sloped to drain the stable, and it was reinforced to carry the animals' weight. The powder-room (D in fig III/17) held a hundred shot, ammunition for the 18-pounder. There was stowage for forage, stores, and water sufficient for fourteen days' operations (E in fig III/17).

Swedish army commanders did not like Chapman's proposed horse-carrier; they wanted a vessel which could transport fifty horses. Chapman protested on several occasions that the military authorities' demands were impractical, but his protests were ignored, and he was instructed to design a vessel to their specifications. Chapman complied, and designed a much larger vessel; fig III/18 shows the profile and deck plan of the ship

that satisfied the army's demands. The larger horse-carrier was hooker-rigged, and had these dimensions:

Length	124 feet (36.83 metres)
Maximum beam	28 feet (8.32 metres)
Draught	6 feet (1.78 metres)

This vessel was to have twenty pairs of oars, rowed by eighty men (two at each oar), and thirty more seamen were necessary to complete the crew. She was armed with four 12-pounders, two on the forecastle and two on the poop, and swivel guns could be placed wherever necessary on the upper deck. There was stowage for one month's supply of fodder for the horses, but no fresh water was provided for the animals as

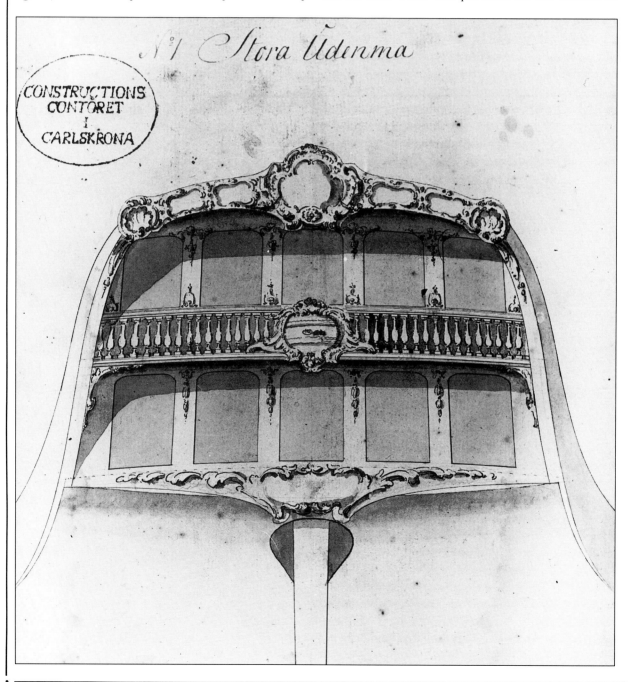

Fig III/9.
Chapman's design for the stern
of the Turunmää
(Sjöhistoriska Museum, Stockholm).

Fig III/8.
Chapman's design for the stern of
the large Udenmää
(Sjöhistoriska Museum, Stockholm).

the mildly saline water of the Finnish skerries was considered adequate. Watering troughs were provided in the horses' stalls and water was supplied through hatches on the upper deck. There were doors hinged to the stem, so the horses could be led aboard on retractable ramps and taken down to the orlop deck, where there were twenty-five stalls. Chapman estimated that the horse-carrier needed eighty pounds of ballast beneath each stall. The deck plan (fig III/18) shows the different compartments and their uses.

According to the late F Neumeyer's article in *Tidskrift-i-Sjöväsendet* (1942), some of these horse-carriers were built for the Inshore Fleet in 1791: unfortunately, he does not state where these vessels were constructed or how many there were. They were probably built in small Finnish yards, but these yards were not named and any records describing or referring to them have been lost.

Both Chapman's knowledge of the Finnish coast, acquired in his timber-cruising days, and his ideas about tactics suitable for skerry warfare are reflected in his three classes of artillery-landing craft. In a letter of 28 November 1775 to Colonel Ankarsvärd, Chapman suggested that the best way to sink an enemy who ventured into the skerries was to lure him into a narrow passage and trap him there, incapable of withdrawal. Caught between shoals and rocky shore by a Swedish skerry frigate, the enemy ship could be sunk at leisure by land batteries and ships stationed on both sides of the narrows.

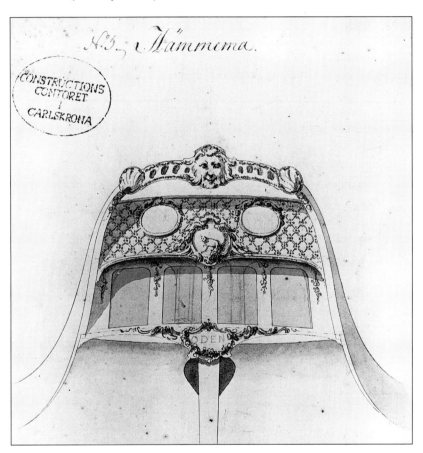

Fig III/10.
Chapman's design for the stern
of the Hemeenmää
(Sjöhistoriska Museum, Stockholm).

The first artillery-landing craft Chapman designed, Type A, was a lug-rigged vessel bearing two 12-pounder field guns on her stern (fig III/19). The guns were landed from the stern on a ramp, then both ship and gunners could be protected in their work by her three swivel guns. The ship's dimensions were:

Length	58½ feet (17.37 metres)
Maximum beam	11½ feet (3.42 metres)
Draught	2½ feet (0.74 metres)

She was manned by a crew of thirty-seven, who handled her thirteen pairs of oars. On his drawings of this craft, Chapman indicated that she could carry water and stores for eight days.

The two other types were, in fact, large open boats, sloop-rigged with lateen sails and fitted with oars which were probably their principal means of propulsion. Type B had a fixed 18-pounder in the bow and a movable 12-pounder in the stern (fig III/20): the 12-pounder had a gun carriage which allowed it to be landed from the stern. The hull was built so as to enable the gun to be hauled down into the hold for stability when the boat was under sail. The dimensions of Type B were:

Length	60 feet (17.82 metres)
Maximum beam	12 feet (3.56 metres)
Draught (fully loaded)	2¾ feet (0.81 metres)

Fig III/11.
Inshore Fleet: a model of the
Turunmää Lodbrok
(Sjöhistoriska Museum, Stockholm).

Type C (fig III/21) was a little larger, with the following dimensions:

Length	63½ feet (18.86 metres)
Maximum beam	13½ feet (4.00 metres)
Draught (fully loaded)	2¾ feet (0.81 metres)

She had a crew of fifty-five, and was powered by ten pairs of oars, two men to each oar. She carried two 18-pounders, two swivel guns, and the same quantities of stores and water as a Type B sloop. The gun mounted on the stern could be fitted with wheels and landed for use ashore.

Three days after Chapman had finished the drawings for these craft, the king approved them, on 20 January 1776. The King-in-Council authorized the release of funds for the construction of four sloops to carry 18-pounder guns, and eight to carry 12-pounders. Henrik af Trolle, the new commander-in-chief of the Inshore Fleet, congratulated Chapman, writing on 29 January 1776, 'Now we can damn well be as strong as our neighbour in the skerries, since these new weapons do not cost much money, and don't require many men.'

In June 1776, Chapman was able to show the king one of the new sloops in action. Here is Chapman's account of the demonstration:

When construction of nine gun-sloops was finished, I armed one of them, and proceeded up to Vaerten [a small body of water north of Old Stockholm] where the

Fig III/12.
Inshore Fleet: a model of the
Hemeenmää
Styrbjorn (Sjöhistoriska Museum, Stockholm).

king came aboard. I rowed and fired the gun, made land, lowered the ramp, went ashore with the gun, and advanced, firing all the time. Thereafter, I retreated, firing all the time until the gun was back in its place on board the sloop.

Chapman's demonstration proved how easily these new vessels could be used in amphibious warfare, and King Gustaf III was so impressed that he promoted Chapman to the rank of lieutenant-colonel in the new Inshore Fleet, and raised him to the nobility. These particular craft and the other gun-boats with fixed guns complemented the inshore frigates, with their lighter draught and greater manoeuvrability. They were to play an important role in the 1788–1791 war against Russia.

The second battle of Svensksund brought a successful end to this war (see Chapter Eight), but it also brought an end to the construction of ships for either of Sweden's two fleets. Chapman, however, continued to design different types of auxiliary vessels for the Inshore Fleet, although his appointment as chief of naval construction ended in 1793. An example of his work in this period is the oddly rigged battery-transport vessel (fig III/22) intended to carry six field guns, four below deck. An interesting feature of this design, dated 1799, is the galley in the transport's bows. No transport of this class was ever built, for Sweden ceased building ships because of a shortage of money — the French Revolution had put a end to the subsidies which had come from Louis XVI (see Chapter Four).

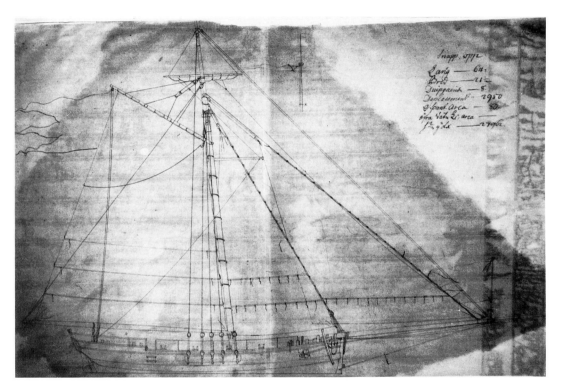

Fig III/13.
Sail plan of the cutter Snapp-Opp
(Royal Society of Naval Science).

HOSPITAL SHIPS

Both the Main and Inshore Fleets suffered a high rate of sickness, and the Royal Swedish Navy set out to improve its hygiene and medical services, for the notoriously dangerous conditions discouraged enlistment. Health problems were much worse in the Inshore Fleet because its ships were so cramped; the smaller vessels were not even equipped with galleys, so the ship's company had to eat cold food at sea, and sick men could not be kept aboard. There was a pressing need for special vessels to accommodate the sick and surgeons to treat them, especially during the war with Russia. More than thirty British and German barber-surgeons were engaged.

The first ship converted to a floating hospital was the galley *Ivan Benlös*, got ready for the 1788 campaign. (Her name rendered into English translates as *Ivan Legless*, a little too appropriate.) A few Roslag cutters were also adapted, each accommodating twenty-six patients and two barber-surgeons. The Reverend J Wetterdahl described in his diary the appalling conditions the wounded endured in these converted vessels. Men who had survived amputations were left lying in their own blood and filth, so close to one another that they could not move. There were no trained attendants to care for them, and most died.

Chapman approved the drawings for an armed hospital ship prepared by an assistant constructor, Eric Henning, in 1806. (At this time af Chapman was

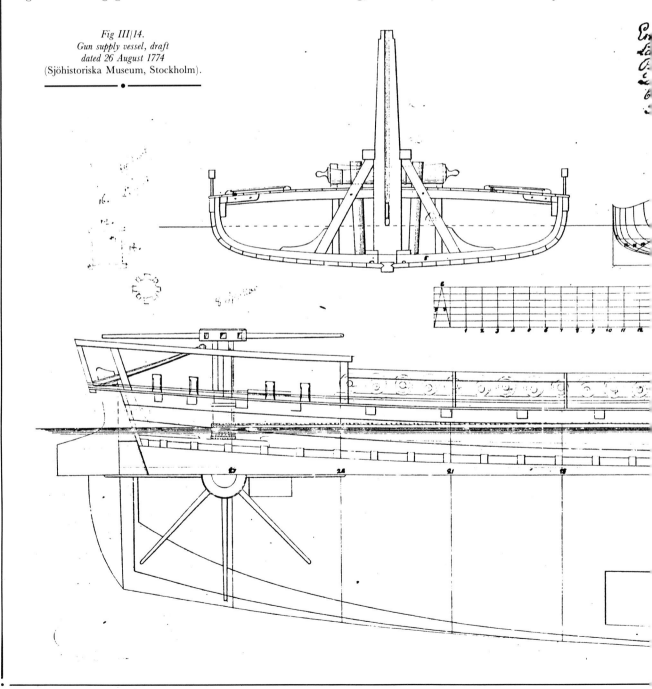

*Fig III/14.
Gun supply vessel, draft
dated 26 August 1774
(Sjöhistoriska Museum, Stockholm).*

eighty-six years old and suffering from a shaky hand, able to write only on a slate.) Each Division of the Inshore Fleet was to have a hospital ship (figs III/23 and 24). The dimensions were:

Length	77 feet (22.87 metres)
Maximum beam	18 feet (5.35 metres)
Draught (fully armed)	$5\frac{5}{8}$ feet (1.67 metres)

Because of the need for open spaces below decks, the hospital ship could not be built with a longitudinal bulkhead like the water-carriers. Chapman proposed to strengthen the keelson by adding a five-inch-square timber, which he thought was enough to prevent strain on the hull when the ship was fully loaded. She was sloop-rigged, with wheel steering and thirteen pairs of oars, each of which needed two rowers. Her complement of forty-two consisted of one captain, one sailing master, twenty-eight seamen, one barber-surgeon, one apothecary, seven hospital orderlies, one writer, and two cooks.

The hospital ship was heavily armed, there being no scruples against attacking the wounded in the days before the Red Cross. She carried four 6-pounders, two on each side, and four 3-pounders, two mounted on the forecastle and two on the stern. She had a magazine, stocked with powder and forty shot. Although there were two cooks in the crew, there seems to be no galley in the design. During the 1788–1791 war, some small merchant vessels had galleys installed, but no plans of

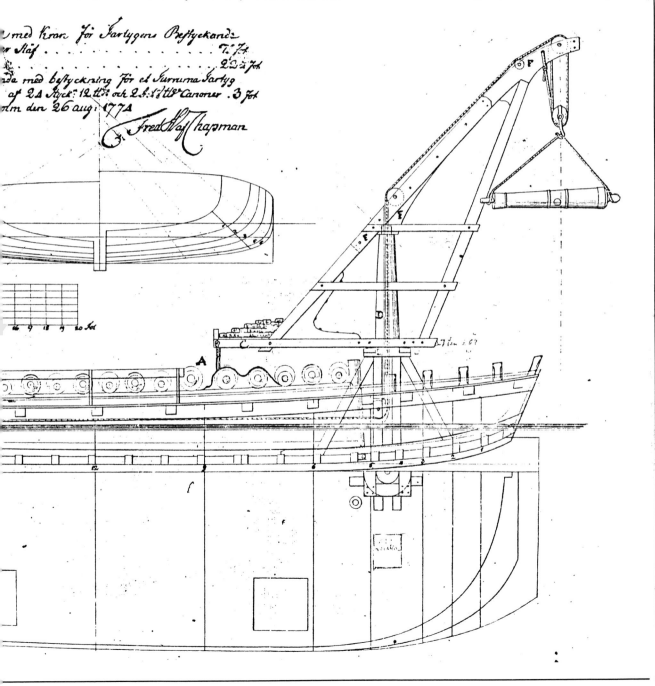

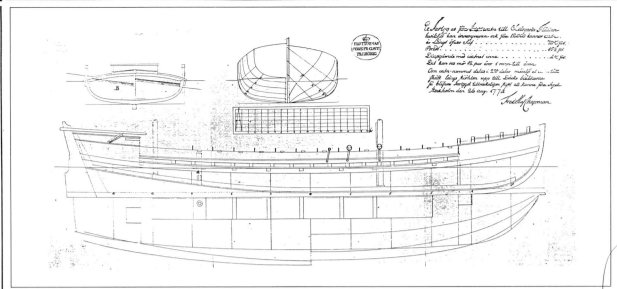

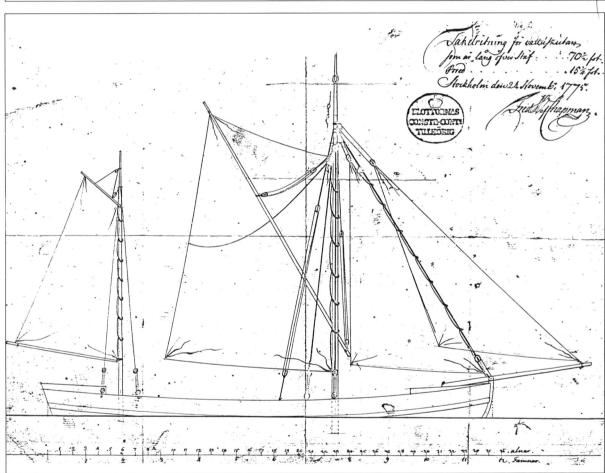

Fig III/15.
*Freshwater-carrier, draft
dated 26 August 1774
(Sjöhistoriska Museum, Stockholm).*

Fig III/16.
*Freshwater-carrier, sail plan
dated 24 November 1775
(Sjöhistoriska Museum,
Stockholm).*

such a vessel still exist. The hospital ship's specifications stipulate that all her hatches were to be oaken, and she was fitted with cots for the patients, with nine-inch spaces between them. There were instructions for the surgeons, too: they were to do all their amputations on the forecastle. (For many years after af Chapman's day, the operating rooms in Swedish hospital ships were still designated 'amputations rooms'.) The surgeons were not given private quarters, and presumably they shared the master's cabin. There is no record of any ship of this design having been built, but it is known that the converted Roslag cutters were used again as hospital ships in the 1809 war against Russia.

CHAPMAN'S INFLUENCE ABROAD

The navies of other powers were influenced by Chapman's designs for the Inshore Fleet. Muskein, a Belgian officer who had served in the Swedish navy from 1788 to about 1795, obtained (probably illegally) copies of drawings of Chapman's gun-sloops, horse-carriers, and troop-carriers, and passed them to the French authorities, who ordered craft based on Chapman's designs to be built in French yards in 1796. After Napoleon Bonaparte took command of the French armies, construction of Chapman-designed shallow-draught vessels was accelerated for the proposed invasion of Britain. The 26-volume *Victoires, Conquêtes,* by an anonymous group of French naval officers and scientists, discusses

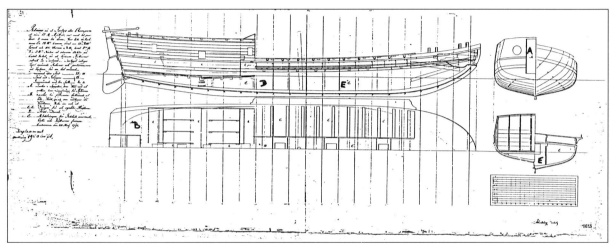

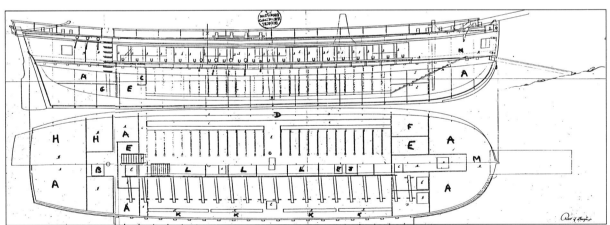

Fig III/17.
Armed horse-carrier for 12 horses,
draft dated 30 May 1791
(Sjöhistoriska Museum, Stockholm).

———— • ————

Fig III/18.
Armed horse-carrier for 50 horses,
profile and deck plan
(Sjöhistoriska Museum, Stockholm).

———— • ————

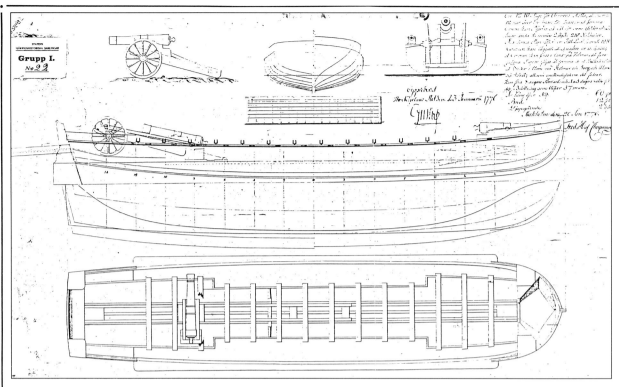

Fig III/20.
Draft of the Type B
artillery landing craft and gun-boat,
dated 20 January 1776.
Gustaf III's approval is dated
three days later.
(Sjöhistoriska Museum, Stockholm).

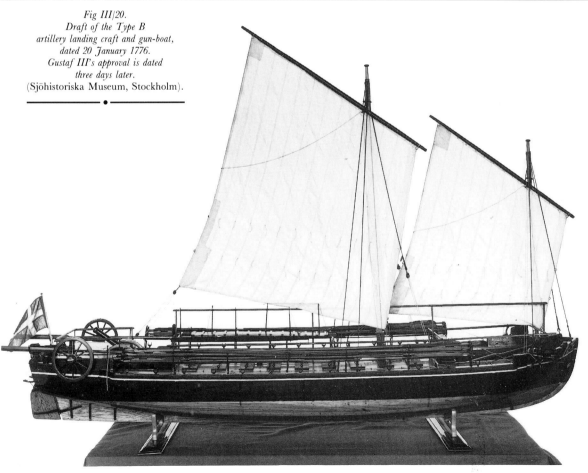

Fig III/19.
A model of the Type A
artillery landing craft and gun-boat
(Sjöhistoriska Museum, Stockholm).

the types of vessels Napoleon needed for his British venture, referring to 'bateaux à la Muskein', and 'bateaux cannoniers à la suèdois'.

Muskein brought to the French admiral Truguet not only drawings of the sloop classes, but also drawings of a bomb vessel and skerry frigates; he was very interested in the Chapman designs, because they had been tested and proved successful in the Russian–Swedish War of 1788–1790. In April 1798, using ships built after Chapman designs, Muskein launched an unsuccessful invasion of the Saint Marcouf Islands, which Admiral Sir Sidney Smith had seized and fortified for Britain in 1795. Muskein tried to use the same cutting-out tactics which he had probably learned with Sidney Smith, when both were serving in the Royal Swedish Navy.

Chapman's drawings of gunboats and the artillery-landing craft came into Danish hands through the Swedish Lieutenant Dahleman, in 1799. Denmark built similar craft, which were used in the so-called Gunboat War against Britain, from 1807 to 1814. A painting by the Danish artist Mølsted, owned by the Queen of Denmark, depicts the capture of a British brig by gunboats based on Chapman designs. Imperial Russia acquired not only some copies of Chapman drawings via Denmark, but also some Chapman-designed ships, after the surrender of Sveaborg in 1809.

The auxiliary craft and gunboats actually built to Chapman's designs were used very successfully in the campaign which ended at Svensksund in 1790, where

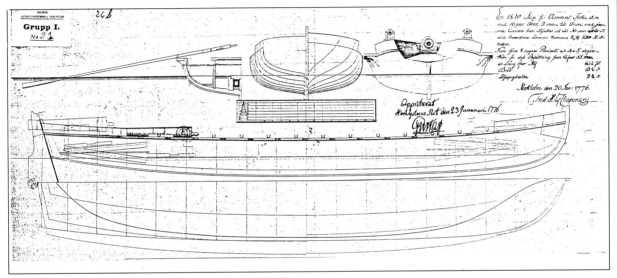

Fig III/21.
Draft of Type C artillery
landing craft and gun-boat, dated
as the Type B.
Note that wheels were fitted to
the after gun for landing
(Sjöhistoriska Museum, Stockholm).

the Swedish Navy almost destroyed the Russian Navy. The Chapman gunboats were modified later for different conditions, and continued in the service of the Royal Swedish Navy for almost eighty years. Only the coming of steam ended their working lives.

PERFORMANCE OF THE INSHORE FLEET

Were the auxiliary craft good sea-boats? In May 1790, after the second battle of Fredrikshamn, a Beaufort scale Force 10 storm hit the fleet, giving the auxiliary craft an excellent test of seaworthiness. All the fleet-train vessels apparently rode out the storm without difficulty.

It is difficult for modern scholars to determine just how fast any of the Inshore Fleet craft could manoeuvre, either under sail or oars, or both. Major Jonas von Wright kept a journal in the spring and summer of 1790, which describes the galleys which served in that campaign. Wright was in the forty-oared galley *Västergötaland*, and his log suggests that her average speed was $1\frac{1}{2}-2$ knots. Doctor Christoffer Ericsson of Helsingfors prepared a table to show the daily wind conditions, arrival and departure times in the Finnish skerries, and the distances covered, based on Wright's log, and the reports contained in the Åbo journal. Ericsson's table indicates that the maximum speed attained by galleys under oars and sail in a Force 10 gale was about 3 knots. It is likely that the auxiliary vessels, such as the water-carriers, field-artillery-car-

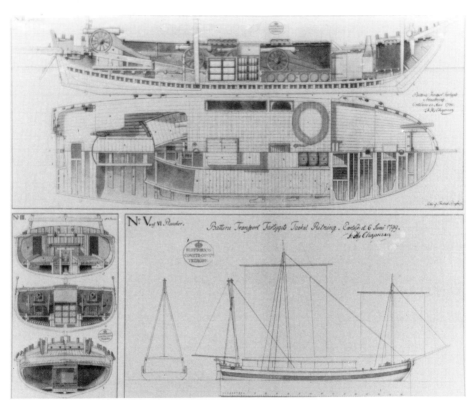

Fig III/22.
Chapman's proposed battery-transport,
draft dated 26 June 1799
(Krigsarkivet, Stockholm).

riers, and horse transports, would have sailed about the same speed as Wright's galley.

The ranges of the various calibres of guns were approximately as follows:

12-pounder	295 yards (270 metres)
18-pounder	306 yards (280 metres)
24-pounder	544 yards (497 metres)
36-pounder	575 yards (526 metres)
Mortar	500 yards (457 metres)

The Turunmää frigate's 12-pounder could fire about 14 rounds in 25 minutes. Some of the gun sloops were fitted with ovens to heat their shot.

Did the Inshore Fleet, a mixture of heavy frigates, open-oared vessels, and unusual artillery craft, do the job for which it was designed and built? Admiral Sir Sidney Smith of the British Royal Navy, who served in the 1788–1790 war against Russia, observed that the Inshore Fleet had particularly dangerous weaknesses in its tactical conception. He considered it folly to work the slow, oared frigates with the more mobile sloops and gunboats, believing that light units could not be efficient, when their average speed was reduced to protect hybrids which could not sail well and could be rowed only with difficulty. Smith highly approved of Chapman's gun-sloops and boats particularly appreciating them during operations against Trångsund. He despised galleys, considering them uneconomical. Existing correspondence between Smith and Chapman

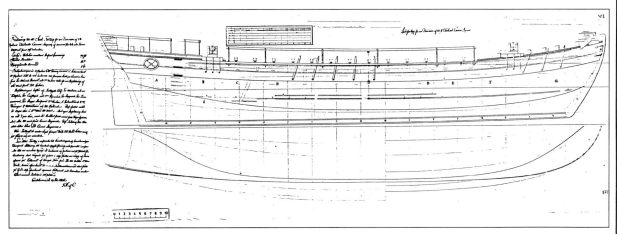

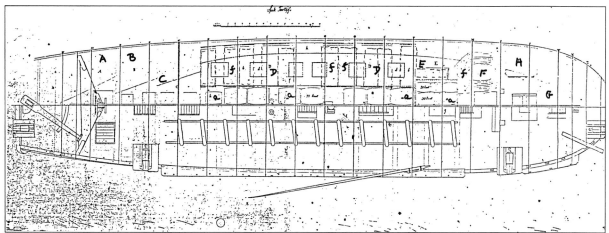

Fig III/23.
Armed hospital ship suitable
for supporting twelve gun-boats,
draft dated February 1806
(Sjöhistoriska Museum, Stockholm).

Fig III/24.
Deck plan of hospital ship.
A = Apothecary's cabin. B = Magazine.
C = Stores. D = Sick bay, 20 cots.
E = Space for 4 patients. F = Cable tier.
G = Space for Masters. H = Bread and vegetable store.
a = Freshwater storage. F = Cot for sick
(Sjöhistoriska Museum, Stockholm).

shows that they met, but does not reveal whether the two discussed shipbuilding.

In the light of Sir Sidney Smith's criticisms it is perhaps significant that the Inshore Fleet won its greatest victory — at Svensksund in July 1790 — defending prepared positions against an ill-organised and precipitate Russian attack. In this case it was the Russians and not the Swedes who suffered from the very varied handling qualities in the ships of their inshore flotilla (see Chapter Eight for details).

The auxiliary and line vessels of the skerry fleet were bulky and difficult to operate, but it was generally recognized that the Swedish ships were more manoeuvrable than the Russians. Chapman's special knowledge of Finland's inner waters, probably acquired

while timber-cruising, undoubtedly equipped him to design ships adapted to the needs of a military command operating in the skerries. Throughout his life he continued to be involved with the Inshore Fleet.

Fig III/26.
Sergal's Sveaborg monument
to Field Marshal Augustin
Ehrensvärd, the founder
of the Inshore Fleet
(author).

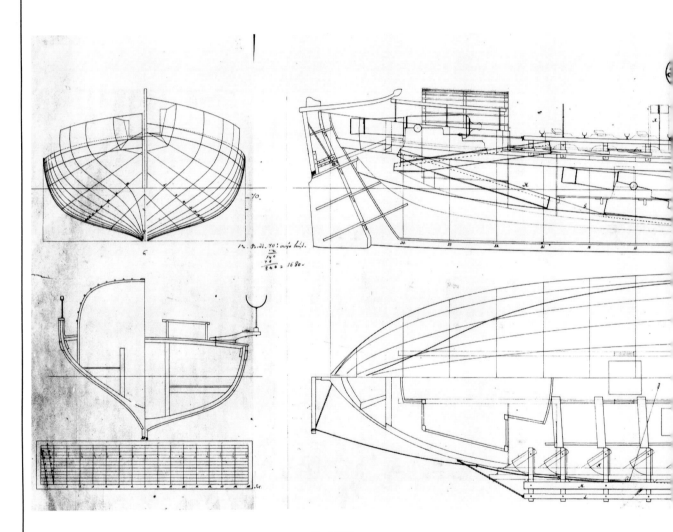

Fig III/25.
Profile and line draft of
proposed decked gun-sloop, dated 28
April 1791 for West Coast.
Length 76 feet, beam 15 feet,
draught 4.6 feet. Armament at bow and stern,
one 24-pounder gun
(Krigsarkivet, Stockholm).

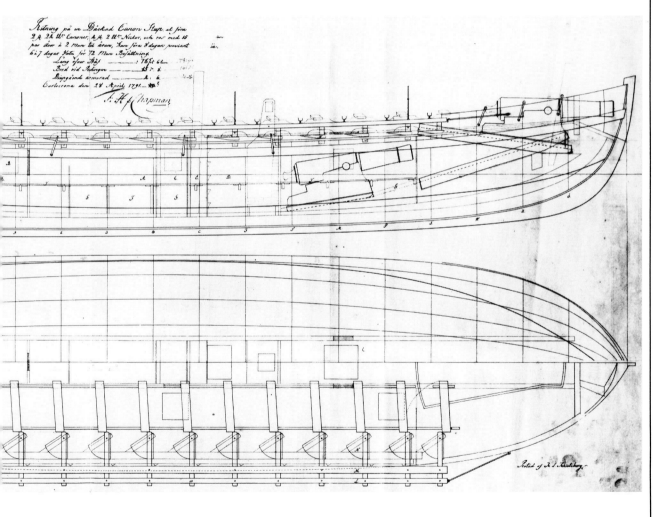

Fig IV/2.
Model of the Adolph Fredrik
(Sjöhistoriska Museum, Stockholm).

Four
THE YEARS OF TRIAL: 1764–80

Chapman returned to Stockholm in 1764. Before leaving the Sveaborg dockyard, he arranged for the construction of a mast crane, a storage building, workshops, and shelters for masts and oars. He also supervised the completion of two dry-docks, one to hold four ships of the line, and the other for storing twenty-two smaller craft in the winter. His move to Stockholm took him away from the Finnish skerries, but Chapman remained responsible for building ships for the Inshore Fleet. In Stockholm he found the opportunities to use the knowledge he had acquired from his studies in mathematics and physics in Britain, and his experience in France.

This was the beginning of Chapman's period of fulfilment and triumph. He finished his famous *Architectura Navah's Mercatoria*, served on royal commissions overseeing naval construction, published several scientific papers and was elected to the Royal Academy of Sciences, managed a shipyard in Stockholm, and, finally, became the Navy's Chief Constructor. However, these years were also marked by constant conflict between the old school of shipbuilders, represented by the Sheldon family and the Board of Admiralty, and Chapman, leader of the new school.

These years were indeed, traumatic for the whole of Sweden. Gustaf III ascended to the throne in 1771, and brought sweeping changes to internal affairs and external relations. In his youth, Gustaf had visited the court of Louis XV, where he was introduced to the *Encyclopédistes* (Diderot *et al*), and *philosophes*, including Jean-Jacques Rousseau. Very much the Enlightenment monarch, as King he encouraged Swedish arts and

CHRONOLOGY	
1764	Appointed member of the Fleet Establishment Commission, and Chief Constructor for the Inshore Fleet at Sveaborg.
1765	Granted eighteen months' leave, moved to Stockholm, and began work on the *Architectura Navalis Mercatoria*.
1768	Manager and part-owner of the Djurgård shipyard, Stockholm, published the *Mercatoria*.
1772	Ennobled
1774	Elected member of the Sculptors' and Painters' Academy.
1775	Published the *Tractat* on shipbuilding.
1776	Elected to the Royal Academy of Sciences; appointed to the Board of Admiralty.
1780	Appointed to the Second Establishment Commission
1781	Appointed Superintendent of the Karlskrona naval dockyard.

sciences. Gustaf was also determined to end foreign interference in Swedish domestic matters. Both Denmark and Russia were working to disrupt Swedish security, hoping to create so much internal chaos that her government would fall apart and leave her vulnerable; a partition of Sweden would have benefited both the other major Baltic powers. Gustaf III had arranged a convention with Louis XV, who gave him enough money to overwhelm his opposition, and pay for strengthening Sweden's land and sea defences.

Gustaf III's reign is often described as part of Sweden's Golden Age, when the arts and sciences flourished. The king stimulated interest in music, fine arts, and the theatre; Bellman, the famous poet and balladeer, enjoyed his patronage and seems to have acted rather like a poet-laureate; he composed a poem for the royal yacht *Amphion*, built by Chapman in this Stockholm period. Chapman was intensely active in all areas of ship construction at this time. Always the innovative designer and astute organizer, he introduced new methods to both the naval architect's office and the shipyard workshop. His mathematical calculations for determining a vessel's stability and sailing qualities in the design stage produced a revolution in an industry hitherto dominated by artisans.

THE FIRST ESTABLISHMENT COMMISSION

In 1764, Chapman was appointed to the Establishment Commission; its final report was submitted in 1768. The membership included two members of the traditional school of shipbuilders — Sheldon and Harald Sohlberg — and a certain Colonel Ehrenbill. In a letter to Sohlberg, after a conversation with Chapman, Colonel Ehrenbill wrote:

> A change ought to be made in our methods of ship construction — Swedish ships have too low displacement tonnage, too great draught — so much that the lower battery deck is so close to the water that no one dares to open the gun ports. When other nations' ships carry topgallants, ours must take three reefs in the main sails. Therefore, in future, ships should be built longer with broader beams and greater draughts.

Sohlberg was dubious at first, but later was converted to the Chapman point of view. Chapman dominated the commission, for the majority decided that shipbuilding could no longer be a matter of guesses and expensive experiments. The commission's report stated that, in the past, hull dimensions were determined by purely arbitrary means, and went on to say,

> Shipbuilding has to become a science based on mathematics. No longer is it possible to demand that the navy's personnel shall be shipbuilders, nor shipbuilders vice versa.

Only Sheldon dissented, and filed a contrary opinion. The Admiralty received the commission's findings favourably, and reported to the Riksdag in March of 1769, '... the marked development in the science of shipbuilding, thanks to the participants' industrious work — no longer should an individual's knowledge be kept secret'. That last comment seems to be directed at Sheldon. The Admiralty recommended that Chapman be kept fully engaged in Crown service, and

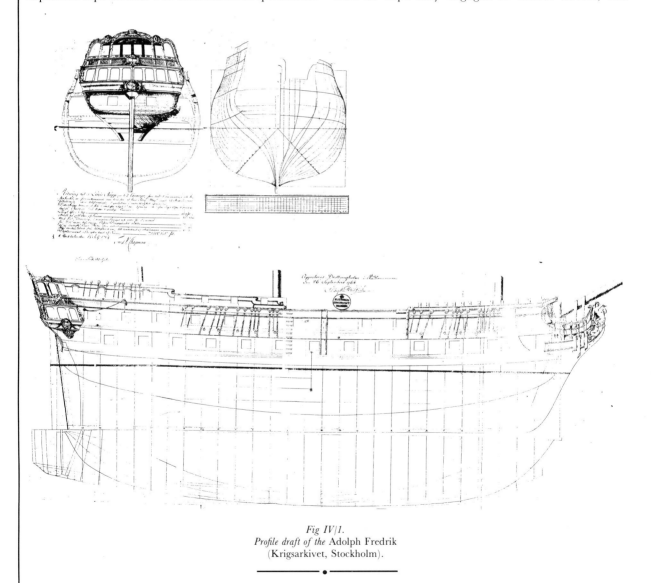

Fig IV/1.
Profile draft of the Adolph Fredrik
(Krigsarkivet, Stockholm).

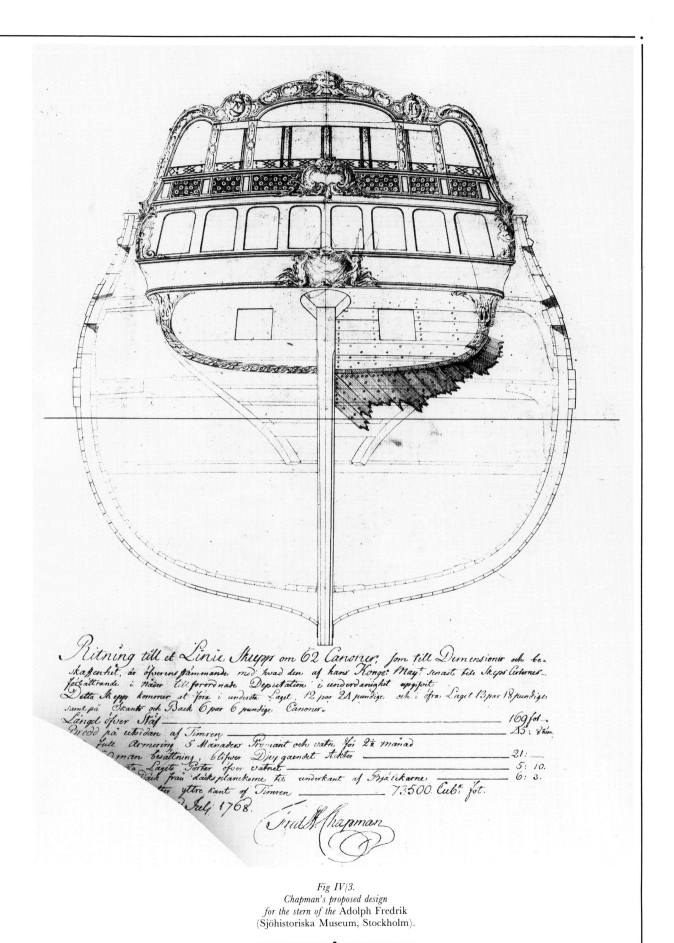

Fig IV/3.
Chapman's proposed design
for the stern of the Adolph Fredrik
(Sjöhistoriska Museum, Stockholm).

Fig IV/4.
Stern decoration proposed by
Rehn for the Adolph Fredrik
(Sjöhistoriska Museum, Stockholm).

commissioned to design and build new ships — two-deckers, more suitable for conditions in the Baltic Sea. The Board had ambitious plans for a new fleet; three-deckers were to be abandoned, and it was hoped that fourteen 70-gun ships, sixteen 60s, and ten 50-gun ships would be built under Chapman's supervision. Unfortunately, this was too much for Sweden's slender purse to bear.

The navy had been sadly neglected before Gustaf III came to the throne. The small appropriations the government did make mostly had to be spent on repairs. In 1979, the Secret Council, an arm of government until its abolition in 1772, ordered the Admiralty to keep as many of the obsolete ships afloat as possible for the sake of appearances. There were always to be twenty-one afloat, but only twelve were actually seaworthy and capable of fighting.

Between 1721 and 1772, France and Russia were, to quote Professor Michael Roberts, 'overt and covert adversaries'. The aim of French diplomatic policy was to block Russian intervention in the affairs of Europe, and France regarded Russian's alliances with Austria in 1726, and Britain in 1742 as impingements on the old world. France objected strenuously to Russia's interventions in Poland in 1730 and 1760, and to the presence of Russian troops on the Rhine, and in 1759 she was able, by firm diplomatic action, to prevent Russia from annexing East Prussia. The object of France's diplomacy in Northern Europe, particularly in Denmark and Sweden, was to check Russia's influ-

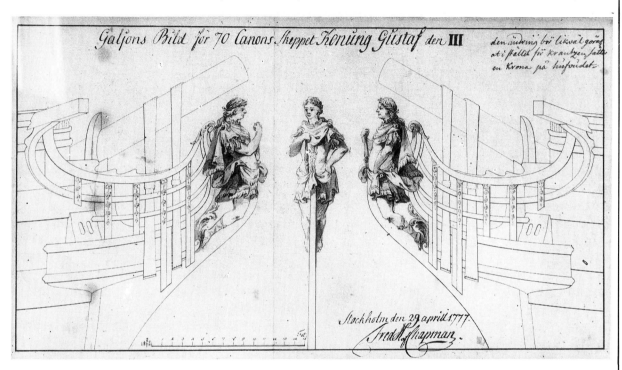

Fig IV/5.
Figurehead for the 70-gun
Konung Gustaf III.
Chapman's note specifies the
replacement of the wreath, as shown
on the drawing, by a crown
(Sjöhistoriska Museum, Stockholm).

ence; to this end, she paid subsidies and made a series of alliances with Poland, Sweden, and Turkey. Only Poland was unable, even with French help, to resist the spread of the Russian Empire, and became a Russian vassal.

To maintain her influence in Sweden, France subsidized one of two factions in the Riksdag, the 'Hats'. The objective of this faction, whose members identified themselves by wearing their hats in the House, was to recover the territory Sweden lost to Russia by the 1721 Treaty of Nystad — Estonia, Livonia, and part of Eastern Finland. France encouraged Sweden to attack Russia in 1741, to regain the Finnish province, but the Swedish army lost the campaign. Sweden was forced to accept the humiliating terms of the treaty of Åbo (1741), by which Empress Elisabeth of Russia forced Sweden to accept her protegé Adolph Fredrik of Holstein as heir to the throne of the childless Fredrik I.

Russia's foreign policy was based upon the assumption that the Russian Empire was surrounded by hostile states. To ensure weakness in Sweden, to protect herself, Russia encouraged certain members of the Riksdag to speak out for an alliance between Sweden and Russia. This group announced its hostility to the French-subsidized 'Hats' by wearing nightcaps, and so are referred to as the 'Caps', and the two factions polarized the Riksdag over this issue of Sweden's relationships with France and Russia, the dominant Continental powers. The Caps might have preferred a British alliance, but the Russians were offering more money — a fact which overcame the traditional Swedish aversion to this old enemy.

Under the Treaty of Nystad, Russia agreed to respect Sweden's Constitution of 1720, which gave almost sovereign authority to the four Estates of the Riksdag, and stripped almost all power from the Crown. Russia also claimed the right to veto any attempts to amend the Constitution, obviously intending to prevent any changes which would harm Russian interests or add any strength to the Crown. The 1720 Constitution made quick action in foreign policy impossible, for the factional splits in the Riksdag gave wide scope for bribery and corruption.

Russia and Denmark were both afraid of Sweden as a military power, though this appreciation was based upon the old memories of the warlike Karl (Charles) XII. In the seventeenth century Sweden had taken the southern province of Skåne and two northern provinces from Denmark. The Danish-Russian treaty of 1765 affirmed the interest of both parties in preserving the Swedish 1720 Constitution; in addition the 1769 alliance of Denmark, Prussia and Russia would consider any modification in the Swedish form of government as a reason for war and for the partition of Sweden to 'rescue' Swedish liberties. An attempt to increase the powers of the executive in 1769 did not pass in the Riksdag. Russia had been aware of it and paid the necessary bribes to bring about the desired rejection.

The Swedish system of government enabled the powers — particularly Russia, France and Britain — to exercise influence by bribery. Britain, which at this time was anxious to make an alliance with Russian against France, believed it could be achieved through an alliance with Sweden, and contributed cash, with Russia, to the Cap faction. The majority of Sweden's citizens resented and were impatient with a regime which was in fact a form of absolutism exercised by groups of corrupt party politicians. In addition, the two parties has shown little interest in taking any measures to alleviate the famines of 1771–72, caused by crop failures. A change which would bring about firm decisions by a new regime was most welcome.

In 1772, the frightening news of the partition of Poland, and the plot between Russia and Denmark to partition Sweden reached Gustaf III, at the same time as Sweden was suffering crop failure and famine. The Riksdag's only suggestion to relieve the parlous state of the nation was to enter an alliance with Russia. Russia was preoccupied with a war against Turkey which gave Gustaf III the time to launch a palace coup in order to force major constitutional changes and prevent this disastrous alliance. Gustaf simply alerted all his forces, especially supporters in southern Sweden and Finland, and loyal members of the army and navy in Stockholm who arrested the Riksdag Secret Council, and proclaimed a new constitution, which affirmed, 'The king shall rule the kingdom, and no other'.

Louis XV of France was Gustaf's closest ally, providing the subsidy which guaranteed the success of Gustaf's royal revolution. Gustaf, needing his approval and continued support to prevent interference from Russia and Denmark, established a semi-despotic regime in the French style in Sweden. Chapman supported the king completely; he stored ammunition for the king's forces in his yard at Djurgård.

Gustaf was fully aware that Russian and Danish intrigues would continue, and he believed it was the navy which would prevent invasion. He was also determined to restore Sweden to the imperial greatness she had enjoyed before the Thirty Years' War. Throughout his reign Gustaf advocated — and paid for — a strong army and navy, and he realized that a powerful High Seas Fleet was essential to guarantee the success of the Inshore Fleet's operations. The High Seas Fleet's purpose was not only to prevent enemy vessels from approaching the skerries, but also to prevent the Russian Fleet from leaving the Gulf of Finland to attack the east and west coasts of Sweden, and keep the Danes in check. Gustaf's French loan was intended to be used to build a new army and navy, and gave Chapman the chance to display his genius.

In 1772, only 7 ships of the line and 4 frigates were

serviceable, and 11 ships of the line and 5 frigates needed major refit. The French subsidies for rebuilding Sweden's defences amounted to 800,000 livres annually, paid for three years in accordance with the Versailles Convention of 1773. Sweden had originally asked for twice as much. The king agreed to raise an army of 47,500 men and a fleet of 21 ships of the line, 8 frigates, 30 galleys and 2 barges. Sweden was under no obligation to use these new forces in the defence of France. The French were aware that the money could be diverted to other projects, and consequently demanded guarantees that the subsidies would be used only for defence.

As a result of the Establishment Commission's report, Chapman received a contract to complete the drawings for one 60-gun and two 70-gun vessels. The ships were built at Karlskrona by the shipwrights Sheldon and Sohlberg. None was completed before 1774. It had been the Swedish practice to leave hulls on the stocks for two or three years to allow the timbers to dry out, which may have been one reason for the delays in completion of the three ships, but another was probably the Sweden's economic situation.

The three ships and their dimensions are given in the table overleaf.

The gun ports of the *Fredrik Adolph* were 1.73 m above the waterline. Figures IV/1–2 show the appearance of the *Adolph Fredrik*.

Fig IV/6.
Drawings of the octagonal
sawmill designed by Chapman for
the Djurgård yard
(Sjöhistoriska Museum, Stockholm).

NAME	Fredrik Adolph	Adolph Fredrik	Gustaf III
LENGTH	169 feet (50.19 metres)	174 feet (51.67 metres)	174 feet (51.67 metres)
BEAM	42 feet (12.47 metres)	46 feet (13.66 metres)	46 feet (13.66 metres)
DRAUGHT	21 feet (6.24 metres)	21 feet (6.24 metres)	21 feet (6.24 metres)
NO OF GUNS	62	70	70
DATE OF LAUNCH	1774	1775	1777

Fig IV/7.
A rather crude model of the Turunmää
Lodbrok (Sjöhistoriska
Museum, Stockholm).

The *Adolph Fredrik* was built under the direction of Sheldon, who took it upon himself to increase the beam by 2 feet (60 cm) and the *Fredrik Adolph* and *Gustaf III* were built by Sohlberg. Chapman resented the Admiralty's decision that Sheldon and Sohlberg were to carry out the building of the three ships. These were the first major war vessels designed by Chapman, and the first to which he applied the scientific and mathematical principles acquired from studies in Britain and France. Appendix 5 contains examples of buoyancy calculations made by Chapman possibly for the *Gustaf III* and the *Adolph Fredrik*.

Chapman designed the decoration for the stern of the *Adolph Fredrik* (fig IV/3) but a more elaborate one was prepared by the Swedish artist Jean Erik Rehn (fig IV/4). It is not known which of the two designs was finally chosen by King Gustaf III, but he would have probably chosen the Rehn design — it would have been more in keeping with his personality.

The figurehead of Gustaf III was supposed to represent the king in Roman dress with a wreath on his head. The carving was, however, a disaster. When King Gustaf visited Karlskrona in 1777 on a tour of inspection, accompanied by Chapman, he expressed his displeasure when he discovered that one side of the figurehead did not match the other. The king remarked, 'Is that really meant to be me?' Chapman replaced the wreath with a crown, but it made only a very slight improvement (fig IV/5). As a result the king issued an order that, 'No other artists were to be engaged to provide ornaments or paintings with which naval vessels were to be decorated, other than those who were members of the Royal Academy of Painters and Sculptors or recognized and approved as such by the Academy'. Figureheads of Swedish naval vessels were to remain crude carvings until Johan Törnström was appointed official figurehead carver to the navy by Chapman in 1781.

The *Fredrik Adolph* was subject to trials in the Baltic in 1776. Chapman was on board as a member of the trials commission. The naval cadets made up part of the ship's crew. The commander was Erik Klint, later to be a member of the 1779 trials commission. His report states that 'the ship manoeuvred fairly fast'. The Sheldon-built ship, the *Adolph Fredrik*, was found to sail less well.

THE DJURGÅRD YARD, STOCKHOLM

Chapman had requested release from the Crown's service on his return to Stockholm in 1765 because, to quote his autobiographical notes, 'I was dissatisfied with the preposterous organization at Sveaborg (Finland) and the royal dockyards in Sweden, where ships cost 10 percent more to build than they should. In England they have less trouble to maintain a fleet of 150 ships than we have to maintain 15'. One of the

reasons for his decision was that he was not allowed to build the two 70-gun, and the 60-gun ships for which he had prepared the drawings. The request for complete release was denied. To quote the document, he was granted 'leave of absence to attend to his personal affairs'. The leave conditions required Chapman to continue to design vessels for the Inshore Fleet and the Crown was prepared to pay him a retainer for this purpose.

In 1768, Chapman acquired an interest in the Djurgård Yard. A syndicate, headed by Wahrendorff of the Åkers Gun Foundry and a director of the Swedish East India Company found the capital; Chapman was to provide the technical knowledge, and reorganize the activity. The yard was not only to build merchant vessels, but also naval craft on contract. He moved into a house close by the yard (it still stands and is now the head office of the Tivoli amusement park) with, according to Admiral Tersmeden's memoirs, a mistress-cum-housekeeper, Elisabeth Lindberg, by whom he had a son and a daughter, and his nephew Lars Bogeman. Chapman also moved the scale models of each type of ship which he had constructed into his new home.

The reorganization of the yard included the construction of an octagonal sawmill building designed by Chapman (fig IV/6). He replaced the customary two-man saw pit operation with a circular saw placed in the centre of the building. The saw was operated by men pulling a rope. It could work simultaneously on eight different sawing positions (two parallel to each other from different positions), from which the building's shape originated. The timbers were passed by the saw on traverse carriages — three are shown in the drawing. The building's floor was about 4 feet above the ground; nine windows and a belfry surrounded by a balcony completed the building. The bell called the labourers to work, at 4am in summertime, and also indicated the end of the working day — 8pm in summer, dusk in winter. The equipment at the Djurgård yard included cauldrons for pitch, a copper steam vessel about 12 metres long, fitted with an iron door at each end, with a furnace below, also an iron pot mounted in a brick wall with a tin steam vessel. The knees and frames were heated with the aid of steam and afterwards were bent to the desired shapes.

Equally important were the three fitting out quays, 56 metres, 37 metres and 36 metres long respectively. The width of each was 10 metres, 10 metres and 8 metres. The longest was adequate for the fitting out of new vessels and the repair of the old. Sheer legs were to provide the means to careen ships.

Some fifty ships, including auxiliary craft, were built for the Inshore Fleet during the Chapman period of management. These included for the Inshore Fleet: the Udenmää, *Torborg* and *Ingeborg*, the Pojanmää, *Brynhilda*, the dispatch vessel *Lovisa*, as well as gun-sloops, mortar-vessels and water-carriers and the inshore frigate (Turunmää) *Lodbrok*. The *Lodbrok* (figs III/11 and IV/7) was the first of a series to be provided with cross bracing between the deck beams and the floors, providing greater longitudinal strength to prevent sagging. She was named after a mythical Nordic king at the suggestion of Ehrensvärd, her dimensions and armament being as follows:

Length overall	124 feet (36.83 metres)
Beam	28 feet (8.32 metres)
Draught	10.6 feet (3.15 metres)
Armament	
12-pounder guns	22
18-pounder guns	2

The *Lodbrok* was provided with nineteen pairs of oars, each to be manned by four men. Chapman designed the figurehead (fig IV/8) for this vessel as he had for all vessels built for the Inshore Fleet. As a result, he was elected a member of the Royal Academy for the arts in 1774.

The *Lodbrok* was the subject of a charge brought against Chapman that he had built an unsuitable vessel, but Ehrensvärd, the commander of the Inshore Fleet, refuted the accusation. Possibly the command of the High Seas Fleet, jealous of the greater attention placed by the Crown to the needs of the skerries fleet and, moreover, smarting over the placing of Inshore Fleet under the command of the army, were responsible for the bringing of the charges against Chapman. Chapman went on to design four frigates for the Inshore Fleet for service in Finland, the *Sigurd Ormöga*, the *Björn Järnsida*, the *Ragvald* and the *Sällan Värre*.

The methods of payment used for the construction of vessels for the Inshore Fleet were similar to those of the twentieth century; one-third was paid when the contract was signed, one-third when all frames were raised and the hull had been fully planked up, and the final instalment of one-third was made on completion (authorized at the meeting of the Rikdag immediately following the delivery date). However, the continuous shortage of funds increased the time of payments for the inshore frigates to be spread over a period of three years plus interest at $4\frac{1}{2}$ percent on the first three payments.

Chapman's connections with the Inshore Fleet brought about his 8-page memorandum of 31 March 1773 which sets out in detail the organization, and establishment necessary for the maintenance of the various units of the Inshore Fleet. The following is a summary.

The fleet to be maintained should consist of the following: 12 Turunmää, 5 Udenmää, 10 Pojanmää, 10 reconnaissance craft, 5 dispatch vessels, 28 longboats, 48 large and small sloops, 6 stores vessels and 20 miscellaneous small craft. 2 Turunmää, 1 Udenmää, 2 Pojanmää, 1 dispatch vessel and 1 stores vessel were to be maintained afloat for training and intelligence purposes. All the other vessels were to be laid up either in the dry-docks or ashore. Chapman hoped that by these methods each vessel could be kept as long as possible free from deterioration. To meet the requirements needed to put all the vessels into service, he proposed that the Sveaborg (Finland) dockyard acquire additional facilities, and outlined the procedures for mobilizing the whole of the Inshore Fleet. Chapman maintained that dry-docks ought to be built to hold ten Turunmää and four Udenmää vessels, and an additional dry-dock into which Turunmää frigate could enter fully armed for repairs to the vessel's bottom. He proposed that the dockyard should have covered slipways to accommodate two Pojanmää, three reconnaissance and four stores vessels, which should not be moved from place to place in peacetime. Two slipways, in Chapman's opinion, were necessary because ships operating in the skerries often ran ashore in the many narrow passages and would need repairs. There were to be several sheds for the longboats, cutters and the 48 sloops and 20 miscellaneous craft. The size of the sheds were to be tailored to the dimensions of the various craft to be stored.

Chapman emphasized the need for sheds, each about 130 feet long and 100 feet wide, with three rows of shelves, for the storage of masts and spars. (He considered a sail loft necessary for the manufacture, repairs and storage of sails and set out the dimensions of a building suitable for that purpose.) Buildings were also necessary for the storage of rigging materials, block and tackles etc. In addition, buildings and sheds for the repair of gun carriages, a smithy, a cooper's shop and storage for water barrels were also very important for the maintenance of the fleet. The stocks of pine for repairs would also require some sort of shed. Chapman estimated that it was only possible for the dockyard personnel to work a full 12-hour day for 100 days. He stated that two pairs of sheer legs and two mast cranes ought to be erected, and the position of these two pieces of equipment should be located in such a way that two ships could be handled at the same time. He pointed out that the vessels kept afloat would have to be careened at stipulated intervals for bottom-cleansing and recommended storage locations be established close to the water for 1000–4000 iron weights, or 'pigs', to be used as ballast. It should be possible to provide service for two ships at once, and storages for ships' anchors and guns should be close to the water for ease and speed in handling. He also wanted a rope-walk with the equipment to tar rope. His memorandum includes as well outlines of the terms of reference for the dock-master and the stores-master.

Chapman proposed the following procedures in respect of rigging, armament and stores be followed in the event of a national emergency when the fleet had to be fitted out and made ready for sea. After floating, the vessels should (1) take on board ballast, (2) set up masts and spars, (3) be rigged completely, (4) take on board anchor cables, (5) cat the anchor on the bow, (6) take on board gun carriages, (7) take in guns, round shot and pertinent tackle, (8) load stores, water and firewood, (9) take on board and bend sails, (10) load gunpowder.

He did not consider it necessary for the larger of the Inshore Fleet's frigates to be under cover for storage. He recommended that their sides and decks be tarred annually and that certain planks from the sides of the vessels be removed to ensure good ventilation.

Chapman's proposals were implemented by 1780 when fourteen of the larger vessels were placed in storage in the dry-docks at Sveaborg. The memorandum gives a clear indication of Chapman's organizational abilities, based upon his overseas experience, his service in Finland, and his management of the Djurgård yard.

The Djurgård yard built several small merchant vessels during its Chapman period, including a cat ship the *Baron v Höpken* (fig IV/9), the barque, *Hertigninnan af Södermanland* and the *Sveriges Lycka*. Since some of the directors were associated with the Swedish East India Company, two ships to Chapman's designs were ordered from the yard in 1767 and 1779 (the *Cron Prins Gustaf*, fig IV/10 and the *Konung Gustaf den Tredje*, fig IV/11). The two ships, whose details are given overleaf, were possibly the first merchant vessels designed in

Fig IV/8.
The Lodbrok's *figurehead*
(Sjöhistoriska Museum, Stockholm).

NAME	LENGTH OVERALL	BEAM	DRAUGHT FORE	DRAUGHT AFT	TUMBLEHOME	ARMAMENT
Cron Prins Gustaf	157 feet (46.63 metres)	41 feet (12.17 metres)	20 feet (5.94 metres)	22 feet (6.53 metres)	3 feet 9 ins (1.11 metres)	28 guns
Konung Gustaf III	161 feet (47.82 metres)	43 feet (12.77 metres)	—	22 feet (6.53 metres)	3 feet 6 ins (1.04 metres)	18 guns

accordance with scientific principles and mathematics. Fig IV/12 shows the division of the accommodation space aft between the ships officers, supercargoes and other officials. It is interesting to observe that the chaplain was provided with twice as much space as the ship's surgeon.

Jacob Wallenberg, chaplain of the company's *Finland*, built some five years earlier than the *Cron Prins Gustaf* in the old style, wrote the following about the two ships which left for Java on 26 December 1769, the *Crons Prins Gustaf* arriving nine weeks ahead of the *Finland*. 'The *Finland* is like an old pot-bellied archdeacon who will not be hurried, rocks over the waves with a continuous movement. The *Gustaf* on the other hand, rolled on and was out of our sight after two days.' It seems likely that Chapman's application of scientific principles in the construction of *Cron Prins Gustaf* was a good reason for the faster passage to Java.

The city of Göteborg's library contains a description (Document 10/1158 DS 40) which specifies the material and the quality thereof which Chapman was to use in the construction of an East Indiaman. The document is undated but its reference to the number of lasts (a Swedish measure of capacity), suggests it referred to the construction of the *Konung Gustaf III*. The document stipulates, amongst other items, that the builder should use French glass for the windows of the great cabin. The launch of the *Konung Gustaf III* in 1776 called for a great celebration. The king, queen, queen mother, and the King's sister Sophia, came to the yard in state with a military escort. The ship was launched with the king and Chapman on board. Those present placed in the belfry of the saw-house sang Bellman's 'King Gustaf's Skål', accompanied by an orchestra. Bellman read an ode in Chapman's praise. The shipbuilders provided a supper for the royal party and refreshments for the other guests and employees. Dancing went on during the whole night. On this occasion, Chapman probably did not wear his patched hooded working jacket with its leather reinforcement at the elbows, which was part of his normal working dress.

The *Konung Gustaf III* and the *Cron Prins Gustaf* made voyages to China for the Swedish East India Company for twenty-six and twenty years respectively. Chapman was to design two more ships for the company during his Karlskrona years (1781–1803). These two ships were probably the first merchant vessels built in accordance with Chapman's scientific methods.'

MEMBER OF THE BOARD OF ADMIRALTY 1776

In 1735, the Riksdag (the Swedish parliament) had given the Admiralty full control over the Navy and set out its new responsibilities. The Admiralty was located in Karlskrona some 300 miles (500 km) from Stockholm. Over a period of time, changes and modifications had occurred in its terms of reference; consequently, there was uncertainty as to the nature of its activities and organization. As a result of dissatisfaction with the Board of Admiralty, the government set up a commission to inaugurate new economic and reporting procedures, giving the admiral superintendant of the dockyard greater powers, but stressing that the Admiralty was to be responsible for the implementation of naval policy, and should also try to increase its number of ships. The terms stated that the ships should 'have similar merits as regards stiffness, to carry sufficient sail, have adequate height for gun decks, and have good features as regards sailing, good steering and speed.' The stipulations included the ships not having too great a draught and being as strong as possible in order to carry heavy guns; moreover, old ships were to be kept afloat for the sake of appearances.

In 1772 Gustaf III's Sinclair Commission revised the Admiralty's terms of reference. It contained some sixty-two provisions. Amongst them were requirements to present an annual budget, to make known its views about new construction and to keep itself informed of naval and maritime developments in other countries by sending personnel abroad for this purpose. An example of the information gathered is contained in Sorell's report of 1774, following a visit to the naval dockyards of Brest and Toulon. Sorell observed that the height of gun ports above the waterline in new construction was to be 5 to 8 feet, the main powder magazine was now placed aft rather than midships, and a small powder magazine was retained in the forepeak. As a result of the information, the Swedish Navy adopted the same practice. Sorrel had some discussions about ventilation and the stowage of anchor cables and noted that the French used stone ballast and that their principal source of oak was Italy. Some ninety officers served in the French fleet during the American War of Independence; thirty served in the British fleet and one served in the Maltese galley fleet from 1774 to 1777.

The Board was to maintain close relations with the army to ensure it was kept abreast of the development and purposes of the Inshore Fleet. The new Board of Admiralty was to consist of a chairman, two admirals, two civilian counsellors. Where a special commission was to consider reports, all flag officers were to attend. The admirals commanding the fleet, and the Karlskrona dockyard were soon replaced by Privy Counsellor Sparre. Chapman in his report on the Karlskrona situation recommended that funds should be used to build new ships rather than be spent on costly repairs to old vessels. He proposed one new ship be built annually and one old one scrapped. He observed that the dockyard's workshops were in poor condition and naval stores were non-existent. He added, 'An evil spirit has entered into the shipbuilding activity'. Chapman's remarks were probably directed at the two principal opponents to his new shipbuilding methods, the shipwright Sheldon and Admiral Tersmeden. The King, incidentally, had appointed Tersmeden dockyard superintendant as a reward for his support in the 1772 coup.

The King again sent Chapman and two privy counsellors, Scheffer and Sparre, to inspect the Karlskrona facilities. the King approved their recommendations for new storehouses, hospitals, ammunition, and the placing of the oak timber ashore under a roof to prevent rot. At the time of the King's approval of these proposals, Counsellors Scheffer and Sparre obtained consent for the construction of the Chapman-

Fig IV/9.
A model of the cat Baron v Höpken
designed by Chapman and built
at the Djurgård yard
(Sjöhistoriska Museum, Stockholm).

designed 60-gun ship, the *Wasa* (fig IV/13). Sheldon was to build this ship in Karlskrona according to Chapman's drawings. It was also decided that there should be no new construction until the *Wasa* had undergone trials in competition with the other vessels of the fleet. Consequently, the completion of the *Hedvig Elisabet Charlotta*, constructed by Chapman to be stiffer than the *Adolph Fredrik*, was delayed. If the *Wasa*'s trials were successful all 60-gun ships would be built thereafter in accordance with Chapman's designs. Chapman's drawing (fig IV/14) for the *Wasa* is dated 2 June 1777 and King Gustaf's signature of approval is dated 10 October 1777. The dimensions of the new ship were as follows:

Length	162 feet (48.11 metres)
Maximum beam	45½ feet (13.51 metres)
Maximum draught (full load)	19¼ feet (5.71 metres)

Armament
Twenty-six 24-pounder guns on the gun deck
Twenty-six 18-pounder guns on the upper deck
Eight 6-pounder guns on the quarterdeck

The ship was designed to carry stores for 5 months and water for 2½ months. *Wasa*'s crew would number 490.

Chapman intended the *Wasa* to be much stiffer than the two ships, the *Fredrik Adolf* and *Adolf Fredrik*. To obtain the greater stiffness, reduction in draught and

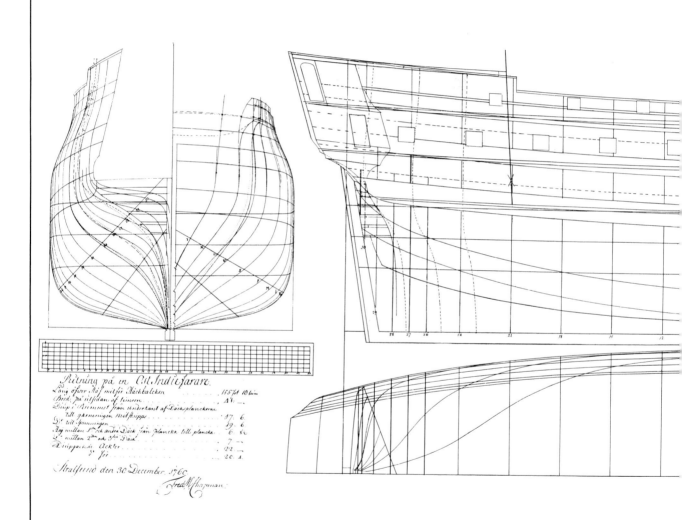

to minimize leeway when tacking, he lowered the new ship's superstructure. That decision caused complaints from the ship's officers who resented the absence of the more commodious quarters of older vessels. The *Wasa*'s hull was launched after six months and she was ready for sea by the summer of 1778. The opportunity to test her sailing qualities and compare these with those of earlier construction occurred in the spring of 1779.

The period of intrigue by the opposition to Chapman's new methods now came to a head. The old guard comprised the chief shipwright, Sheldon, supported by Admiral Tersmeden in particular, and by most of the other flag officers. Chapman was supported by General Admiral af Trolle, but also had a political advantage over his opponents because of his friendship with those members of the court closest to the King.

The inauguration in 1779 of neutrality patrols in the North Sea to protect Swedish trade provided an opportunity of testing three Chapman-designed vessels, including the *Wasa*, against Sheldon's the *Sofia Magdalena*, the ship favoured by the commander of the fleet (fig IV/15). The Board of Admiralty issued an eleven-page document of instructions to Admiral Grubbe, who was to head the commission set up to supervise the trials. The commission included af Chapman, Erik Klint and Colonel Holdt; and the King's brother, Duke Carl of Södermanland, was to command the neutrality squadron. The document, which contains very comprehensive and rigid instructions about the information to be obtained, required observations to be made in

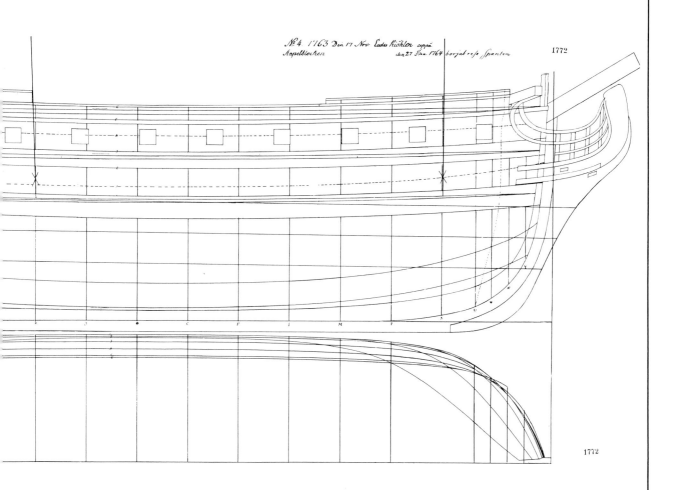

Fig IV/10.
Profile and body plan of the East Indiaman
Cron Prins Gustaf
signed by Chapman at Stralsund
on 30 December 1760
(Göteborg Maritime Museum).

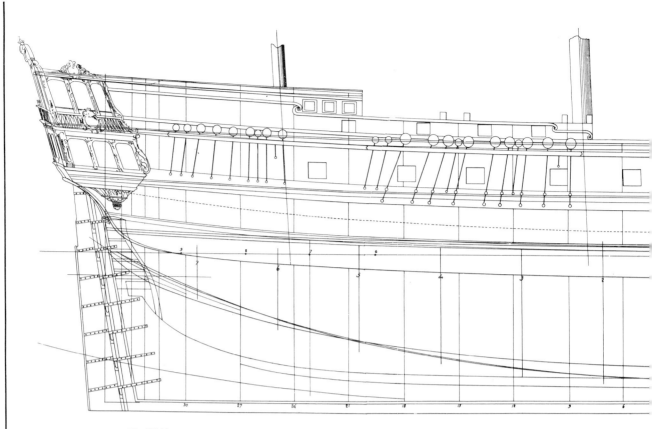

Fig IV/11.
Profile and body plan of the
East Indiaman Konung Gustafden Tredje
(Göteborg Maritime Museum).

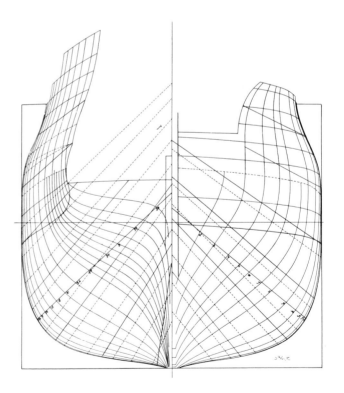

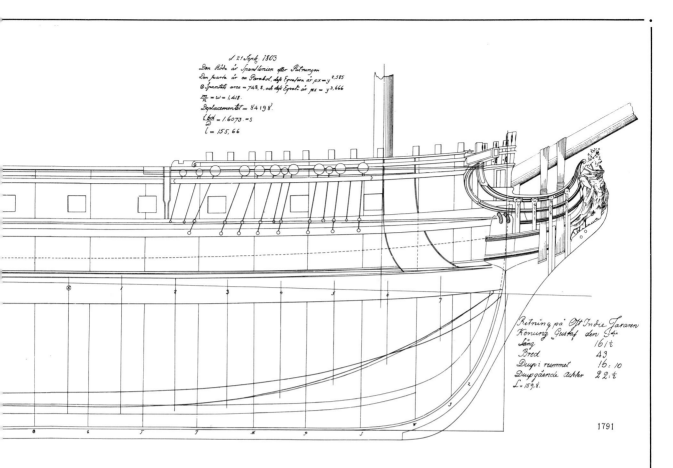

1791

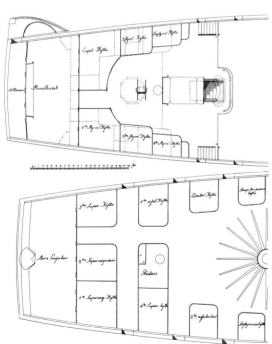

Fig IV/12.
Cabin arrangement plan of the Indiaman
Cron Prins Gustaf
(Göteborg Maritime Museum).

two different sets of circumstances: firstly, to see how each of the three ships behaved under peacetime conditions and, secondly, under wartime conditions. Special consideration was to be given to the comparison between the *Wasa* and the *Sofia Magdalena*, the latter being considered the best sailer in the fleet.

COMPARISONS

The dimensions of the two ships were as follows:

Each ship's sailing characteristics under different conditions and the different sets of sails were to be recorded. The time taken for each vessel to go about was to be carefully noted and each ship's tendencies to luff or fall off to leeward was to be registered for each manoeuvre. In addition, the speed, leeway, extent of rolling, pitching and heeling was to be observed and recorded. The instructions also stated that the neutrality force was to participate with the *Wasa* in

	SOFIA MAGDALENA	WASA
Length overall	174 feet (51.69 metres)	162 feet (48.11 metres)
Maximum beam	44½ feet (13.22 metres)	45½ feet (13.51 metres)
Maximum draught	23 feet (6.83 metres)	19½ feet (5.79 metres)

Fig IV/13.
Wasa, *contemporary model*
(Sjöhistoriska Museum, Stockholm).

68

manoeuvring, firing, and in the chase. The manoeuvrability in the line of battle of the *Wasa* and her opponent was to be noted. The other ships participating in the exercises were to record how the opponents managed to clear two enemy lines. The instructions required the conditions of spars and rigging to be carefully observed. Another important matter to be noted was the extent to which smoke from gun fire cleared from the gun decks. Each ship forming the neutrality force was to keep journals to show times and dates, ships' speeds, courses, drift, wind direction and force, weather conditions, sea conditions and set of sails, position of rudder. In addition, the ships' heeling, drift and pitching was to be measured in degrees. The periods between rolls was to be observed and noted. The times taken to tack, wear and manoeuvre when running were to be entered in the journals (an example of the record for part of August kept by Klint is attached in Appendix 7). In addition to the seakeeping qualities, trials were to be made with a new type of gun carriage known as the traversing slide carriage.

The fact that the *Sofia Magdalena* sailed better than the *Adolph Fredrik* and the *Fredrik Adolph* prompted Chapman to make some investigations. He found that both vessels had been loaded with 1500 pounds of extra ballast (twice as much as he had ordered) and that Sheldon, the builder of the *Adolph Fredrik*, had reduced her designed beam by two feet. The *Sofia Magdalena* had had her bottom cleaned shortly before the trials began, whereas both the *Adolph Fredrik* and the *Fredrik Adolph* had not been in the dry-dock for similar purposes for almost five years. Chapman found other deficiencies — his ships were badly rigged and, in addition, the rigging material was of such poor quality that the shrouds had to be adjusted daily. However, problems also arose with the flagship, Sheldon's *Sofia Magdalena*. She could not make the Drogden passage into the Sound (Öresund) as her draught aft was too great. The crew moved the ballast forward, which made steering almost impossible. As a result, only after considerable persuasion did the pilots finally agree to take her through Drogden into the Sound. When the squadron anchored off Copenhagen, the Danish admiral invited Duke Carl and the ships' commanders to visit the royal dockyard and he particularly asked that 'the able and efficient Chapman be included in the party to explain models which the dockyard had'. No doubt Chapman's reputation, perhaps from his publications, was known to the leading Danish shipbuilders Gerner and Stibolt; the former certainly had copies of Chapman's scientific papers and publications (see page 47, *Danske Orlogsskibe 1690–1860*).

The trials began in earnest on 21 June in an area bounded by Jutland, the Dogger Bank, and the Norwegian coast. As the squadron met with heavy weather in the North Sea, the exercises were limited to several days cruising after which most of the squadron returned to Swedish west coast waters. The Duke handed over the command to Admiral Gerdten in the middle of July after he had signed the report and Admiral Grubbe and Chapman went ashore at the same time. The trials were continued for another month, with Majors Klint and Raab designated to assess the *Wasa*'s performance. (At that time military rather than naval ranks were being used for all officers under flag rank, a system which lasted until the 1820s (see Appendix 8).) Klint was responsible for reporting on the *Wasa*'s seakeeping qualities, sailing and manoeuvrability, and Raab was charged with testing the suitability of her armament and the new type of gun carriages.

The detailed journals maintained by Klint and Raab throughout the trials were entirely responsible for bringing to the fore the *Wasa*'s excellent qualities. The Commission's report dated September 1779, signed by Admiral Grubbe, Major Erik Klint and Colonel Holdt contains the following comments:

> As the most important features of a ship of the line are good defence, be stiff under sail, have high gun batteries, sail well and be exceptional in its motions, the ship which has all these features is the most perfect. When this ship *Wasa* is compared with the *Sofia Magdalena*, it has the same number of guns, higher freeboard and similar stiffness, but does not sail as well as the *Sofia Magdalena* when carrying the same canvas.

The report states clearly that the *Wasa* was in all other respects superior to the other ships.

The trials did not give Chapman the complete triumph he had anticipated. Shipbuilding based on the practical application of theory had not won the desired total victory over shipbuilding based upon experience. Chapman's first initial comments on the report were that:

> if the *Wasa* is lengthened by two feet but keeping the same beam and displacement, then she shall with the same sails, sail as well as the *Sofia Magdalena* without any loss of stiffness or the height of the gun decks. This increase in length will cause little change in the design and will not increase the costs.

The Commission's report was on the whole favourable, but Duke Carl and Admiral Grubbe publicly made it clear that they preferred the *Sofia Magdalena* and spread reports from Karlskrona that the *Wasa* was an unsuccessful ship.

Fig IV/14.
Profile and body plans of the ship of the
line Wasa, *dated 1777*
(Krigsarkivet, Stockholm).

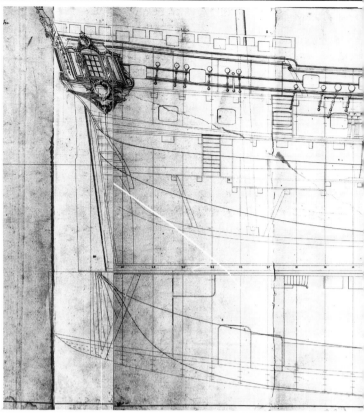

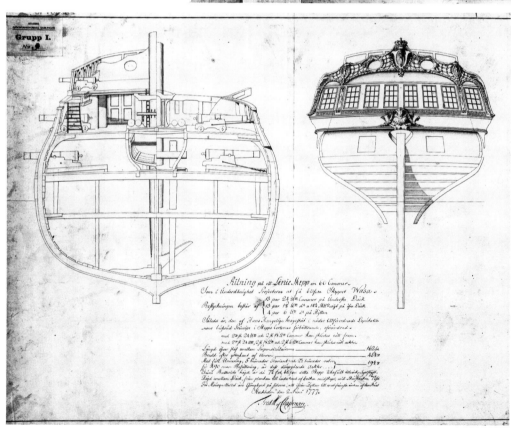

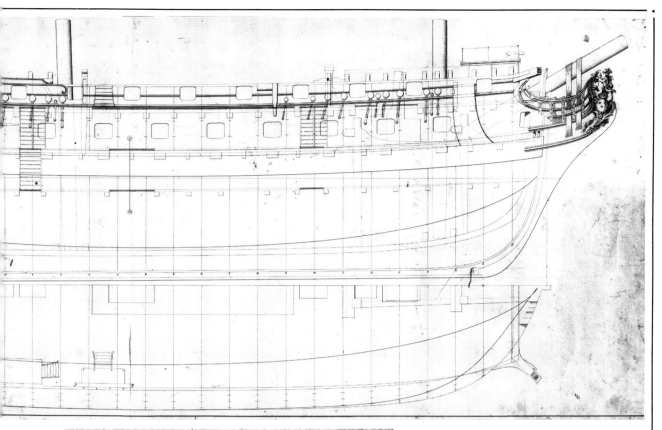

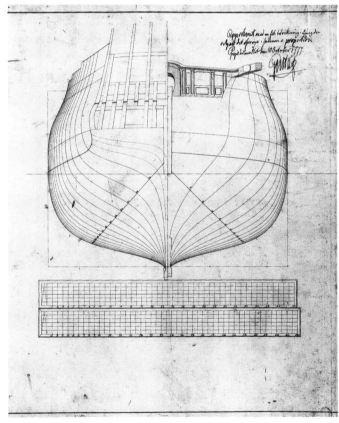

Fig IV/15.
A frame model of Sheldon's Sophia Magdalena
(Sjöhistoriska Museum, Stockholm).

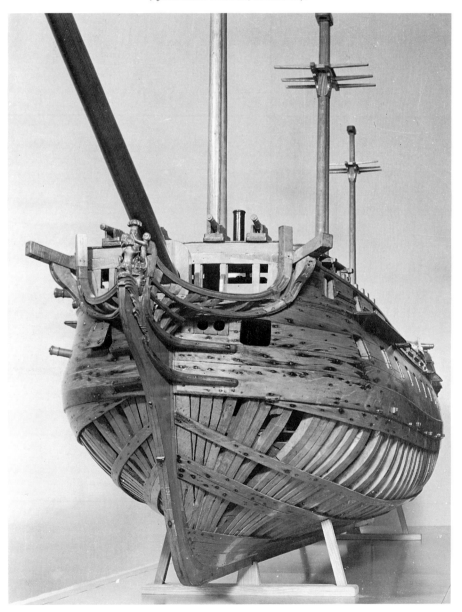

Fig IV/16.
A contemporary partially planked model of the Wasa
(Sjöhistoriska Museum, Stockholm).

Fig IV/17.
Stern view of the contemporary model of the Wasa
(Sjöhistoriska Museum, Stockholm).

Fig V/1.
Frigate *(Merchant Vessels, 1st Class)*, Plate IV

Length between perpendiculars	128ft
Breadth moulded	34½ft
Draught as it is on plan	18ft
Draught laden	19ft 3in
Burthen	276 heavy lasts
Area of the midship frame	438sq ft
Area of the load waterline	3593sq ft
Displacement	37,282cu ft
Total cost of construction	40,597 Krone

Above right is a scale of burthen for the 'frigates' in the Mercatoria
(Sjöhistoriska Museum, Stockholm).

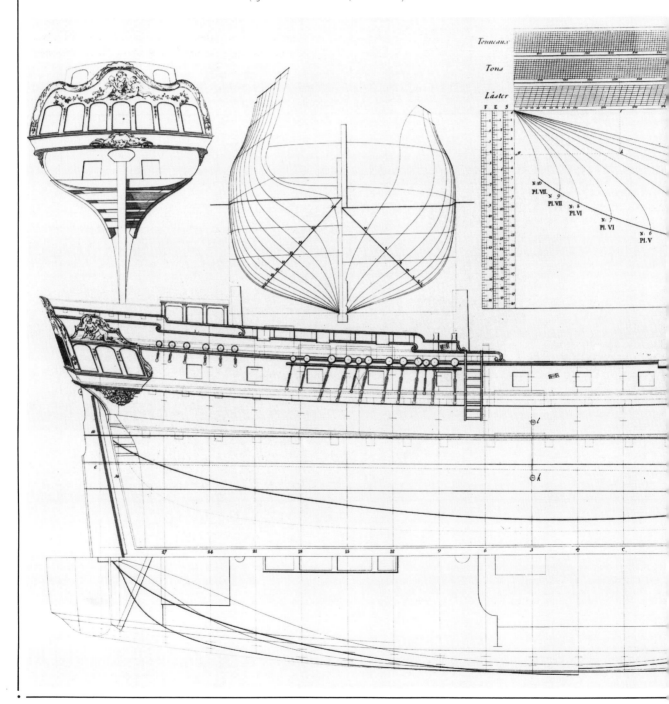

Five

THE ARCHITECTURA NAVALIS MERCATORIA

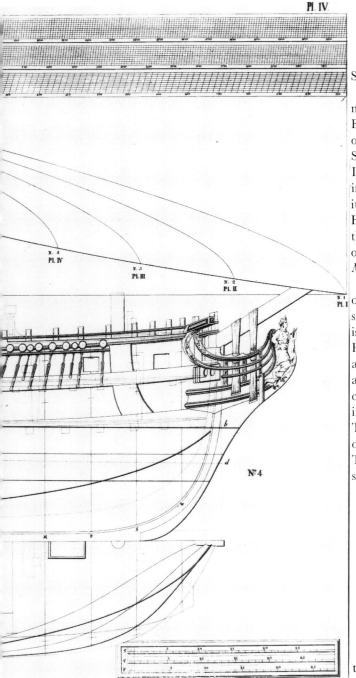

Pl. IV

N. 4
Pl. IV

N. 3
Pl. III

N. 2
Pl. II

N. 1
Pl. I

N.º 4

During the time that I was preparing the drawings for the 70-gun ship *Adolph Fredrik*, the 60-gun *Fredrik Adolph*, and a few years later, the *Gustaf III*, I prepared a work on shipbuilding; the name, *Architectura Navalis Mercatoria*.

So wrote Chapman in his autobiography.

On 8 August 1766, Chapman wrote to the commander-in-chief of the Inshore Fleet, General Augustin Ehrensvärd, asking for one year's extension of the leave of absence he had been granted on his move to Stockholm in 1764. He pointed out that since the Inshore Fleet would not be building anything of importance for some time, he could take the opportunity to 'improve [his] knowledge so to be able to provide His Majesty and the Crown much more useful service'. the 'more useful service' he had in mind was the task of finishing his first masterpiece, *Architectura Navalis Mercatoria*.

This book is a collection of sixty-four engraved plates of ships and boats of all types and sizes. The title page shows Årres' famous view of Stockholm, and the work is dedicated to Gustaf III's brother, Admiral of the Fleet Prince Carl. The only text in the first edition is a systematic list of the contents, in English, French, and Swedish, on three large pages. This list is a comprehensive collection of data about ships and includes a great deal of general economic information. The various types of ships are described by categories of data, with information ranged under headings. There are, for instance, eight categories for merchant ships:

1. Type and rigging of the ship
2. Length between perpendiculars
3. Moulded breadth
4. Draught at full load
5. Tonnage (ie, displacement)
6. Midship frame
7. Total cost
8. Cost per unit of displacement

Most of the engravings measure 82 by 55cms, and there are five principal groups: merchant vessels, vessels for fast sailing or rowing, privateers, a selection of the types of vessels used by various nations, and illustrations of the launching and rigging of ships. The third and fourth groups include heavily-armed merchantmen and naval ships. Each engraving shows particulars of armament; the number of guns, their total weight on deck, forecastle to poop, the number of swivel guns, and the height of gun ports above the water. Also detailed are the number of oars (where applicable), the ship's complement, amount of stores needed per month, and the amount of water required per man per month.

Chapman illustrated eleven different types of merchant vessels and six different shallow-draught craft. As examples of swift sailers, Chapman drew five variations of privateers and eleven different foreign warships. One plate shows twenty-four types of rig. Where there was enough room in the plate, he drew in the appropriate type of gun carriage. Each engraving carries a scale for linear measurement, in Swedish, English, and French feet. Some engravings include a tonnage scale by which the displacement may be calculated.

In most of the plates, Chapman drew two concentric circles in the ships to indicate the centre of gravity and the metacentre — the basic data from which stability is calculated. Each vessel's sheer plan, profile, and midship frame is illustrated. Some etchings show hulls careened — lying over on their beam ends, almost 90 degrees off perpendicular — or at an 8 degree heel.

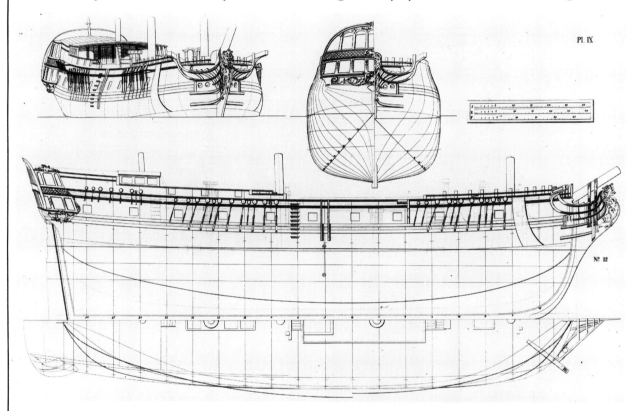

Fig V/2.
Hagboat *(Merchant Vessels, 2nd Class), Plate IX*

Length between perpendiculars	*148¾ft*
Breadth moulded	*37⅝ft*
Draught as it is on plan	*20ft 4in*
Burthen	*389 heavy lasts*
Area of the midship frame	*594sq ft*
Area of the load waterline	*4727sq ft*
Displacement	*61,498cu ft*
Total cost of construction	*70,659 Krone*

Above left is a waterline perspective view of the Hagboat
from starboard looking aft
(Sjöhistoriska Museum, Stockholm).

Fig V/3.
Frigates *(Vessels of War)*, *Plate LV, Nos 9 and 10*
Frigate La Sirenne *(Vessels of War)*

Length between perpendiculars	$131\frac{1}{4}$ *ft*
Breadth moulded	$34\frac{1}{3}$ *ft*
Draught	$15\frac{1}{2}$ *ft*
Displacement	*27,222 cu ft*
Guns	*34*
of which	*26 8-pounders on the deck*
	8 4-pounders on quarterdeck
	and forecastle

Note. *No 9 is the French naval frigate* La Sirenne, *an excellent sailer able to carry a press of sail without too great an inclination.*

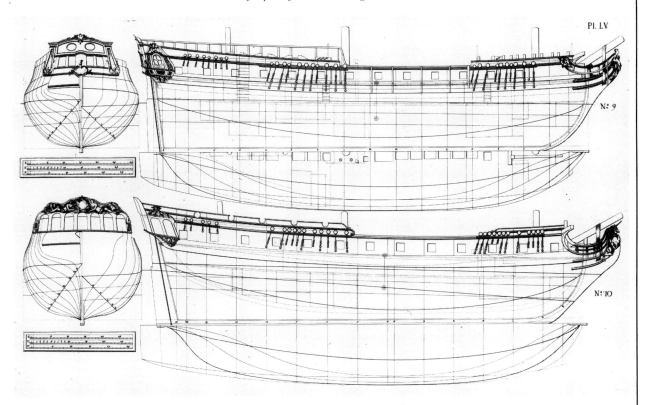

Pl. LV

N.º 9

N.º 10

Frigate the Unicorn *(Vessels of War)*

Length between perpendiculars	$125\frac{1}{4}$ *ft*
Breadth moulded	$34\frac{1}{6}$ *ft*
Draught	$17\frac{1}{4}$ *ft*
Displacement	*27,742 cu ft*
Guns	*34*
of which	*24 8-pounders on the deck*
	10 4-pounders on the forecastle
	and quarterdeck

Note. *No 10 is an English naval frigate, the* Unicorn, *a fast vessel. The line running at an angle up towards the stern is the launching draught of waterline*
(Sjöhistoriska Museum, Stockholm).

Plate XXXVI shows a frigate with diagonal bracing between the deck beams and the floor timbers designed so as to prevent hogging.

Traverse bracing as longitudinal strengthening is a feature in drawings of the lightly-built and relatively narrow Turunmää and Hemenmää skerry frigates. Their long, low hulls were stiffened with a system of diagonal braces placed between the deck beams and the floors, along most of the hull's length, in two lines parallel to and about half-way between the hull's sides and the centreline.

Chapman calculated displacement in cubic feet, and the cubes for the calculations of stiffness by which the metacentric height could be determined. His basic thought was that when a new vessel of a specific cargo capacity was planned, by these tables, the constructor could determine the hull proportions, and find all important relevant data in one place. Chapman's curve system made it possible to calculate, for each draught line, the displacement of a vessel, whether fully-loaded or in ballast. Plate IV (fig V/1) shows the curve, described in British, French, and Swedish length and capacity units, for ten different merchant vessels.

Chapman's objective with the *Mercatoria* was to show, in sixty-four engravings, a synthesis of the results achieved by shipbuilders of many different lands, through hundreds of years of successful traditional design — the best of the era before the application of mathematics and physics to determine the properties of ships. Chapman knew from his experiences as a

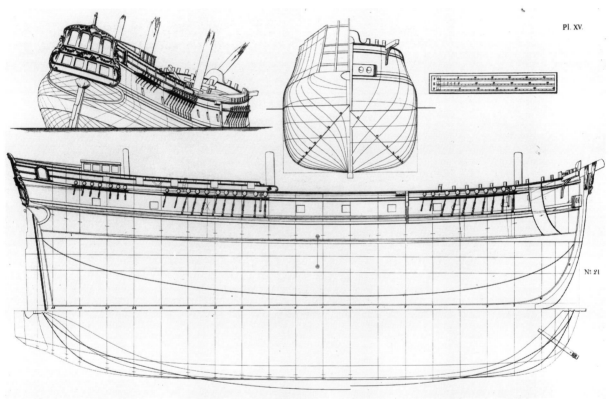

Pl. XV.

Fig V/4.
Cats *(Merchant Vessels, 4th Class), Plate XV*

Length between perpendiculars	*157 ft*
Breadth moulded	*38½ ft*
Draught as it is on the plan	*20 ft*
Burthen	*467 heavy lasts*
Area of the midship frame	*611 sq ft*
Area of the load waterline	*5295 sq ft*
Displacement	*70,682 cu ft*
Total cost of construction	*79,648 Krone*

Above left in a perspective view of the vessel heeling over
(Sjöhistoriska Museum, Stockholm).

shipwright that no ship — especially not an effective warship — could possibly be designed from a simple summary of the dimensions of Europe's best sailing vessels. His argument was that through this procedure, new faults are most often exposed.

French, British, and Dutch vessels dominate the *Mercatoria* because Chapman was most familiar with them, from his studies abroad. There are also drawings of craft from Algiers, Bermuda, Flanders, Malta, Venice, Spain, Greenland, Norway, and Finland, presumably because Chapman saw these types in his foreign travels and in the ports of Scandinavia. The majority of the small cargo and pleasure craft, and perhaps some of the frigates and privateers, are probably based on Chapman's or his colleagues' designs. Exceptions

are the Swedish naval frigate *Jarramas*, and Plate LVII, Drawing No 14, the Ostende privateer frigate *Neptunus*. This is the drawing which Chapman received at the age of ten, from the Flemish shipbuilder Wiederliner.

In 1768, when the *Mercatoria* was first published without any explanatory text, questions arose about its usefulness to shipbuilders seeking to improve their product. Outside Sweden, some considered the *Mercatoria* to be a collection of drawings for experts only, who required no additional explanation. (Röding's *Allgemeine Wortbuch der Marine* of 1793 held that view.) Chapman, however, stated his intentions at the end of his last notice to subscribers:

The promised descriptions of the whole contents, with

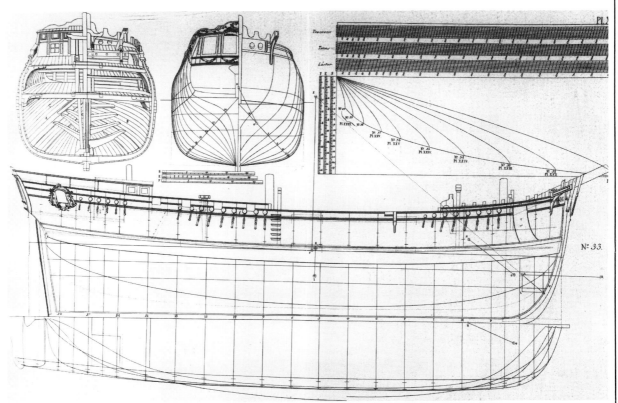

Fig V/6.
Bark *(Merchant Vessels, 5th Class)*, Plate XXIII

Length between perpendiculars	*131ft*
Breadth moulded	*33ft*
Draught as it is on the plan	*17ft 9in*
Draught laden	*18ft 6in*
Burthen	*335 heavy lasts*
Area of the midship frame	*467sq ft*
Area of the load waterline	*3791sq ft*
Displacement	*44,864sq ft*
Total cost of construction	*41,727 Krone*

*Above left is a view looking aft from the midship frame (leftside — A)
and looking forward from the midship frame (rightside — B).*

Above right is scale of burthen for barks
(Sjöhistoriska Museum, Stockholm).

Fig V/5.
Bark *(Merchant Vessels, 5th Class)*, *Plate XXI*

Length between perpendiculars	*155ft*
Breadth moulded	*39ft*
Draught as it is on the plan	*20ft 6in*
Draught laden	*21ft 3in*
Burthen	*521 heavy lasts*
Area of the midship frame	*636sq ft*
Area of the load waterline	*5185sq ft*
Displacement	*71,772 cu ft*
Total cost of construction	*79,473 Krone*

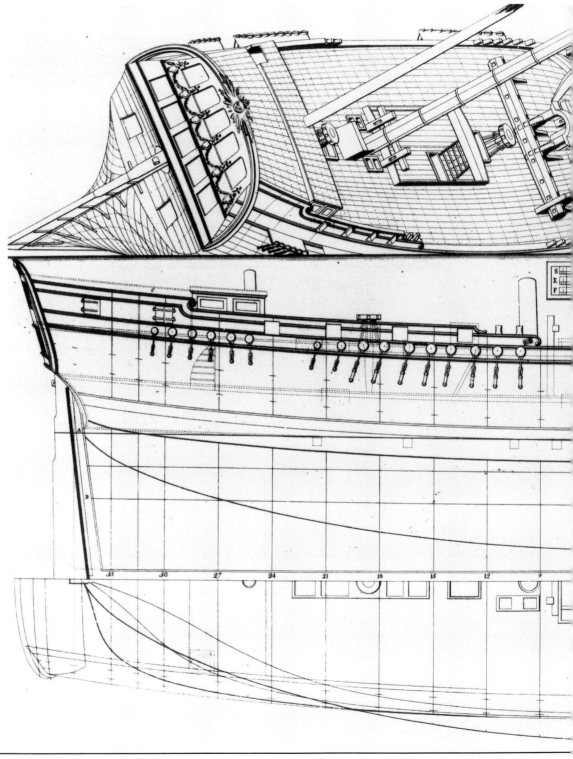

Note. *On the sheer draught, A is the metacentre for waterline A — A, and B*
the metacentre for waterline B — B.
Above left is a view of the deck when the ship is careened
(Sjöhistoriska Museum, Stockholm).

N.º 31

the relevant calculations and measurements, ought to have accompanied the last number. These will now make up a separate volume, but as other work commitments have prevented me, and will continue to prevent me, from fulfilling that commitment, I must humbly ask my subscribers kindly to have patience with that section until next year, 1769.

The promised explanations did not appear until 1775, when his first *Treatise on Shipbuilding* (*Tractat om Skeppsbyggeriet*) was released. Chapter 12 gives explanations for the more important draughts in the *Mercatoria*. According to a letter of Henry Pierrepont of Malmö dated 20 January 1807, a copy of this book was presented to Lord Grenville, the First Sea Lord

of Great Britain, who expressed his appreciation. According to W F Stoot,

> Chapman availed himself of most of the developments of his time, and produced a book that was a great value, and an object lesson for other shipbuilders. It was far in advance of other works of its type produced at this time.

Chapman's opinions about ship construction problems are set out best in the following extract from the *Tractat*:

> It has been the custom in shipbuilding that each tried to do his best, according to his knowledge, to improve the form of ships; where a ship has been built and tested, and

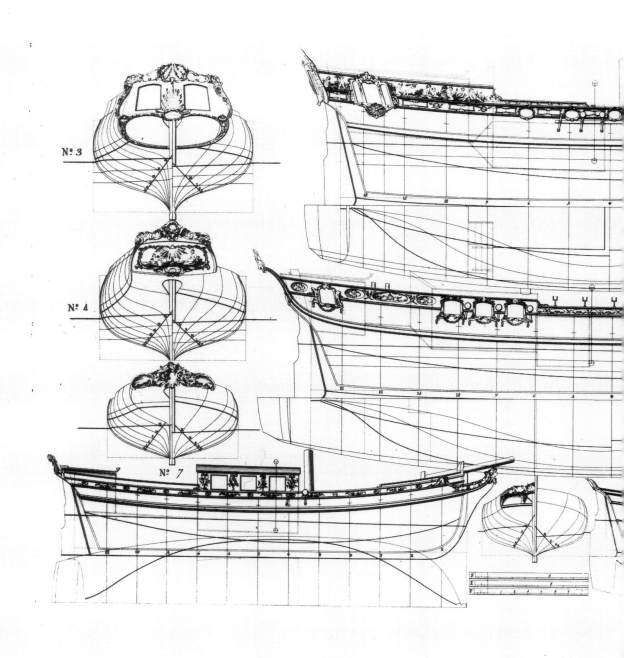

found to have one or other faults, the builder has tried to eliminate these faults when building a second vessel, by changing its form. But more often than not, the second vessel is no better than the first, because the second has other faults. It has even happened that the second ship has similar, and greater, faults than the first. In addition, one has not with certainty been able to determine whether these faults are due to the form of the vessel, or some other circumstances. One discovers that better or worse ships are built by chance, rather than by positive intention, and in consequence thereof, as long as another basis of knowledge for the construction of ships is not available other than experiment and experience, ships are not able to attain perfection beyond that which they now have. It is, for that sake, necessary to find out what it is that will bring that knowledge closer to perfection.

The *Tractat* includes not only explanations of different problems such as the calculation of displacement and centre of gravity, but also Chapman's new method of ship design which he called the Parabolic System (see Appendix 6). Shipbuilders found that for the first time, technical shipbuilding concepts were clearly and systematically defined. For the first time, theoreticians' speculations were converted into usable formulae, and a simple design method was explained, which showed how many features could be computed at the drawing board stage which earlier could be determined only by trial.

The *Tractat* includes Chapman's methods for calculating cargo capacity by the factors of the vessel's length, beam, average draught, and a constant for vessels of beamy or narrow shape. After the publication of the *Tractat*, the old Swedish method of calculating capacity fell into disuse. Chapman's fundamental rule was officially adopted in a 1778 Order-In-Council, which ordered that displacement would be calculated

> so that the vessel's length, beam, and waterlines' heights brought down fore and aft are multiplied together and divided by 112. If the ship be full at extremities, by 110, if it be lean, by 115. The quotient is the burden in lasts.

As a result of this piece of work, Chapman was elected to the Royal Swedish Academy of Science.

The *Tractat* was translated into French in 1779, into English by the Rev James Inman and Dr Wooley, Director of the School of Naval Architecture at Portsmouth, in the early 1800s, and into Russian by Sivers in 1836. Apparently, it was not translated into German until 1936.

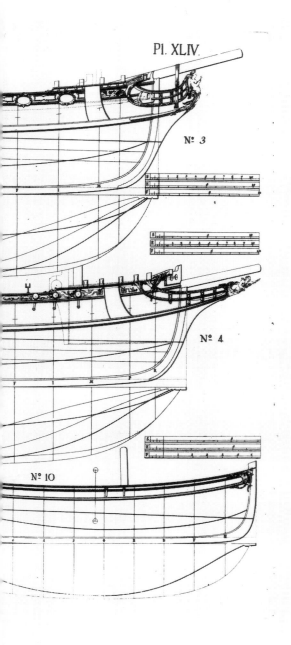

Fig V/7.
Yachts *(Pleasure Vessels — for Sailing)*, Plate XLIV

No 3 Yacht	
Length between perpendiculars	*54ft*
Breadth moulded	*17½ ft*
Draught	*6½ ft*
Displacement	*1420cu ft*

No 4. Schooner	
Length between perpendiculars	*64ft*
Breadth moulded	*17ft*
Draught	*6ft*
Displacement	*1594cu ft*
Pairs of oars	*6*

No 7. Yacht	
Length between perpendiculars	*32ft*
Breadth moulded	*10¼ ft*
Draught	*3½ ft*
Displacement	*250cu ft*

No 10. Yacht	
Length between perpendiculars	*24ft*
Breadth moulded	*7⅝ ft*
Draught	*2½ ft*
Displacement	*160cu ft*

(Sjöhistoriska Museum, Stockholm).

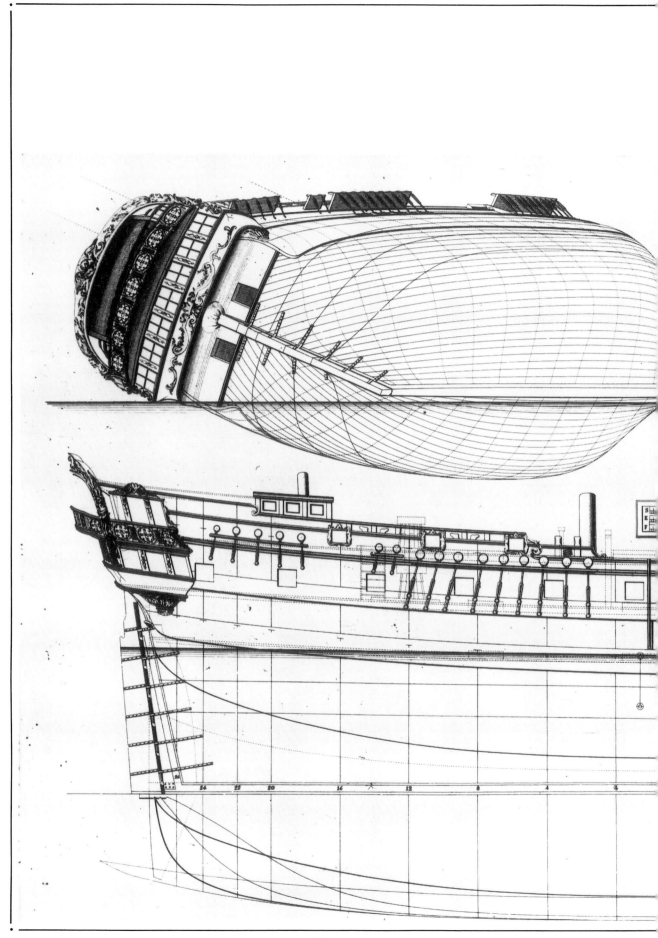

Length between perpendiculars	$135\frac{1}{2}$ ft
Breadth moulded	$34\frac{2}{3}$ ft
Draught	$19\frac{3}{4}$ ft
Burthen	314 heavy lasts
Displacement	52,333 cu ft

Above left is a view of the ship careened
(Sjöhistoriska Museum, Stockholm).

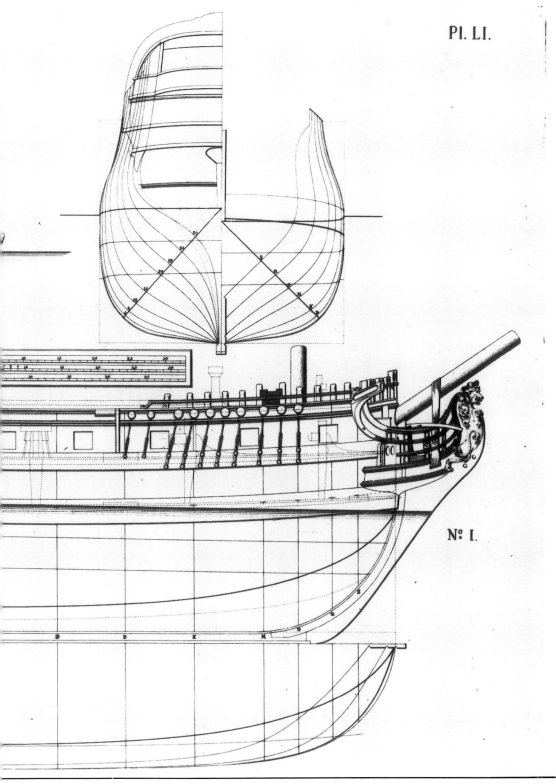

Pl. LI.

Nº I.

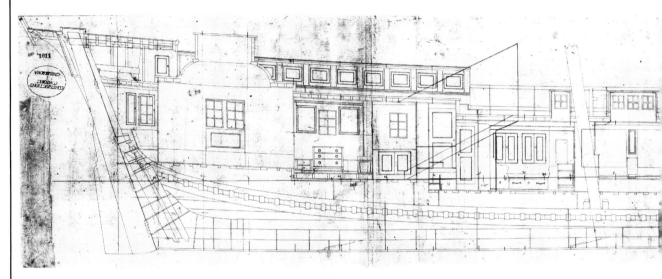

Fig VI/1.
Internal profile of the yacht Amphion
(Krigsarkivet, Stockholm).

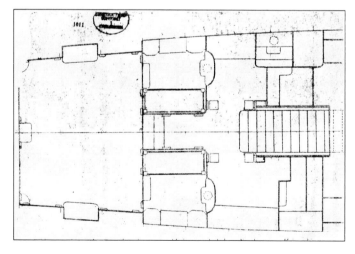

Fig VI/2.
Royal yacht Amphion,
division of space in the royal apartments
(Krigsarkivet, Stockholm).

Six

THE ROYAL PLEASURE CRAFT

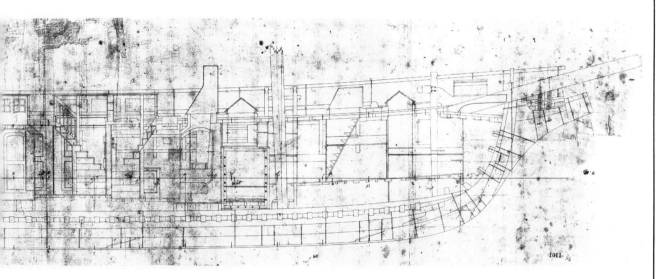

French culture and the luxury of the Versailles court made a great impression on Gustaf III during his stay in France in the 1760s. Louis XV owned nine richly decorated small craft, which were kept at Versailles. Gustaf III wanted similar craft for use at his Drottningholm Palace, as well as a yacht for cruising in the Swedish and Finnish skerries. In 1784, the King visited Venice, where he saw the city's fantastic water fête and took a trip on the Adriatic in richly decorated gondolas. All this made a deep impression, and he conceived a desire to have craft like the gondolas for sailing the confined waters of the Djurgård park. By this time, Chapman was Sweden's leading naval architect, and was already in Crown service. The King ordered him to build pleasure craft for the court, and as a result Chapman designed six boats for Gustaf III and one for his son, Gustaf IV. These yachts reveal the flexibility of Chapman's talents.

In August 1777, Gustaf III approved a Chapman design for a schooner (fig VI/1), 110 feet long and $22\frac{1}{4}$ feet in beam. In letters dated 5 September 1777 and 15 January 1778, Gustaf ordered the Treasury to pay out money to the Djurgård yard 'for a schooner building for us'. The final payment was made in July 1778. The royal schooner-rigged yacht *Amphion* made her maiden voyage that summer. The Chapman drawing describes this vessel as a 'Turunmää vessel for His Royal Majesty to use on Lake Mälar.' Gustaf III reduced the heavy armament Chapman proposed, ordering that only swivel and saluting guns be installed. Built for both rowing and sailing, the *Amphion* was a very poor sailer. Her original schooner rig was changed to a brigantine rig in 1779, but she remained Chapman's least successful yacht.

Fig VI/2 shows the division of space for the royal apartments — note the heads provided on the port side close to the companionway and in each of the royal sleeping cabins. Further aft was the great cabin, which served as an audience chamber, conference room, and dining room (fig VI/3). (Most of the great cabin (fig VI/4) and the stern of the *Amphion* is preserved at the National Maritime Museum at Stockholm.) Chapman was responsible for both the interior and exterior decoration of the yacht, which illustrates his artistic side perfectly, no doubt cultivated during his years in France. He worked in the style of decoration known in Sweden as 'Gustavian', and seems to have been greatly influenced by the famous Swedish artist Jean Eric Rehn.

The rectangular great cabin has four windows in

the stern and two on each side. Seats were built into each side and in the stern. An oval skylight was installed, a cupola with a lantern light. The areas between the windows were decorated with emblems of the arts and sciences, in red-shaded gold against a blue sky. In the roof, the *Amphion*'s lyre swings under a light cloud. The principal colours used in the great cabin were grey, gold, and crimson. All the carving was gilded. The yacht's richly decorated stern taffrail is in the form of a gilded head and a sunburst surmounted by Gustaf III's cipher and two shields showing the minor national coats of arms (fig VI/4). Ehrensvärd had submitted a design for the stern, which included the sunburst motif. No doubt Gustaf III approved of the association with Louis XIV and ordered the

sunburst's inclusion in the final design. The carvings under and over the stern windows belong to the Rococo style, and all the carving on the stern was gilded. The remainder of the stern was painted blue. The *Amphion*'s figurehead, carved by Per Ljung, represents Zeus's son Amphion, the bearer and spreader of culture, with his lyre.

Gustaf III used the *Amphion* as his headquarters ship in the 1788–90 war between Sweden and Russia. In 1790, Gustaf convened in the great cabin the council of war which decided to attack the Russian fleet in the second battle of Svensksund, Sweden's greatest naval victory. It was also in the great cabin, on 17 August 1790, after the signing of the Treaty of Värälä, that Gustaf III bid his officers farewell.

Fig VI/3.
Royal yacht Amphion,
great cabin as preserved at the National
Maritime Museum in Stockholm
(Sjöhistoriska Museum, Stockholm).

The *Amphion* was present at the battles of Fredrik-hamn Viborg, and both battles of Svensksund. She was almost captured at Viborg, where she sailed so badly that the court had to abandon her. Her captain, Lieutenant Eschelsson, refused to give her up or destroy her, in spite of the fact that the High Seas Fleet and the Inshore Fleet had left the battle area. He managed to haul her around the outer point of the Viborg approaches by cables fixed ashore, then hoisted sail, passed under the Russian guns, and made good his escape. On her return to Stockholm, the *Amphion* was hauled ashore for repairs. Carvings by Lars Lindgren replaced the figurehead's arms and lyre, which had been shot away at Viborg.

The *Amphion* served as flagship for the fleet from 1850 to 1858 and as an accommodation ship until 1885, when she was broken up. Luckily, when her operational days were over, some unknown person preserved the stern, the figurehead, the cupola, the skylight, most of the carvings in the great cabin, the beds from the royal sleeping cabins, and four mahogany columns. When the Maritime Museum at Stockholm was built in 1938, on the advice of its architect, Professor Ragnar Östberg, the *Amphion*'s stern was given pride of place in the new building.

When Gustaf III and his suite abandoned the *Amphion* at Viborg, they escaped in the royal galley *Serafims-Orden* (fig VI/8). This galley was built for Gustaf III's predecessor, Adolph Fredrik, in 1719. She was rebuilt at Stockholm between 1769 and 1772, and

Fig VI/4.
Royal yacht Amphion, *stern*
(Sjöhistoriska Museum, Stockholm).

broken up in 1832. Gustaf made his June 1777 state visit to Catherine II at St Petersburg in *Serafims-Orden*. Chapman probably was involved in her reconstruction, but no evidence is available to confirm this. Here are her particulars:

Length	137 feet (40.69 metres)
Beam	20.5 feet (6.09 metres)
Draught	7.4 feet (2.20 metres)
Displacement	235 tons
Oars	22 pairs
Complement	220 men

Armament
One 24-pounder
Two 8-pounders
Twenty-five 3-pounders

The *Serafims-Orden*'s name refers to the highest Swedish order, the equivalent of the British Order of the Garter, usually granted only to royalty.

Chapman designed a variety of royal pleasure craft, though only two, the *Amphion* and the Royal Barge *Wasaorden*, were built under his supervision at the Stockholm yard. The *Wasaorden* (fig VI/9–13) was designed and built at the Djurgård yard in 1774, from drawings completed by Chapman's young pupil J Neuendorf. Chapman built another, similar, barge at the same time, for Prince Heinrich of Prussia. The *Wasaorden* was built entirely of oak, with iron nails. Her particulars were:

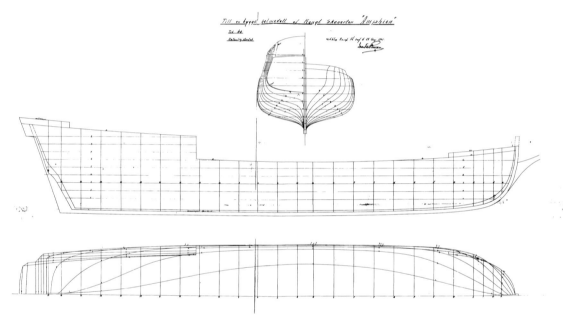

Fig VI/5.
Royal yacht Amphion,
drawing of lines and body plan for the
construction of a model, dated 1901
(Krigsarkivet, Stockholm).

Length	58 feet 4 inches (17.32 metres)
Displacement	106 cubic feet
Beam	10 feet 3 inches (3.04 metres)
Draught	4 feet (1.19 metres)
Complement	2 officers
	1 petty officer
	18 rowers

The *Wasaorden* was originally equipped with two masts for lateen sails as an experiment, but this rig was a failure.

The outer planking and superstructure were painted white, and the inside of the planking, the cabin's interior, and the exterior roof were painted blue. The scantlings were varnished, and the carvings mounted on the bow, stern, and cabins were gilded. Gustaf III's cipher on a blue shield was attached to the bow and stern pieces, and surmounted by gilded crowns. Attached to the centre of the cabin roof was a large crown on a red cushion with gold tassels, and a carving of the Swedish minor coat of arms (three crowns representing the three kingdoms which were united to form Sweden) was mounted on the ceiling. All the decorative carving, inside and outside, was covered with gold leaf. The cabin had windows, including two in the doors. Gustavian-style sofas were placed on each side of the cabin. Its curtains were dark blue damask, woven in Lyons with a motif of the minor coat of arms.

For almost a hundred and fifty years, the *Wasaorden*

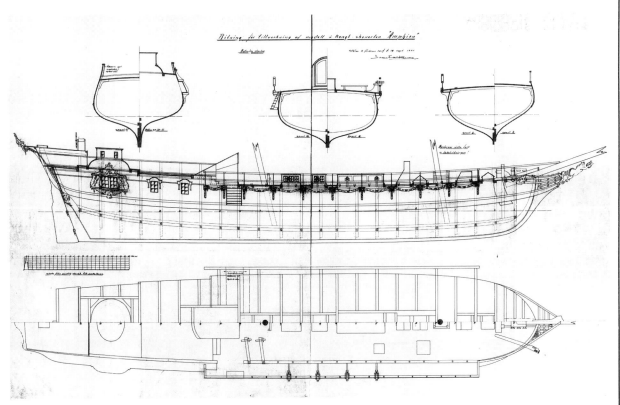

Fig VI/6.
Profile and deck plan of Amphion
taken from the original drawings
and prepared for the making of a model, 1901
(Krigsarkivet, Stockholm).

was used by visiting dignitaries, including Tsar Nicholas II, Kaiser Wilhelm II, and President Poincaré of France. She was destroyed in the Stockholm dockyard fire of 1921, but fortunately, her movables (carpets, cushions, oars, and boat hooks) were stored elsewhere and survived, as did much of her hardware and her tiller, which came through the fire. A public appeal raised funds to build an exact replica of this last royal craft from Chapman's drawings and the many photographs available. The building committee ordered that the replica be built with the same techniques and materials used in the construction of the original vessel.

As Chapman's drawings did not provide sufficient detail of the ornamentation and sculpture, Ragnar Hjört, an architect, designed the patterns and supervised the carving with Professor Curman's advice. Two sculptors were engaged. They made a few changes in the decoration; the cipher of Gustaf V replaced that of Gustaf III on the prow and stern, and the badge of the House of Wasa, the wheatsheaf, is shown immediately below. Portraits of Gustaf III and Gustaf V, framed in gold, hang in the cabin whenever the *Wasaorden* sails. A cylinder containing a scroll of the names of the subscribers to the reconstruction fund is kept in a locker in her stern. Ash oars were made to replace the original heavy pine oars, which are now in the collection of the National Maritime Museum at Stockholm.

In spite of delays caused by a shortage of suitable

Fig. VI/7.
Royal yacht Amphion, *the fully rigged model made from the plans reproduced in Figs VI/5 and 6*
(Sjöhistoriska Museum, Stockholm).

oak planking, the replica was finally completed in time for the opening of the new Stockholm City Hall in 1923. The greatest surprise was that the carpets, curtains, and cushions from the original *Wasaorden* fitted the replica exactly (fig VI/12). Carl XVI Gustaf and Queen Sylvia sailed in her from Skeppsholmen to the palace on their wedding day in 1976 (fig VI/13), and the *Wasaorden* has carried Queen Elizabeth II and the Duke of Edinburgh twice, in 1964 and 1983, from the Royal yacht *Britannia* to the Stockholm Palace to meet Sweden's royal family (fig VI/11).

The only change in the decor and fittings of the replica has been the replacement of the original curtains in 1982. The original curtains finally fell apart, after more than two hundred years of wear. The Swedish Navy discovered that the Lyonnais weavers were still in business and still had the patterns, and were thus able to make a complete new set. The royal barge *Wasaorden* is now safely stored, when not in use, in an unheated concrete building.

Chapman designed four other pleasure craft for Gustaf III. Although these were not built during his Stockholm period, I believe it is appropriate to discuss all Chapman's designs for the Royal Court Yacht Squadron at the same time.

In 1782 at Karlskrona, Chapman designed and built two similar small yachts, the *Amadis* for the king, and the *Esplendian* for Prince Carl (fig VI/14). Their particulars are given on page 96.

Fig VI/8.
Royal galley Serafims-Orden
(Krigsarkivet, Stockholm).

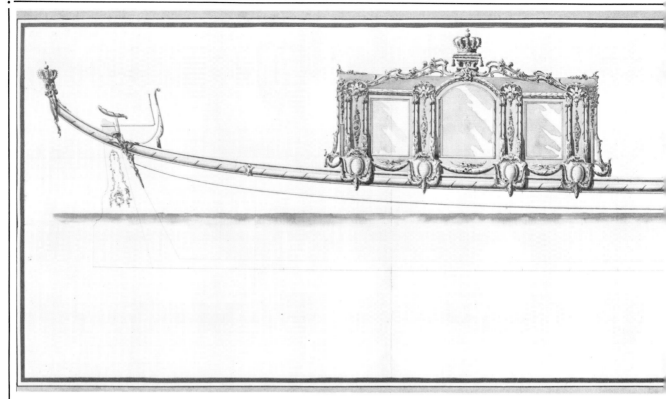

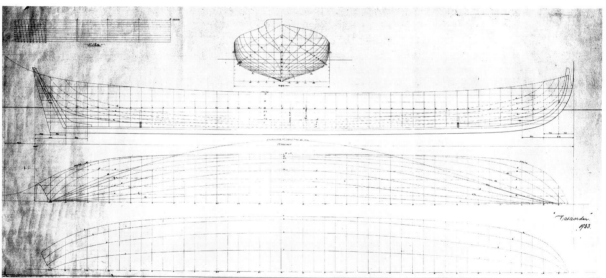

Fig VI/9.
Royal barge Wasaorden, *lines plan*
(Krigsarkivet, Stockholm).

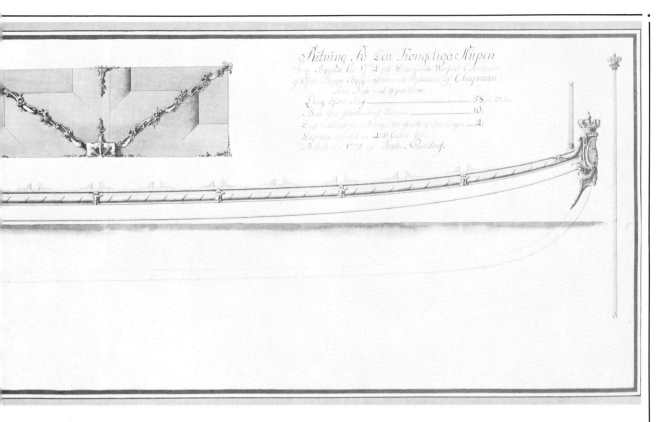

Fig VI/10.
A modern reproduction of the original
sheer plan of the Wasaorden
(Sjöhistoriska Museum, Stockholm).

Fig VI/11.
The replica royal barge Wasaorden
with HM Queen Elizabeth
and Prince Philip on board, May 1983
(Svensk Pressfoto AB).

Length	56 feet (16.63 metres)
Beam	19.3 feet (5.73 metres)
Draught	6 feet (1.78 metres)
Displacement	85 tons
Oars	4 pairs

Armament
Eight 2-pounder swivel guns

The drawing shows that the yachts' spaces were organized, from bow to stern, as crew space, galley, anteroom, saloon, royal apartment, and main cabin. The design of the two yachts proved highly successful. In a letter to Chapman of 6 September 1782, Lieutenant F Waldén described a voyage from Karlskrona to Stockholm:

I have never sailed such an excellent sailer as the *Amadis*. I put to sea in a half gale, and in the afternoon had to take two reefs in the main sail, which went fine. I passed all other sailing vessels that I could see, and in two days arrived at Dalarö, in four days to Stockholm all in the inside belt of the skerries, anchoring at night. We arrived [at] Stockholm at 3pm Monday. The King came on board [from] a dinghy which he steered himself. He sailed the yacht the next day. The yacht is stiff, and in general has good features. I have been commanded to stay with her, but had hoped to avoid this. The ship's christening took place today.

The *Amadis* and the *Esplendian* were transferred to the Inshore Fleet from the Royal Yacht Squadron in

Fig VI/12.
The replica royal barge Wasaorden:
the ornate furnishings and decoration of the cabin
(Reportagebild).

1791. Gustaf III used the *Amadis* from time to time during the battles of Svensksund in 1790, dining aboard her the night before the second battle of Svensksund on porridge without milk, and herrings. The *Amadis* was discarded in 1838.

The *Esplendian*, re-rigged for the occasion, appeared at the 1832 opening of the Göta Canal, which connects the Baltic to the North Sea. Berger's painting of the ceremony shows the *Esplendian*, with King Karl XIV Johan standing at the stern, being drawn into the lock at Mem by the directors of the Canal Company. A crowd of four hundred was present to watch, and later to feast on the company's bounty. Each lock of the canal was opened with similar pomp and ceremony, attended by the king in the *Esplendian*. This occasion

was the highest point of the *Esplendian*'s career, however; in 1869 she was converted, and ended as a lightship at Falsterbo. She was broken up in 1873.

Chapman designed and built two small pleasure craft for the court in 1787. The 'gondolas' (rowing boats) *Delfinen* and *Vildsvinet* (fig VI/15) were richly decorated about the stern with carving, with an effect like a combination of fishes' and peacocks' tails. The figureheads are the dolphin and the wild boar for which the boats were named. In this period, Chapman acquired a collection of Chinese watercolours showing different types of river craft; the similarity of the dolphin and boar figureheads to figureheads in a Qing Ming celebration scroll by Qin Ying clearly shows the source of Chapman's inspiration in this project. The

Fig VI/13.
Royal barge Wasaorden *with their Majesties*
King Carl XVI Gustaf and Queen
Sylvia on board on the occasion of their wedding
(Pressens Bild AB).

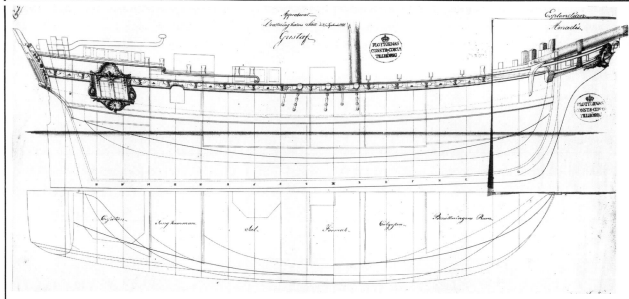

Fig VI/14.
Official drawing of the royal yachts
Explendian *and* Amadis
(Sjöhistoriska Museum, Stockholm).

Fig VI/15.
A photo taken in the 1950s of the gondola Delfinen
In the background is the
Swedish coast defence ship Drottning Victoria
(Sjöhistoriska Museum, Stockholm).

two boats are 23 feet long (6.83 metres), and 14 feet (4.16 metres) in beam. The rowers were concealed by screens decorated with painted shields. The Karlskrona dockyard footed the construction bill of 1200 riksdaler when Chapman sent the two boats as gifts to Gustaf III. Both boats are now preserved at the National Maritime Museum at Stockholm.

In spite of restrictions placed on new construction at the end of the 1788–90 war with Russia, Gustaf III ordered Chapman to design a new pleasure craft. Chapman finished the drafts for a new galley (figs VI/17–19) on 5 May 1791. The king approved the drafts at Haga Palace in the same month. The particulars of the proposed galley were as follows:

Length	124 feet (36.83 metres)
Beam	18 feet (5.35 metres)
Draught	6 feet 8 inches (1.98 metres)
Oars	16 pairs, three rowers to each oar
Rig	Three masts, square sails on the main and the fore, and gaff only on the mizzen.

Armament
4 swivel guns

She was to carry eight days' dry provisions for the ship's company, and enough akvavit, bread, and water for twelve days. The records do not suggest that this vessel was ever built. The precarious state of Sweden's

Fig VI/16.
Royal gondola Delfinen
preserved in the Swedish National
Maritime Museum
(Sjöhistoriska Museum, Stockholm).

finances after the end of the war with Russia probably forced Gustaff III to restrain his personal expenditure on such luxuries.

Chapman built one pleasure craft for Gustaf IV, which was used at the Drottningholm Palace on Lake Mälar. She was similar to the dragon-boats which Chapman knew from his collection of Chinese watercolours. The figurehead and stern decorations were found in the Drottningholm Theatre collection some years ago. Fig VI/20 shows Chapman's drawing of the boat, which was said to have disappeared in a flood in 1819.

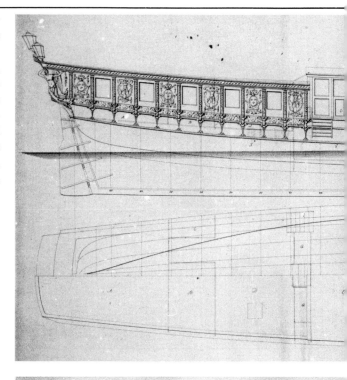

Fig VI/17.
Profile and lines plan of
new royal galley approved by Gustaf III
on 5 May 1791 but never built
(Krigsarkivet, Stockholm).

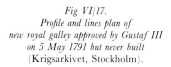

Fig VI/18.
Body plan, section and stem view of proposed royal galley of 1791.

The inscription gives the following detail:
Length 124 feet (36.8 metres)
Beam at waterline 18 feet (5.35 metres)
Draught 6 feet 8 inches (1.98 metres)
To be rowed by 16 pairs of oars 3 men to each sweep
Armament 4 swivel guns
To carry 8 days basic rations for the crew including bread, akvavit and water for 12 days. A supply vessel should accompany the vessel with the crew's main rations with galley and fire wood.
a. Royal cabin
b. Royal sleepoing cabin
c. Garderobe
d. Anti-room
e. Deckhouse
f. Wine store
g. Mess room
h. Rooms for servants
j. Quarters of captain and major domo
k. Water stowage
l. Galley
m. Cook's quarters
n. Court's stores
o. Cable tier
p. Petty Officers' quarters
q. Bread room

signed F H Chapman
(Krigsarkivet, Stockholm).

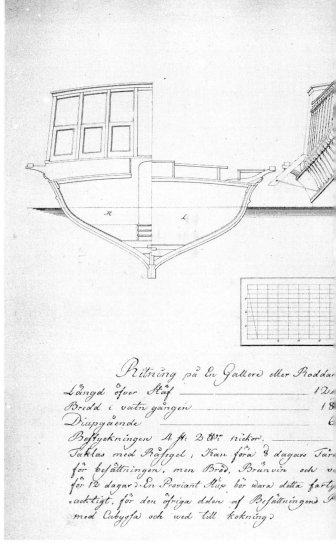

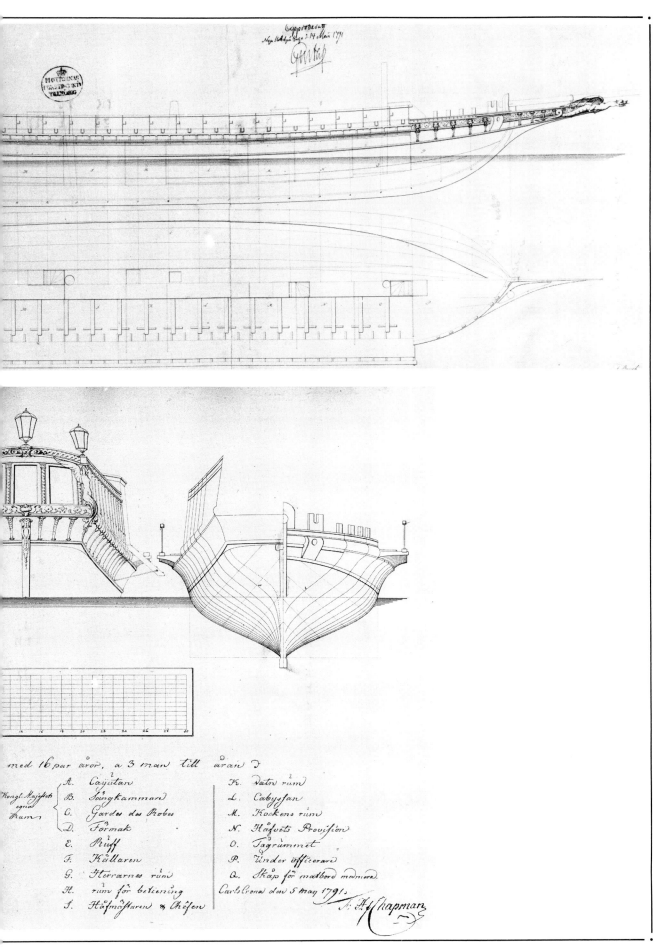

med 16 par åror, a 3 man till åran

Kongl. Majestets
egnat
rum
{
A. Cajutan
B. Sängkammare
C. Gardes des Robes
D. Förmak
E. Ruff
F. Källaren
G. Herrarnes rum
H. rum för betiening
I. Hofmästaren & Chefen

K. Watn rum
L. Cabyssan
M. Kockens rum
N. Hafvets Provision
O. Tagrummet
P. Under officerare
Q. Skåp för matbord mdmira.

Carlscrona den 5 may 1791.
F.H. Chapman

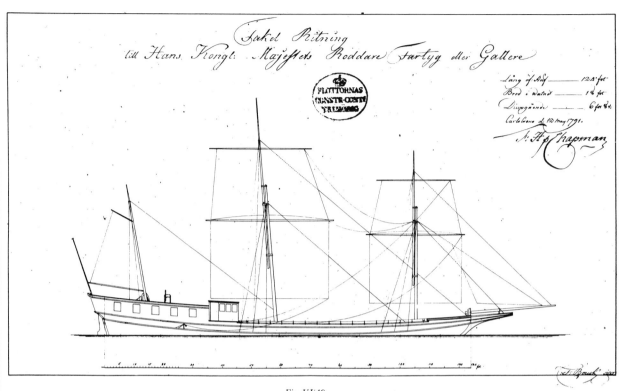

Fig VI/19.
Proposed new royal galley 1791: sail plan
(Krigsarkivet, Stockholm).

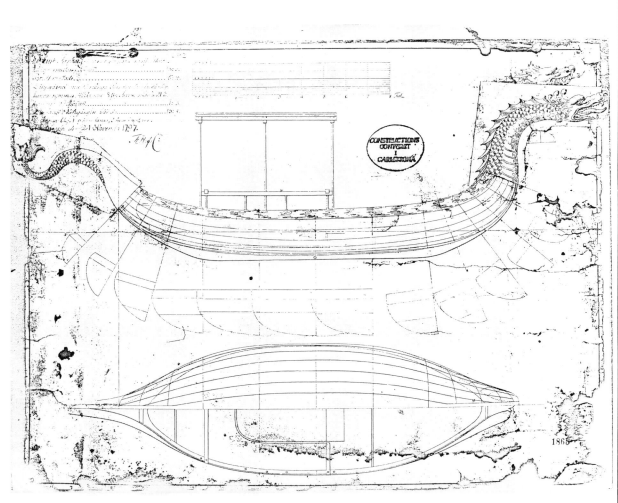

Fig VI/20.
Pleasure craft designed for Gustaf IV
by Chapman for use at Drottningholm
(Sjöhistoriska Museum, Stockholm).

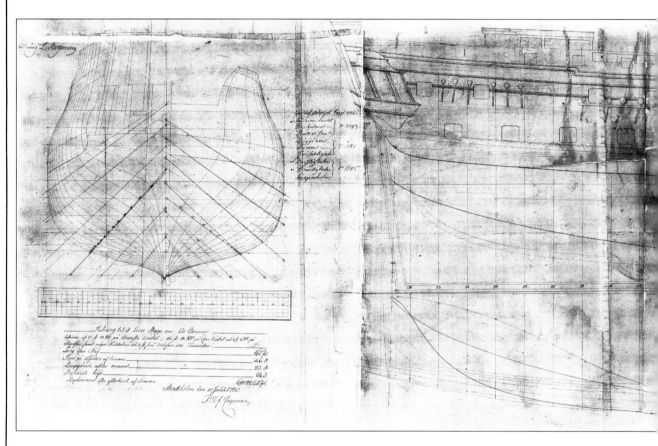

Fig VII/1.
Original sheer draft of the
Kronprins Gustaf Adolph *(improved* Wasa*).*
The plan is damaged and does not reproduce well
(Krigsarkivet, Stockholm).

Seven

THE YEARS OF
TRIUMPH
1780–92

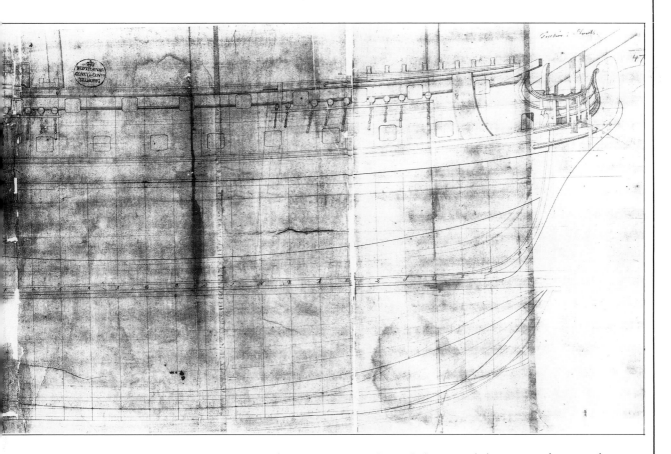

The king's new commission, established in the spring of 1780, was to determine which types of vessels should make up the new fleet. G C Ehrensvärd, at Gustaf III's court, wrote in his diary on 3 April 1780 that

> The commission [comprised of] Duke Carl, Counsellors Sparre and Scheffer, General Trolle, Chapman, [and] Admirals Falkengren, Nordenacker, and Cederström was to make comparisons between Chapman's drawings [and] those of the old ship construction.

They were also to determine whether 'Swedish envy will cause the discarding of the best projects'. Both Chapman and Gilbert Sheldon were to present pro-

posals, and the commission was to become the scene of the major battle between the old and the new shipbuilding techniques.

Gilbert Sheldon knew little of mathematics and physics, and his method for determining a ship's length was probably to multiply the number of guns on one side of the lower gun deck by the most suitable space between the guns, and then add a certain percentage for the forepeak and the extreme stern section. He gave no consideration to the weight of the guns. Sheldon probably calculated the beam in the formula of the time by dividing the estimated length first by three, and then by four. He would add the two results, and then divide the sum by two, producing the maximum beam. Thus, if the length of a ship was to be 168 feet, division by 3 would give a quotient of 56, the division by 4 a quotient of 42. Sheldon would adjust this final figure to suit his hunches, taste, and experience, and consequently, his ship's draught and sailing capabilities would be evident only upon completion. Chapman's enemy, Admiral Tersmeden, advised Gilbert Sheldon to feign illness to avoid appearing before the commission, and to send instead his son Francis, who was well versed in his father's views. Gilbert Sheldon knew he was incapable of defeating Chapman in debate, so he agreed.

The designs of the vessels Chapman offered to the commission were derived from mathematical calculations and consideration of the vessel's purposes, length of sea time, the weight of ammunition, guns, and stores she was expected to carry, and the size of her complement. Chapman designed his ships specifically for service in the shallow waters of the Baltic approaches, and so he had produced a collection of good sailers, handy and easy to steer. But the admirals on the commission refused to approve Chapman's designs, and Chapman savagely attacked Gilbert Sheldon's submissions. Francis Sheldon entered a strong written protest to Chapman's critique, complaining bitterly that his father's drawings had not been filed

> for the Honourable Colonel and Knight af Chapman's sole scrutiny, neither could my father ever have imagined that the honourable Colonel and Knight should wish to assume the sole right to criticize my father's official tasks, which, long before the Honourable Colonel and Knight's time, won a reputation which cannot now be disputed.

Francis Sheldon's protests were swept aside on the hearing's third day, when Trolle astounded the commission by producing a comprehensive plan for the composition and construction of the new fleet. This was something of a pre-emptive strike by Chapman, for he had collaborated with Trolle. Trolle had written to Chapman only a few days before the commission met:

> Please send me today the following information about your planned 60-gun ship. I need it for the 'opus' which I intend to present at the next session. It will be [made so] clear that you will, I hope, be satisfied as well with my whole opus. I need specifications of the timber required for the ship's sides, and in summary, the main points which ought to describe the vessels' features, so that one will wish to order such a vessel. We shall win — you alone ought to have the honour — my task depends on you — keep well.

Trolle's plan urged the commission, when determining the types of ships to be built, to consider in addition Sweden's geographical position. The ships should be built only for use in the Baltic and North Sea, having regard to the strength of Sweden's neighbours and the objectives of Sweden's naval operations. These, Trolle maintained, should be offensive, 'If we are at war with Denmark, take Norway at Copenhagen. If we are at war with Russia, be able to destroy Kronstadt and the Russian fleet.' The new fleet, Trolle continued, should consist of ships with uniform characteristics, namely twenty-one 60-gun ships of the line, fifteen heavy and six light frigates. The new fleet would replace most of the existing fleet which comprised a collection of miscellaneous ships, some over sixty years old. The ships of the line should not carry more than 60 guns so that they could be employed in both the Baltic and the North Sea, which were the only areas Sweden would possibly wage war.

> These ships would gain in stiffness: be able to carry as heavy guns as larger vessels and have the great advantage of having the lower gun deck high above water. Many centuries of experience has taught us that the Baltic is shallow. A 60-gun ship can be of service in those areas where a 110-gun ship cannot move ... sources of ship timber in Europe for the construction of large ships are becoming exhausted: the major powers have begun to reduce the size of their ships for that reason, although some of us demand larger vessels.

Trolle proposed that the new fleet be ready in seven years and should cost no more than the annual appropriations for the navy, unchanged since 1772. He continued:

> If we agree, the best ship constructor which can ever be obtained — af Chapman — should prepare the drawings for the new ships. The new ships should be the improved *Wasa* class. All this ought to be carried out to the letter ... otherwise the whole matter remains on paper and that is no way to defeat the nation's enemies.

The plan was accompanied by detailed estimates for new construction, requiring an annual appropriation of 18 barrels of gold. In addition, a table prepared by Chapman to show the estimated service lives of the existing fleet was filed in support of Trolle's proposals.

Trolle's plans astonished the commission whose reaction was mixed. At first the admirals refused to approve Chapman's drawings and apart from Falkengren, who was not anxious to quarrel with af Trolle, opposed Trolle's proposals, but Duke Carl, who presided as chairman, was eventually persuaded to give his support to Trolle's reform party which gained the majority on the commission and carried the day. Gustaf III approved Trolle's plan on 6 June 1780. He promoted Trolle to the rank of general-admiral and appointed him commander-in-chief of both the Inshore and the High Seas Fleets. The king also placed Chapman at Trolle's service.

The plan required one year for the purchase of timber and for its drying and Chapman stressed the importance of seasoning timber to minimize rot. He considered the time stipulated by the king for the construction of the new fleet far too short but he was forced to comply with the king's orders. The cost of one new 60-gun ship was equal to the then current total annual cost of Sweden's civil administration.

Although the king appointed af Trolle commander-in-chief of both fleets, he retained Wrangel as commander of the High Seas Fleet and Tersmeden as admiral superintendent of the Karlskrona dockyard. Wrangel was so upset at the promotion of af Trolle that he was apparently unapproachable for several days. The king included in his orders to the two admirals an instruction 'to furnish Colonel af Chapman all the assistance which you are able'. Chapman was now forced to work alongside Admiral Tersmeden, who had denounced af Trolle's programme as ridiculous, and who had, some years earlier, strongly criticized Chapman's revolutionary construction of the Inshore Fleet. In particular, Tersmeden had disagreed with Chapman's rigging plans for the skerry frigates, maintaining that Chapman was no seaman. Perhaps this was the king's reason for the division of responsibilities, which put Tersmeden in charge of rigging and armament, and Chapman responsible for construction of the ships' hulls. Chapman reacted adversely to the division of responsibilities: 'ships and sails are two

Fig VII/2.
Gustaf Adolph *model: a close-up of*
the forecastle
(Sjöhistoriska Museum, Stockholm).

Fig VII/3.
A fully rigged waterline model of the ships of the Gustaf Adolph
class. Note the very plain stern decoration
(Naval Museum, Karlskrona).

inseparable things, like birds and their wings. They make up a single body or machine. Accordingly, the constructor ought, when he prepares a draft of a ship, also make the drafts of the sails, types and sizes.'

Tersmeden, a rake and a gambler whose interests were primarily in pleasure, was hardly the co-operative and congenial colleague desirable for Chapman, who normally worked sixteen hours a day summer and winter, and whose only interest was the improvement of the sailing vessel. Naturally there was considerable friction between the two and Trolle had to get the rake and egoistic scientist to agree to work together. On one occasion Trolle had to intervene between Chapman and Tersmeden about the contents of their activity

reports because Chapman had included in one of his particulars of tasks which had been performed by Tersmeden. After some argument with Chapman, Trolle succeeded in persuading his friend to delete those items which should only feature in Tersmeden's report. Chapman was not inclined to give credit to his associates for good work where he could take it himself. Finally, in 1782, after a stormy audience with the king in which Tersmeden complained that Chapman thought too much about the royal wishes and too little of the durability of the ships, Tersmeden retired in return for a handsome ring and the promise of 6000 riksdalers in severance pay. The amount was later reduced to 3000 riksdalers on account of the nation's financial problems, caused in part by the rearmament

Fig VII/4.
A broadside view of the same model.
The rounded corners of the gunports are a
characteristic feature of Chapman's designs
(Naval Museum, Karlskrona).

programme. Chapman was made superintendent of the dockyard and a year later (1783) was promoted to the rank of rear-admiral, but without the pay of that rank (a practice of promotion to higher rank without the additional pay was used in the Swedish Navy even in the present century).

Although he was glad to be promoted to flag rank, Chapman was anxious to acquire the emoluments belonging to his new rank — like all true Yorkshiremen he had a great interest in 'brass'. His opinions about a promotion without an increase in salary reached the king through his friend, af Trolle. The king is reported to have replied, 'I see with distress he is a man like any other and although ... it costs those who rule much worry — keep him happy with fine words ...

and blame my absence abroad ... when I come back to Karlskrona, I shall find many good reasons to surprise Chapman. I shall be glad to have something left in my bag to give him.' When, a year later the king returned from Italy and visited Karlskrona, he made Chapman a Knight Commander of the Wasa Order and authorized the payment of a rear-admiral's salary.

The design of the new ships of the line (fig VII/8) was to be an improvement of the *Wasa* type, with the following dimensions and armament:

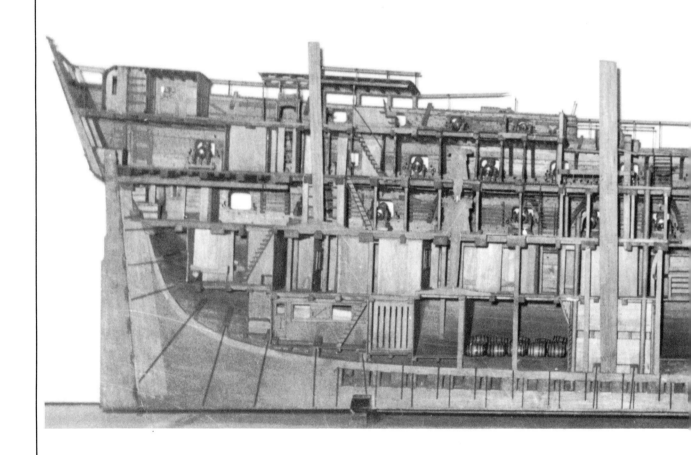

Length overall	166 feet (49.30 metres)
Beam	45¾ feet (13.59 metres)
Max draught full load	19½ feet (5.79 metres)
Height of gun deck above water	7⅓ feet (2.18 metres)
Tonnage	2000
Complement	Total 564 (7 officers, 2 officer cadets, 33 petty officers, 522 other ranks)

Armament	
Twenty-six	24-pounders on gun deck
Twenty-six	18-pounders on upper deck
Eight	6-pounders on quarterdeck

Prior to the outbreak of war with Russia it was intended to replace all the 24-pounder guns with 36-pounders, and to install the Aschling Chapman traversing slide gun carriage. Chapman wanted to reduce the weight of guns and believed that a 36-pounder gun with a shorter barrel would be as effective as the 24-pounder guns with longer barrels. The trials at Kaknäs and on board the *Gustaf Adolph* proved that the 36-pounder gun's maximum range was about 680 metres, and the 24-pounder gun's maximum range about 643 metres. However, the recoil of the 36-pounder gun was much heavier than the 24-pounder's. The admiralty planned to equip all the fifteen 60-gun ships of the line with 36-pounders to be placed on the lower tier, and to move the 24-pounders to the upper deck. It ordered

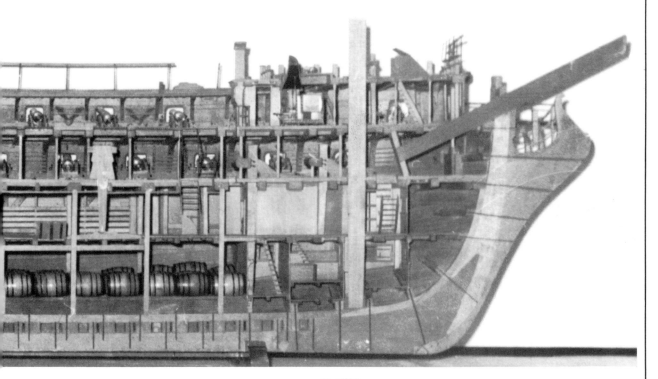

Fig VII/5.
A sectional half-model of the ships
of the Kronprins Gustaf Adolph *class,*
showing internal construction and fittings
(Naval Museum, Karlskrona).

390 36-pounders, and 420 24-pounders, but delays in delivery resulted in only six of the new ships of the line being armed with the heavier guns in time for the war.

Ten ships in all were eventually built in accordance with the same drawings and Chapman's parabolic method (see Appendix 6 for description). They were 19 metres longer than the *Wasa*, had a sharper stern but the same beam and draught. The *Wasa*'s design had been criticized because of its low bulwarks, her commander complaining that they provided insufficient protection for the crew manning the guns on the upper deck, so the bulwarks were raised slightly in the new ships. The total cost of each fully completed 60-gun ship was estimated to be 78,000 riksdalers.

The particulars of the larger frigates (fig VII/6)

were as follows:

Length overall	156 feet (46.33 metres)
Beam	40 feet (11.88 metres)
Draught (full load)	17½ feet (5.20 metres)
Tonnage	1360
Height of gun deck above water	7 feet (2.10 metres)
Complement	342

Armament
Twenty-six 18-pounder guns
Fourteen 6-pounder guns

The 18-pounders were replaced with 24-pounders

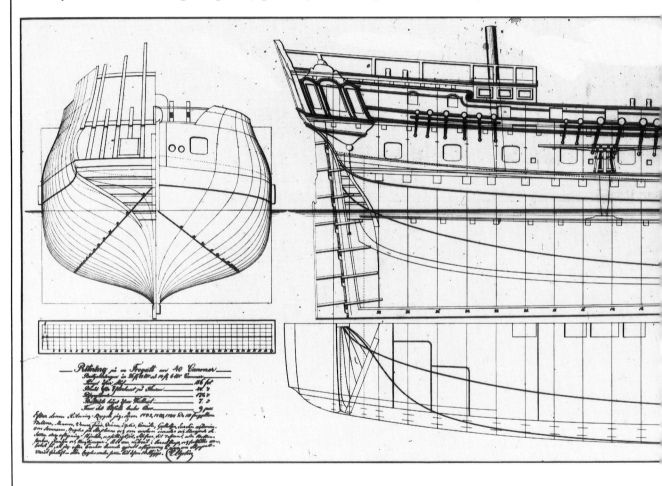

before the outbreak of the 1788 war with Russia. The estimated total cost of each fully fitted ship was 41,000 riksdalers.

The small frigates' dimensions and armament were as follows:

Length overall	139 feet (41.28 metres)
Beam	36½ feet (10.84 metres)
Draught (full load)	15⅚ feet (4.70 metres)
Height of gun deck above water	6¾ feet (2.00 metres)

Armament
Twelve 24-pounder guns
Ten 4-pounder guns

The estimated total cost of each completed vessel of this class was 34,000 riksdalers.

All three classes of vessels were designed to carry five months' stores, and water for two and a half months.

As mentioned earlier, the navy considered the *Wasa*'s upper works insufficient for the crew's protection. Chapman gave the new series of ships of the line higher bulwarks which enabled a gangway of three deck planks width to be fitted at the ship's side. These gangways connected the forecastle and quarterdeck. The forecastle planking was fixed to the deck beams and all ropes for the headsails and anchor catting gear were handled from that deck; the purpose of these gangways was to allow the crew to move quickly from one part of the vessel to another. Chapman extended

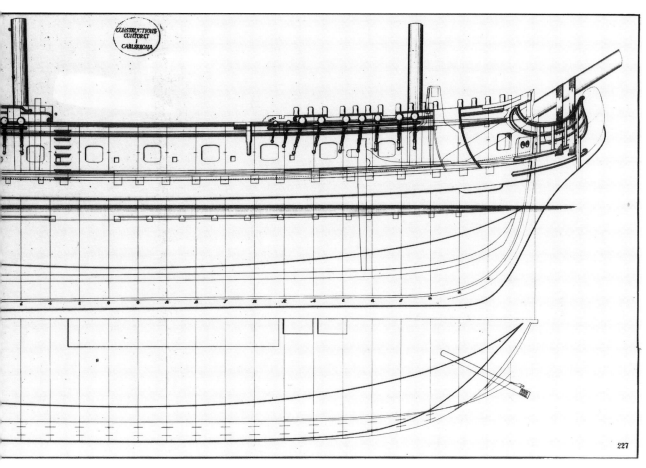

Fig VII/6.
Original sheer draft for the Bellona *class frigates*
(Sjöhistoriska Museum, Stockholm).

the quarterdeck almost to the main mast and eliminated the poop deck which had been a feature of older vessels of this size. Other improvements were to increase water storage by allowing more space in the hold for barrels, and arranging for the magazines to be lit from outside by lamps with reflectors. The new ships were to stow the anchor cables amidships on the orlop deck between the main mast and the main hatch as Chapman believed that moving the cable aft would help reduce the vessels' pitching. The *Wasa* draught (fig IV/14) shows the anchor cable stowed in the hold aft of the fore mast while the cutaway model of the new series (fig VII/5) shows the anchor cable stowed amidships on the orlop deck. Stowage of shot and powder remained unchanged.

Trolle agreed to Chapman's proposals that all the ships of the line be built entirely of oak. The frigates on the other hand were only to be built partially of oak with the outside planking from the keel to the wales and the ceiling to be constructed entirely of pine. Trolle agreed that where curved oak was unavailable, knees be made from root pine. Chapman proposed pine be used extensively in repair work on older vessels. He pointed out that although the estimated life of a pine-built ship was only two-thirds of an oak-built vessel, the costs were one-third less.

Trolle proposed that the new ships be sheathed with iron, since he considered copper sheathing to be too expensive. The type of sheathing used on the larger Swedish ships up to 1780 consisted of a layer of tar

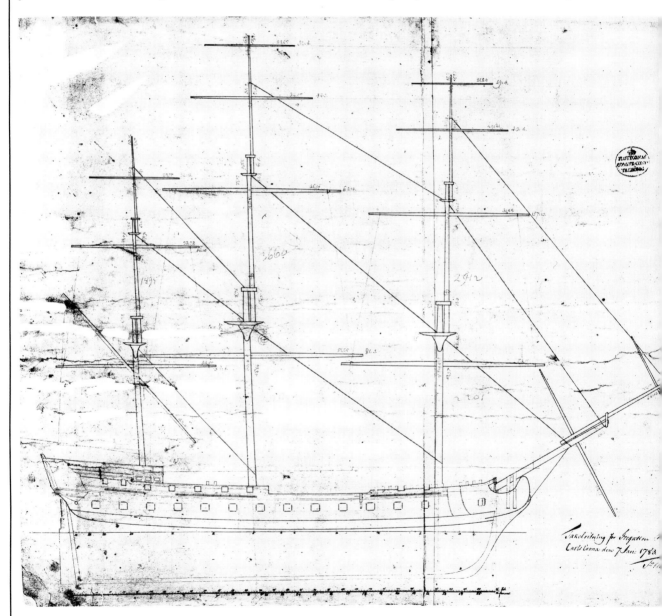

and cow hair covered by thin planking. However, not-withstanding the costs, two frigates and a cutter were fitted with copper sheathing for voyages to the Swedish West Indian colony of St Barthelmy in 1784 and 1785. The frigate *Diana* which made a voyage to the Mediterranean in 1787 was also copper-sheathed.

Copper sheathing seems, however, to have been more extensively used because Chapman made a request to the King in a dispatch dated 2 September 1790 for permission to remove copper sheathing from five ships, including the frigate *Sprengporten*, because of the reaction of the iron fastenings to copper sheathing. As the Baltic is free of the teredo or ship worm, the removal of copper sheathing was not impractical. However, in the 1809 combined operations with British

Fig VII/7.
Bellona *class frigates:*
sail plan
(Sjöhistoriska Museum, Stockholm).

copper-sheathed ships in the Baltic against Russia, it was apparent that the British ships sailed faster than the Swedish vessels — although a contributory factor was the superior seamanship of the experienced British crews. There are apparently no records to show whether Trolle's proposals for iron sheathing were ever implemented even on an experimental basis.

DOCKYARD BUILDINGS

In his autobiography Chapman states that he promised Gustaf III to complete three ships of the line and three frigates annually, provided that he was allowed one year in which to prepare the final drawings, assemble material and organize labour resources both for ship construction and dockyard improvements. Already in 1777, Gustaf III had approved the construction of new buildings in the Karlskrona dockyard for the storage of ammunition and naval equipment which had been recommended by the Sparre, Scheffer, and Chapman investigating committee. Chapman was now to be responsible for the extension of the dockyard's facilities. Thus, from October 1780, Chapman became involved in the provision of additional shipbuilding slips, also in the construction of administrative building stores, workshops, a museum, and repairs to the dry-dock gates. All were necessary for the construction and maintenance of the new fleet. Chapman designed five of the buildings for the dockyard. He planned, with the aid of Extra Lieutenant Mechanicus Lidström, an additional four-storey building to be known as No 1 Store (figs VII/11 and 12). The construction took from 1781 to 1784. The building, which still stands, was to house the equipment for twelve ships of the line, and was divided vertically into as many sections, one for each ship, except for the basement which contained two circular beds on which hempen cables could be coiled down and which had a drainage system to carry off water seepage. The second floor was to hold spars and all standing and heavy rigging, and the third was to contain running rigging, sails, hammocks etc. C August Ehrensvärd changed the exterior design on his return from Italy, which shows the influence of Italian renaissance architecture. Chapman designed the interior, in which the partitions between four sections were stone fire walls without openings. He gave his reasons in a letter to Ehrensvärd dated 6 March 1788:

> In my memorandum, I did not state the reasons for lining the armoury with stone. The reason is that if the walls were built of thin planks an evil individual on a dark night could cut a hole in these planks and thrust in fire, and since the buildings contents are flammable, everything would be destroyed; the stone walls prevent this happening.

When the king during an inspection tour saw the building, he is reported to have said, 'Is it really only of stone? The costs were so high I could have believed it was built of silver.'

Chapman designed the guardhouse at the entrance to the dockyard, a fire station, the rigging building and a small workshop for the figurehead carver, Törnström, which still stands today (fig VII/13). He also designed the museum and hiring hall building (fig VII/14). It has a Doric temple façade of stone with the pillars made of wood and a gable bearing Gustaf III's cipher. A clock tower, in the Swedish eighteenth century manor house style, crowns its roof. This façade was superimposed upon a very ordinary two-storey stone house. The upper floor of the building was to contain not only some hundred models made by the Sheldons, but also Chapman's own collection which he had sold to the crown. Tersmeden has described the collection in his memoirs as follows:

We made a tour to see the new models which have been made in accordance with Chapman's drawings for a frigate and a ship of the line to the scale of $\frac{1}{2}$ inch to the foot together with their rigging and armament — all admirably made. Also under construction are two half-models to show the division of space between the keel and the quarterdeck. Six craftsmen are employed here daily. No other dockyard in Europe has such a collection of models of ships used in Europe or Asia.

Fig VII/8.
A framing model of the frigate Bellona
on the stocks
(Naval Museum, Karlskrona).

The lower part of the building was used as a hiring hall for dockyard labour and for the enrolment of naval personnel. Chapman arranged for the construction of a slip and building for boat construction, a new forge and buildings to house the labour employed in the yard, as well as schools and a hospital.

In 1780, Chapman designed for himself and his closest colleagues a two-storey house, with two wings to be built of wood in the eighteenth century Swedish manor house style. The house, with its sixteen rooms, two wings and outhouses, was to be erected adjacent to the outside walls of the dockyard. Trolle approved the proposal and required Tersmeden to supervise the construction. The latter's comment was: 'I am taken aback by the pretensions he has to live so grandly in contrast to what I have seen in England, Spain, and Holland. And I am lost in thought, how dangerous it is when artists are raised up to an unusual status from their proper stations.' The house is still occupied by the dockyard superintendent (fig VII/15). The main reception room, which is a good example of Gustavian interior decoration, is decorated in light blue and silver, with the portraits of all Europe's rulers of Chapman's time on the walls. Incidentally, Chapman's walking-stick-cum-chair used when making his rounds of the dockyard, is still preserved in this house.

Lidström, under the general supervision of Chapman, designed a special building and the equipment for

Fig VII/9.
A fully rigged waterline model of the frigate Bellona,
very similar in style to the
Gustaf Adolph *model in Figs VII/3 and 4*
(Sjöhistoriska Museum, Stockholm).

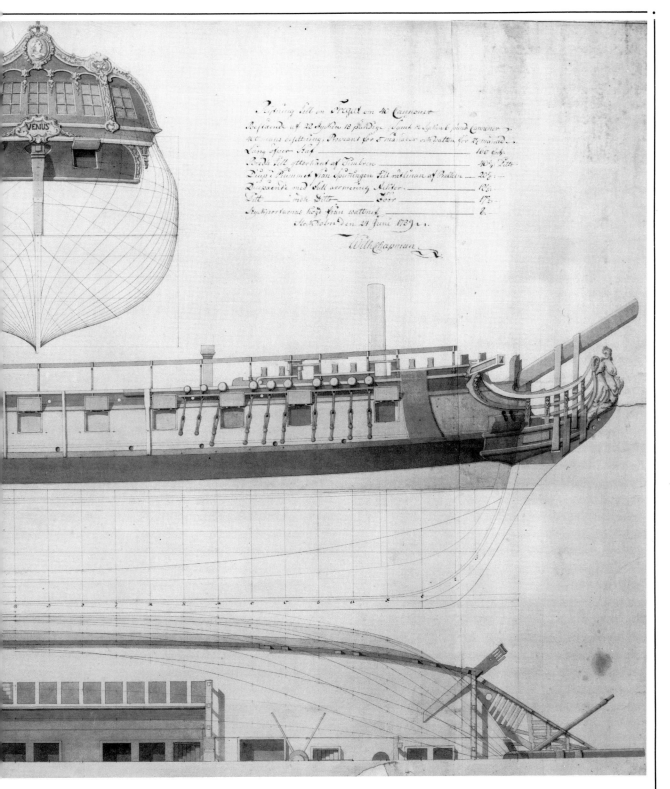

Fig VII/10.
By way of contrast with the above, this Danish drawing of the
frigate Venus *(a sister of* Bellona*) is dated 1789 so shows the ship as*
completed. The decorative work is noticeably
more elaborate, and the stern and quarter galleries more
conventional
(Rigsarkivet, Copenhagen).

à grinding mill (fig VII/16). The building, completed in 1782, was octagonal in shape and similar to the sawmill which Chapman designed for the Djurgård yard, Stockholm. To operate the machinery, a horse on the upper storey walked a circular track harnessed to a shaft which turned a large wooden cog wheel on the floor below. The cog wheel, through a train of wooden gears, operated eight grinding stones, drills, and lathes fixed on the lower floor. The machinery was used extensively for block-making and the grinding of block sheaves. The records show that eight covered saw benches were erected for straight and curved lumber, as Chapman apparently did not consider it necessary to construct a mechanical sawmill similar to the one built for the Djurgård yard; perhaps he believed that either the available funds could be used for other more productive purposes, or that there was sufficient labour available to continue with the old saw pit methods.

THE GREAT SHIPBUILDING PROGRAMME 1782–85

Chapman was successful in obtaining some 170,000 cubic feet of oak (45,000 cubic metres) from the Crown-owned forests. About 1800 soldiers were employed to carry out the felling. He also obtained additional supplies of oak from Poland and Swedish Pomerania. As regards supplies of timber from Swedish private sources, Chapman insisted that the vendors be paid in cash instead of promissory notes, but he preferred for economic reasons to use the Crown resources wherever possible. He wrote:

> All this brings one to the conclusion that such a task required annually certain quantities of many different types of materials — such an extensive operation cannot work smoothly without a fixed work plan or regulations which should always be before one's eyes. And he who objects to such a plan's inauguration must be very ignorant of that which concerns a navy's perpetual maintenance.

It is difficult to determine the size of the dockyard work force during this period of intensive activity. (Karlskrona was at this time Sweden's third largest city having a population of about 11,000.) In 1784, about 1150 personnel were employed in the dockyard amongst which there were about 550 carpenters, 300 bolt- and nail-makers, mast-makers, sawyers and bridge-builders. Two regiments of marines were stationed in Karlskrona, and all the personnel of at least one of them were employed in the new construction programme. Some 800 men of the Helsingland regiment, a force normally stationed in the northern part of the country, were marched to Karlskrona in 1780 to work in the dockyard. About 100 long-term convicts were employed in the anchor forge as Swedish criminal law of the day often sentenced those convicted of serious crimes to long or life terms at hard labour in the forge. The dockyard authority paid no wages to these unfortunates. This method of manning the forge lasted until the middle of the nineteenth century. It is interesting to note that Gustaf III permitted the immigration of skilled Jewish tradesmen at this time. One, Fabian Philip, was allowed to settle in Karlskrona to open a factory to weave sail cloth for the fleet, and by 1786 Philip had eighteen looms working and some 300 women spinning linen.

All those working in the dockyard were subject to naval discipline — a situation which lasted until 1919. A worker who was absent for one day without permission was treated as a deserter and became liable to imprisonment. Punishment for smoking in a forbidden area was two to four days' arrest; the unfortunate smoker was sentenced to be locked up during non-working hours. An armed escort would take the miscreant in the morning to his place of work, and return him to his cell when the working day ended — and, of course, he lost his pay during his imprisonment. Carpenters, sail-makers, riggers, rope-makers, who normally served afloat, were employed in the construction of the new fleet and on the many other dockyard construction projects. In 1782, Chapman forced the pace of ship construction to such an extent that Sundays became an ordinary working day in spite of objections from the Church. To encourage rapid completion of the shipbuilding programme and the construction of the new buildings, Chapman instituted a system of bonus payments which he called 'discretions'. For example, in March 1784 he promised the builder of the hiring hall and museum, a bonus of 8 ducats for the erection of the framework by mid-May and, an additional 8 ducats if the building, including floors, windows and columns, was completed by mid-July in the same year: it was. Chapman maintained that every 100 riksdalers paid out in bonuses resulted in a saving of 1000 riksdalers to the Crown. In his report to Trolle, he emphasized that these payments to the labour force were essential if the programme was to be completed within the time frame laid down by the king.

In 1781, when af Trolle and Chapman took over effective management of the Karlskrona dockyard, there was only one incomplete ship on the stocks, namely the *Hedvig Elisabet Charlotta*, a sister ship to the *Wasa*. In a letter to af Trolle in 1782, Chapman wrote that he had paid shipwright Uhrun $66\frac{2}{3}$ riksdalers as a bonus for having completed the *Charlotta* before the end of August of that year. To speed up the completion of the new construction, Trolle reduced the amount of repair work by discarding some of the older vessels, which released additional labour for the new construction.

The 60-gun ships and frigates were built together, one on each type of pairs of neighbouring slips. Vessels

Fig VII/11.
Karlskrona dockyard No 1 store building
designed by Chapman
and Ehrensvärd, seaward view
(Naval Museum, Karlskrona).

———————•———————

Fig VII/12.
Karlskrona dockyard No 1 store
building, land view
(Naval Museum, Karlskrona).

———————•———————

of each type were built to one standard set of drawings for which Chapman had a series of templates made. To speed up the work of making the templates, which were vital to the building programme, he promised shipwright Pousset a bonus of 20 ducats if he and his force completed them by the end of May 1782. The promise of the bonus had its effect and the templates were completed by the required date. The timbers were cut in accordance with the templates and then brought to the yard and stored close to the slips where they were to be used. The special curved timbers for the stern section and the extreme forward part of the bow were cut and shaped in accordance with special moulding cradles which were placed close to the building slips (fig VII/17 is a photograph of two models of these moulding cradles held by the Naval Museum at Karlskrona).

This system introduced by Chapman was an early form of prefabrication of ships, as impressive in its way as the mass-produced Liberty ships of Henry Kaiser almost 160 years later. Chapman made some savings by constructing masts of several pieces of pine which were skilfully coaked and scarfed together. Chapman, always concerned with cost reduction, maintained that by this method he had saved the Crown one-third of the usual cost of masts made in the royal dockyard.

The French Government, which had advanced monies for the intensive naval programme, seems to have kept an eye on its progress. Baron Evert W Taube wrote to Chapman on 4 April 1781:

Fig VII/13.
Karlskrona dockyard's Törnström's
figurehead workshop designed by Chapman
(Naval Museum, Karlskrona).

His Majesty has instructed me to request you to send him one of the most fine examples of your work which His Majesty wishes to send to the French Minister for War, the Marquis de Castries. His Majesty has also instructed me to ask you if there is any drawing or description of the dockyard buildings in Karlskrona, if so, His Majesty also wishes to have it.

Over the three years, 1782–85, ten ships of the line and ten frigates were built. The hulls were built up to the wales and then launched (fig VII/18) and the rest of the construction was carried out afloat. Thus a ship of the line and a frigate were laid down at the same time and would be launched on the same day. The following table of construction dates of the twenty ships shows that the building period of the first six ships averaged 122 days, and the remainder about 52 days, which suggests that Chapman's prefabrication methods were very successful.

The choice of names of the ships of the line was a form of praise for Gustaf III. The following interpretation can be given to them in translation. *Crown Prince Gustaf Adolph* [rules the] *Fatherland* [with] *Affection, Justice, Virtue* [and] *Honour,* [chooses] *Prudence, Audacity, Manliness* and *Bravery* [as his advisers]. The names of the frigates were taken from the classical antiquity which were of great interest to the eighteenth-century Swedish intellectuals.

Chapman gave orders that the timber used for the construction of the twenty vessels should not be given

Fig VII/14.
Karlskrona dockyard, hiring hall and
Museum building designed by Chapman
(Naval Museum, Karlskrona).

Ship of the Line	Frigate	Keel laid, Stem- & Stern-posts Raised	Dates Launched	No of Days on Slips
Kronprins Gustaf Adolph	*Bellona*	18.7.1782	6.11.1782	111
Fädnerslandet	*Minerva*	6.11.1782	31.3.1783	145
Ömheten	*Venus*	31.3.1783	19.7.1783	110
Rättvisan	*Diana*	19.7.1783	2.9.1783	45
Dygden	*Fröja*	1.5.1784	6.7.1784	66
Äran	*Thetis*	6.7.1784	28.8.1784	53
Försiktigheten	*Camilla*	28.8.1784	23.10.1784	56
Dristighenten	*Galathea*	23.5.1785	7.9.1785	45
Manligheten	*Euredice*	9.7.1785	31.8.1785	53
Tapperheten	*Zemire*	31.8.1785	21.10.1785	51

Fig VII/15.
Karlskrona dockyard, superintendent's
house designed by Chapman
(Naval Museum, Karlskrona).

the customary smooth finish. 'These ships' he is reported to have said 'are there to be shot to pieces'. As a result of the pace of construction being continuously increased to meet the royal wishes, in the case of the frigate *Euredice*'s planking, for example, the bark was not completely removed.

Af Trolle was able to report to the King on 7 November 1782:

> Yesterday morning the 60-gun ship *Kronprins Gustaf Adolph* and the 40-gun frigate *Bellona* were launched, ready after four months of construction. At 1pm on the same day the keels, stem- and sternposts of the 60-gun *Fädnerslandet* and the 40-gun frigate *Minerva* were laid and raised, for which vessels all frames and other timbers were sawn and fitted

in the same four-month period . . . which has never before occurred at your Majesty's dockyards.

Chapman, referring to the payment of bonuses to the dockyard workforce in a letter to af Trolle dated 7 February 1782, pointed out that this was the only way to encourage the dockyard personnel to work quickly. He added that he believed if he was not able to offer bonuses for fast completion of ships and buildings, the dockyard workers would return to their former inefficient ways. He is reported to have said, 'In the event I am not provided with funds for this purpose and the old ways return then I shall be unhappy and die.'

Trolle sent Chapman's letter, together with his own

Fig VII/16.
Model of grinding mill and drill stands
designed under the direction of
Chapman for the Karlskrona dockyard
(Naval Museum, Karlskrona).

Fig VII/17.
Models of bow and stern moulding cradles
designed by Chapman for the major
shipbuilding programme
(Naval Museum, Karlskrona).

covering letter, to the king. Trolle wrote praising Chapman's unselfish efforts, and stating that he used his own funds to pay bonuses for the completion of the *Hedvig Elisabet Charlotta* so that it could be ready for sea by the spring. Trolle mentioned Chapman's loss of the Djurgård shipyard salary as a result of his move to Karlskrona, and that Chapman's removal expenses had not been paid. He also stressed that the payment of bonuses was unavoidable during a period of labour shortages. Trolle recommended that Chapman should be paid an additional 666⅔ riksdalers a year so long as the new construction programme was continued. The King agreed, and authorized Chapman's salary increase to become effective from 22 March 1782. In November 1782, the king wrote a letter of praise to af Trolle and Chapman:

> The management by which the work at the dockyard is continued, we attribute not only to your supervision, but also to Chapman's zeal and insight and we have to attribute your efforts to our fleet's growth. We instruct you to forward to Chapman an expression of our particular and gracious satisfaction with what we consider the remarkable diligence towards the work and the honourable affection for our service.

The king had issued a royal decree that no figure-heads or decorations were to be fitted to the ships of the Royal Navy without the approval of the Royal Academy of Painters and Sculptors. This decree, as mentioned earlier, was the result of the king's displeasure at seeing a lopsided figurehead supposed to represent him on the *Konung Gustaf Adolph*. It therefore became important to find a skilled artist to carve the figureheads for the new fleet. Trolle wrote in a letter dated 26 February 1781, 'The navy has needed for some years a clever sculptor who has the ability to make shapes and human likenesses for galleys and warships from 10 to 14 feet in height — there seems to be no one in Sweden, perhaps we should initiate a search in Hamburg.' C A Ehrensvärd, Chapman's friend replied, that he would search for a sculptor. It seems that one Törnström, a pupil of J B Masreliez of France, had completed some carvings for the Chapman-built ships at the Djurgård yard, and carvings for the Royal Palace in Stockholm. Masreliez had trained Törnström as a wood carver and cabinet maker, but the latter had no formal training at the Academy of Art. Chapman most likely encouraged him to move to Karlskrona where he became the dockyard's carver. From time to time Chapman drew sketches of the figureheads he considered appropriate for each ship; Törnström was to make wax models from these sketches, which in turn were sent to the king and the Admiralty in Stockholm for approval. Chapman on one occasion accused Törnström of delays in completing a wax model, stating it was an easy feat to make a wax model from a drawing. Törnström rolled the model into a ball of wax and suggested that the dockyard superintendent should try himself. Chapman failed and returned the ball of wax to Törnström and is understood never to have complained again. Törnström could take up to two years to complete a figurehead out of oak on the heroic scale required for the ships of the line and as a result many of the ships were without figureheads. It was rumoured that Ehrensvärd's wife was a model for either the frigate *Euredice*'s figurehead (fig VII/20) or the medallion on the stern. As neither Chapman nor Törnström had visited Greece or Italy, the figures represented by the carvings hardly corresponded with the classical styles. Törnström was initially paid on a piece-work basis, and when naval construction ceased in 1790, making a living to support his ten children became far from easy. However, he was able to get work for local churches. Many of Törnström's figureheads are preserved at the Naval Museum, Karlskrona and in the National Maritime Museum, Stockholm.

In March 1784, Chapman's great friend and supporter, af Trolle, died suddenly at the age of fifty-four from a cold, presumably followed by pneumonia. Chapman was reported to have cried like a child on hearing the news. King Gustaf was in Italy at the time of af Trolle's death, but he had provided for emergencies by leaving letters to be opened by the Privy Council's chairman, Counsellor Creutz, if such events took place. Creutz called a meeting of the Privy Council, and broke the seal of one of the king's letters which directed that C A Ehrensvärd, then thirty-nine, was to be appointed as fleet admiral in succession to af Trolle. Chapman was pleased with the appointment since he had got to know the young Ehrensvärd when serving under his father with the Inshore Fleet at Sveaborg. Although he was a trained officer of the Inshore Fleet, Ehrensvärd's true interests lay primarily in the arts, which he had studied both in Italy and France. His sketches and his studies on the philosophy of art are still highly regarded in the Nordic countries.

King Gustaf visited Karlskrona in 1781 to inspect the neutrality squadron before it set sail for the North Sea. He came again to Karlskrona in September 1784 to see the progress made in the construction plan, and to determine if Ehrensvärd had been the best choice to succeed af Trolle. He never possessed the same confidence in Ehrensvärd that he had in af Trolle. Gustaf asked Chapman's old enemy Tersmeden if he 'did not consider that the dockyard work is now being expedited with greater speed'. Tersmeden is reported to have replied, 'Almost too fast, because a fleet built of raw timber and in such haste can only result a similarly quick destruction.' Tersmeden also complained that the new types of ships had not been properly tested through sailing trials, but the prinicipal trial sailings in the North Sea were not planned to take place until 1787. In spite of Tersmeden's gloomy predictions, many of the vessels and frigates were to last eighty years before being broken up.

The King-in-Council considered the dockyard's annual report for the year 1784 in March of 1785. After examining Ehrensvärd's report, the King is reported to have remarked, 'The new construction is not being carried out in accordance with His Majesty's instructions and thus the true interests of the state; Chapman left to himself has only extended his cares to ship's hulls without bothering about other matters which pertain to the ships' serviceability.' That Chapman wished to complete the construction of buildings (storehouses etc) for the navy, the king found to be natural but 'he asked the fleet-admiral to quench the rear-admiral's desire for building in the less important areas, but to draw out full benefits of that which belongs to the main objective'. The fact is that when the king began his war with Russia in 1788, there were severe shortages for which Ehrensvärd and Chapman could perhaps be held partly responsible, but neither of them was privy to the date of the king's intended declaration of war against Russia. Two other reasons were the king's sudden decision to mobilize the fleet in 1788, and the king's lack of understanding of the necessity for the extra stores, ammunition, and reserve equipment required to support a navy in wartime. The other reason for the deficiencies in naval stores and trained personnel, was the precarious state of Sweden's

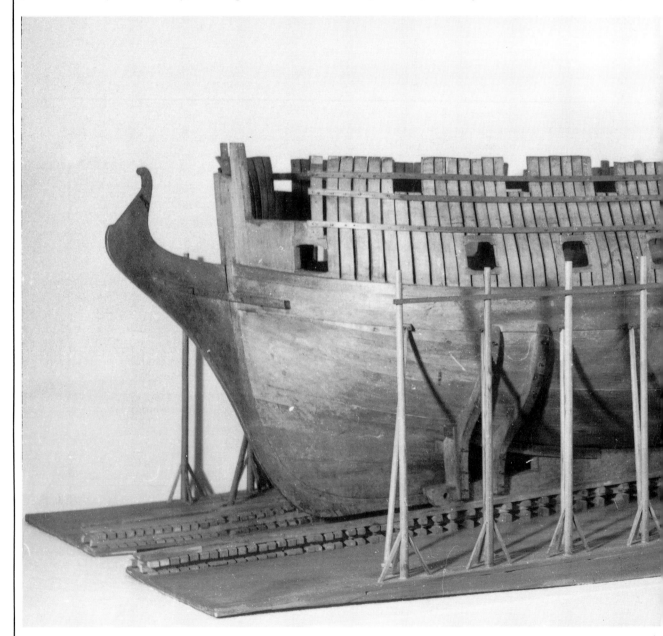

finances. A further factor was Gustaf III's lack of appreciation of the importance of well-trained officers or men.

Trolle's master plan for the large fleet encoutered severe difficulties in 1786 because the state of the kingdom's economy (the result of crop failures in the years 1780–84) could not allow it, in spite of French subsidies, to carry the heavy burden of the planned defence expenditures. The Minister of Finance, Lilljecrantz, recommended a reduction in expenditures in all areas. He was even so bold as to suggest economy in the king's own expenditures, but Gustaf III refused to agree to any limitation being placed upon his spending. Lilljecrantz was thus forced to recommend a reduction in the defence outlays, and the navy was to bear the brunt.

In September 1786, the king set up a committee to examine the naval administration, its members being Chapman, Ehrensvärd, Lilljecrantz, Carlsson (Deputy Minister for War), and Toll. The last-named was a former army officer who was responsible for the reform of the army and who enjoyed the king's confidence. The report, completed by 12 October, stated that Trolle's original plan could not be fully implemented. The committee found that the causes were neither the results of bad management nor miscalculations but 'for reasons unforeseen' — in other words the crop failures which had reduced the state's internal revenues. The committee reported, in part: 'During the past five years 2,330,000 riksdalers have been spent on the navy's

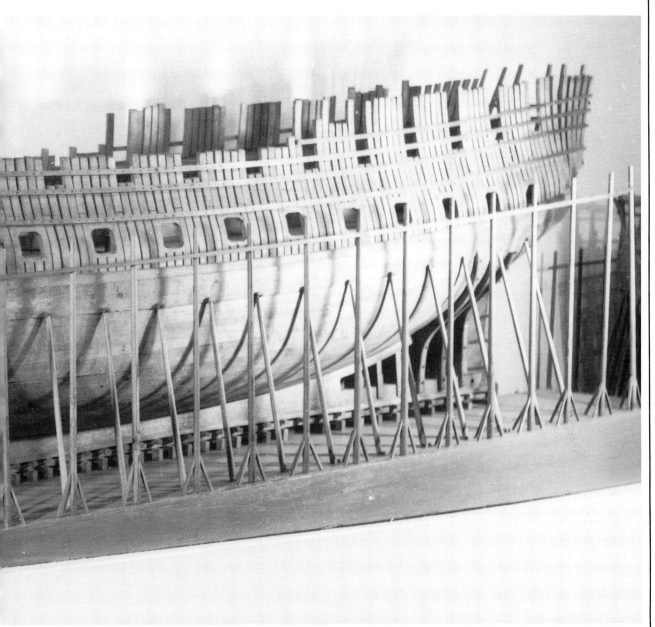

Fig VII/18.
A model of a Gustaf Adolph *class 60-gun ship ready for launching, although the topside is still unplanked*
(Naval Museum, Karlskrona).

ships and dockyard buildings; an additional 2,400,000 riskdalers are required'. The king was satisfied that 'the best management has taken place for the past outlays and the work has proceeded with energy'.

The report emphasized that the fleet in the years 1763–80, which had cost the same amount in total, had produced only seven ships of the line, one frigate, and some fifty-two small craft. However, in the five years to 1786, ten ships of the line, ten frigates, arsenals, storehouses and workshops had been completed. The king again visited Karlskrona in 1786, but before the royal visit Chapman's enemies were not idle, starting a rumour that he was to be dismissed. The 82-year-old Sheldon, formerly chief shipwright, wrote and circulated a disparaging broadsheet about Chapman and his knowledge of the shipwright craft. Sheldon's diatribe maintained that Chapman had learnt little about Swedish shipbuilding before he went abroad, but had begun his training with the study of mathematical 'whimsies'. Sheldon maintained that two vessels built by Chapman after his mathematical studies, sank on launch, an accusation without any foundation. The broadsheet attacked Chapman's methods and exalted those of the Sheldons, pointing out the long service of the Sheldon family to Sweden since its arrival in 1655. The king's opinion of Chapman was neither shaken by Sheldon's broadsheet nor by Tersmeden's complaints that the ships were being built too quickly. The king did pause over the costs of the dockyards buildings, and urged Ehrensvärd to persuade Chapman to concentrate on ships rather than on buildings; nonetheless the king awarded Chapman the Wasa Order.

Chapman wrote a fourteen-page letter, dated 25 February 1787, to a senior official of government outlining some of the difficulties which he had experienced in his management of the dockyard. He complained that he had not been informed of the payments from fund allocations made for the construction of the new fleet, and he pointed out that the current practice was at variance not only with the instructions of the fleet admiral, but also with the accounting regulations. There seems to have been differences of opinion about the amount of unspent funds at year ends. Chapman states in his letter that he had asked the fleet admiral a year earlier to consult him when proposing to make payments, and to discuss the reasons for the disbursements: 'After all,' continued Chapman, 'it is the Admiral Superintendent who is responsible for the management and production of the dockyard, and neither the Fleet Admiral nor the Commission.'

Chapman refers in his letter to the payment of bonuses for speedy work. In addition, he draws attention to the fact that he had used his personal funds to purchase hides, lead, and tin from Britain, and oils and hemp from Russia, at no profit to himself. In addition, he made local purchases at lower prices than could be obtained through the normal channels.

Chapman does not demand full reimbursement of his outlays, although he points out it was the usual practice to refund such disbursements. He states he was willing to sacrifice his own property for the sake of his king and country. 'It was I,' he stresses, 'who has done everything possible in six years to build a certain number of ships so that the navy would not deteriorate — this was the first agreement with Trolle who was to be my aid in Karlskrona.' Chapman maintained that he had many 'persecutors' in that city, moreover, his removal expenses from Stockholm had never been paid. He continued that if he had not been so loyal to king and country, he would have stayed in Stockholm, where there were possibilities of making a more remunerative career.

Chapman mentions the construction of his country house at Skärva, a couple of kilometres outside Karlskrona. Apparently his friend Trolle had authorized its construction; the materials came from the dockyard. The letter also indicates that Chapman had some concern for the welfare of the dockyard workers, since he had arranged for some of these, at his expense, to spend a Sunday at Skärva to rest from dockyard activities.

As a result of the commission's report, Chapman submitted a ten-year plan for the completion of five ships of the line, six frigates, additional storehouses and a hospital. The King-in-Council approved the plan, but the lack of funds, and political developments, were to prevent its full implementation.

An admiral's barge named *Gäddan* (Pike or Jackfish) (fig VII/21) was built in 1786. Although the drawings are signed by Chapman's nephew Lars Bogeman, it is highly probable that Chapman not only had to approve them, but also had some influence on the design. Two cutters, the *Tärnan* (Tern) and the *Måsen* (Gull), were delivered to the fleet in the years 1787 and 1788. The *Tärnan* was armed with eight swivel guns and the *Måsen* with twelve. One frigate of the light series, the *Ulla Fersen*, (fig VII/22) armed with 18-pounder guns, was completed in 1789, the second year of the war.

THE PERFORMANCE OF THE NEW SHIPS

How did the new ships and frigates behave at sea in comparison with those built according to the old methods? The first report refers to those attached to the neutrality squadron operating in the North Sea in the year 1781. The commanders of the new vessels now had glowing comments:

All these ships maintain a reputation for quality, and their merits stand out before all foreign ships — English, Danish, and Russian — which I encountered during the patrols. The English Admiral Parker when he saw Your Majesty's ships at Flekerö confirmed with the expression that it was a squadron consisting of the most beautiful ships anyone could desire. He especially, no less than the Danes, liked the ship *Wasa* and her heavy armament, and whatever else was visible to the eye.

Colonel [Captain] O H Nordenskjöld, commanding the *Hedvig Elisabet Charlotta*, the flagship for the neutrality squadron for the year 1782, reported:

The ship sailed exceptionally well, especially when close-hauled, and she has made 8½ knots under jib and topsails. I encountered no ship which I could not overtake. She is in all respects a good seaworthy craft and a good fighting ship.

The logbooks of the 40-gun frigates show that these vessels too were excellent sailers. The frigate *Diana* was sent to Tangier in 1787 on an ambassadorial mission to take gifts to the Moroccan emperor — in effect, payments to ensure that Swedish vessels trading in the Mediterranean would not be subject to the maraudings of his piratical subjects. In April 1787, the *Diana*'s executive officer reported that:

The frigate with the best wind, a fresh breeze, made 13-14 knots; of all the sailing vessels which we have seen, in total about one hundred and fifty which have sailed in our company, none has been able to follow either when

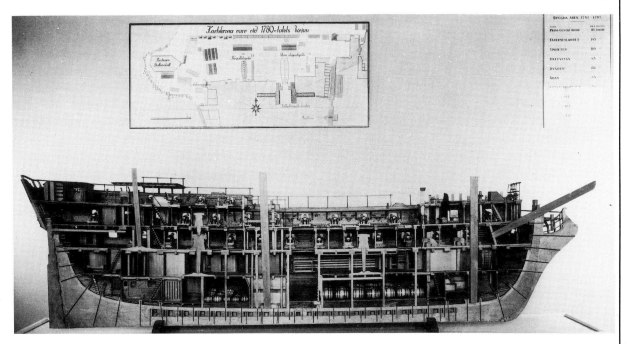

Fig VII/19.
A 1/16 scale model of the Gustaf Adolph
class 60-gun ships displayed below
a plan of the Karlskrona dockyard during
the period of the great shipbuilding programme
(Sjöhistoriska Museum, Stockholm).

sailing close-hauled or running free — the majority have been overtaken in three hours and then hours later again were out of sight — if only it will blow hard because she can withstand much wind.

This officer also made some comments as regards copper sheathing. He wrote: 'Without doubt the use of this expensive invention has greatly contributed to this frigate's furious sailing.'

The most extensive trials took place in the summer and early autumn of 1787 in the North Sea when the *Gustaf Adolph* of Chapman was pitted against the *Sophia Magdalena* of Sheldon. The report to Fleet Admiral Ehrensvärd, dated 28 November 1787, was signed by admirals Wrangel, Tersmeden, Chapman, and Wagenfelt. It was a summary of the ships' journals which reported the day-by-day events in the contest. Here are the particulars of each day of the trials as set out in the report which was a summary of the entries in the logs of both vessels:

JULY

22   Both ships sailed about the same; *Sophia Magdalena*'s angle of heel 9 degrees, *Gustaf Adolph*'s 7 degrees.

23   *Gustaf Adolph* won some cable lengths and sailed closer to the wind.

24/25   *Gustaf Adolph* had the advantage in sailing.

AUGUST

13   *Gustaf Adolph* had the advantage close-hauled in topsail breeze and topgallant breeze.

14   *Gustaf Adolph* outshot *Sophia Magdalena*. Both ships had lee side ports open and the angle of heel was 7 degrees.

15   *Gustaf Adolph* had the advantage in running before the wind in the early part of the day fresh, but later dying away.

16   *Gustaf Adolph* had advantage in sailing before the wind in topgallant breeze.

17   *Gustaf Adolph* had some advantage for beating and sailing close-hauled.

18   *Gustaf Adolph* when sailing before the wind won.
     Sophia Magdalena wins when sailing close-hauled in heavy seas.

19   Heavy swell, light breeze no comparison made.

20   *Gustaf Adolph* superior.

22   Both ships go about well with three or all reefs in the topsails.

23   In a storm, close-hauled both ships sailed well under three staysails. Under fore sails, *Gustaf Adolph* won.

24   Before the wind *Gustaf Adolph* wins.

25   Topsail breeze half wind *Gustaf Adolph* had great advantage.

26   In stiff topsail breeze, *Gustaf Adolph* had some advantage.

27   *Gustaf Adolph* had advantage when sailing close-hauled.

28   High seas, both ships equal-reefed topsails.

29   Becalmed.

30   Seven reefs in the sails, *Gustaf Adolph* had much advantage. *Sophia Magdalena* had to furl topgallants and reef down her topsails. Estimated speeds, the *Gustaf Adolph* $10\frac{3}{4}$ knots, *Sophia Magdalena* $8\frac{3}{4}$ knots.

31   *Gustaf Adolph* had the advantage, again made $10\frac{3}{4}$ knots close-hauled, *Sophia Magdalena* $8\frac{3}{4}$ knots.

SEPTEMBER

1/2   *Gustaf Adolph* had some edge over *Sophia Magdalena* but owing to very light breezes, no comparison was made.

8   No trials.

9   *Gustaf Adolph* had great superiority.

10   In squalls and storms both ships sailed equally well.

11   Light topgallant wind.

12   Topgallant breeze, *Gustaf Adolph* somewhat superior in the forenoon. In the afternoon both ships were about equal.

13   *Gustaf Adolph* superior.

14   Reefed topsail breeze, *Gustaf Adolph* opened lower gun ports. *Sophia Magdalena* not able so to do. At anchor *Gustaf Adolph* to for 7/8 cable, *Sophia Magdalena* to $1\frac{1}{2}$ cable. Both ships rode easily.

15, 16, & 17   Sailed out to sea *Gustaf Adolph* had the advantage.

Found that both ships good warships, also in sailing and manoeuvring and lying at anchor in high seas. The *Gustaf Adolph* is preferred, is a stiffer ship, the lower gun ports are high and thus she can use her guns longer, she carries more provisions and fresh water. In addition, her design provides well for the crew. Under most conditions the *Gustaf Adolph* has been superior in sailing.

A J Wrangel
Carl Tersmeden
Fred H Chapman
J Wagenfelt

Fig VII/20.
Original figurehead of the frigate Euredice
(Sjöhistoriska Museum, Stockholm).

Tersmeden, Chapman's old enemy, had described the meeting of 25 November 1787 where the report was reviewed.

Like all other flag officers, I was called to a morning meeting at Count Ehrensvärd's, where we should examine the trials sailing journals and give our opinions about both ships. I found this ridiculous as His Majesty in public had with much joy talked about the preference for the *Gustaf Adolph*, which probably was based on the journals. Thus our objective today is more or less such a formality that for my part I need no more evidence about the ship *Gustaf Adolph*'s properties than His Majesty had himself already given.

Tersmeden could not fail to notice that the logs of the two ships had been finely bound and that the *Gustaf Adolph*'s journal had been placed on a gilded table under a mirror. He noted with satisfaction that under the table he found a black leather-bound book bearing the title in silver letters *Criticism of Chapman's Shipbuilding* by Clairbois. Tersmeden believed that entries made in the deck log books had been altered on transfer to the fair log books. 'I was able' he said 'to look at the *Sophia Magdalena*'s log books but those of the *Gustaf Adolph* continued to be held by Chapman and Nordenskiöld.'

Tersmeden brought up an incident of 24 July when the *Gustaf Adolph*, in the Baltic in severe weather and high seas with three reefs in the topsails, refused to go about. As a result they had to wear ship, although the

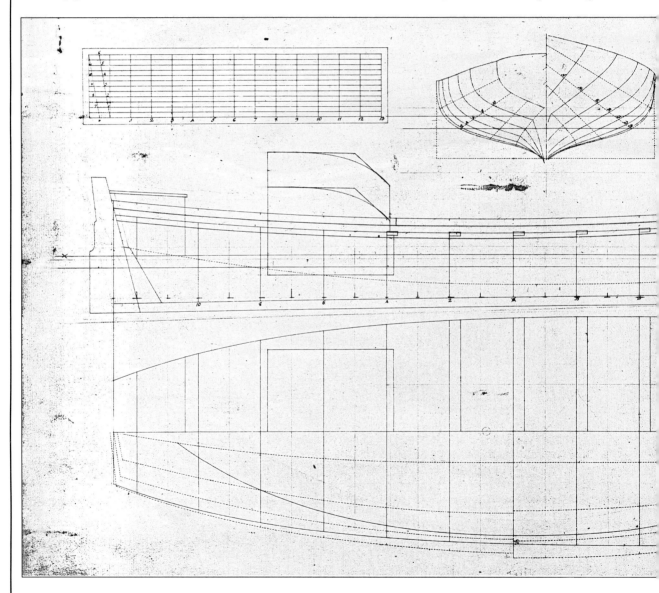

Sophia Magdalena was able to go about without any difficulty. Her refusal has been ascribed to the officers' handling of the ship during the manoeuvre; given that at 10am the same day the ship under the captain's control had gone about quickly, Chapman's supporters were immediately ready to cast the blame on the officers in charge for the failure. 'I brought up other reasons' wrote Tersmeden, 'why the ship had not come about. His Excellency became a little hot and maintained that a ship never refuses to go about unless the officers are at fault, which was clearly so. When Nordenskiöld took over command, she went about.'

Tersmeden, in spite of the evidence from the log books, still remained unconvinced of the superiority of the Chapman-designed ships, but there are still individuals who maintain the earth is flat. Chapman at long last had his triumph over the old school and its adherents. Shipbuilding was no longer to be a 'hit and miss' activity, and the application of scientific methods to the industry became established in Sweden.

PREPARATIONS FOR WAR

The king's sudden command of 19 April 1788 to mobilize the fleet upset Chapman's ten-year plan to complete a new fleet, in part based upon Trolle's original proposals. The king commanded the dockyard and the naval authorities in Karlskrona to fit out twelve ships of the line and five frigates by 30 May 1788. Neither Ehrensvärd nor Chapman knew of the king's intentions to provoke an incident to bring about a state of hostilities with Imperial Russia. Moreover, Ehrensvärd was personally opposed to the king's war policy. He was concerned about the lack of trained personnel to man the new fleet, and just the month before, he had addressed a memorandum to the king stating that if the Crown would neither re-establish a school for officer cadets, nor allocate funds for a training establishment for non-commissioned officers, nor provide funds for exercises, and if the fleet following its completion was not allowed six years' peace, 'that admiral who takes the fleet to sea in its present condition is either an egoist or a traitor to his king and country'. Ehrensvärd's memorandum was not one to enhance his standing with a monarch already determined on a war course. Ehrensvärd and Chapman were kept in the dark about Gustaf III's real intentions as late as mid-May 1788.

The king appointed his brother, Duke Carl, as a commander-in-chief of the navy and the aged Admiral Wrangel as commander of the fleet. Duke Carl had been given the rank of grand-admiral at birth by his father. He was alleged to have confessed to his wife that he did not find it amusing as 'an apprentice seaman to plunge around for weeks on end like a duck on the waves and not see anything but ships, the sky and the sea.' His interests lay in the Freemasons' order and similar organizations. In fact, he had neither the interest nor the required knowledge and experience to fit him to command a navy.

Nevertheless the navy had acquired some seatime experience for extended periods through the neutrality patrols in the North Sea, which began in 1779 when six ships of the line and six frigates were sent out. The number engaged in the patrols was increased to ten in 1783. The objective of the patrols was to prevent the belligerents from carrying out searches of homecoming merchant vessels and to curb the activities of British and French privateers operating in the Baltic. In spite of these patrol activities, the navy lacked well-trained personnel of all ranks. As previously mentioned Gustaf III had, during the American War of Independence, been able to arrange for some of the fleet's younger

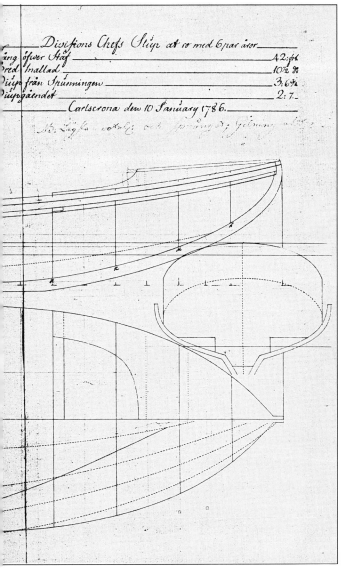

Fig VII/21.
Admiral's barge Gädden *(Pike or Jackfish)*
(Naval Museum, Karlskrona).

officers to serve in the British and French navies. One of these, O H Nordenskiöld, who had done service in both the British and French navies, was appointed captain of the fleet. In spite of training some officers in the fleets of the two largest and most important navies of the day, the number of well-trained and experienced officers was small. The situation as regards petty officers and men was worse. The coastal settlements were obliged to provide seamen for the navy in return for Crown subsidies, as and when required. A proposal made at this time to adopt the British press-gang method of recruitment was rejected. The Danish ambassador to Sweden, who was maintaining a careful watch over Swedish naval activities because of Denmark's close association with Russia and her objec-

tion to a strengthened Sweden, wrote that 'the Swedish crews would consist mainly of farm labourers transformed into seamen by a couple of dips in salt water.'

Chapman had great difficulty in complying with the king's order because, as a result of the 1787 committee's report, the acceptance of Chapman's ten-year plan, and the nation's economic conditions, the majority of the dockyard's skilled tradesmen, including carpenters, had been laid of at Christmas 1787. When the king made the decision to mobilize the fleet, not only was there a shortage of skilled tradesmen to complete the fitting out but the dockyard storehouses contained insufficient quantities of hemp, sailcloth, signal bunting, shot and powder for even a short naval campaign. Some writers, notably the Swedish naval historian

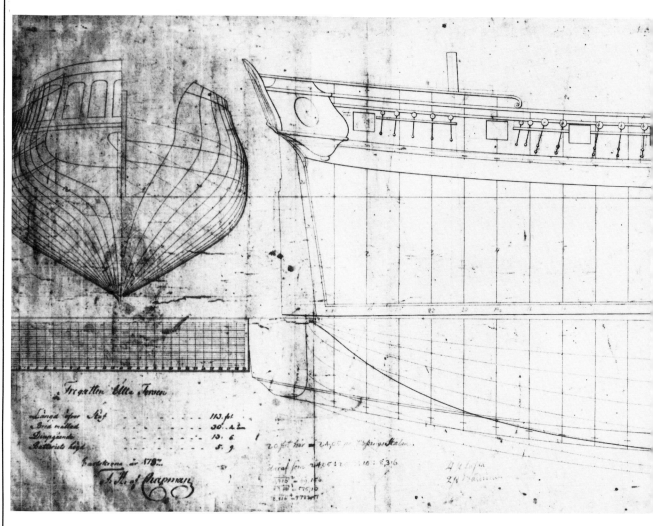

Munthe, have placed the responsibility for the shortages on Chapman and Ehrensvärd, but the evidence suggests that the blame lies elsewhere, namely with Gustaf III. He failed to communicate his intentions sufficiently beforehand to enable his Karlskrona dockyard commanders to acquire the supplies necessary for a naval war.

The king established a special committee to supervise the fitting out of the fleet for the war with Russia. It consisted of the two admirals Strömfelt and Rajalin and Counsellor Matzow, none of whom had any experience in fitting out a war fleet. Furthermore, the comptroller general instructed the committee to be as parsimonious as possible with the nation's funds. One of the first acts of the committee, on 19 April 1788,

was to instruct Chapman to cease work on all new construction and to concentrate on fitting out twelve ships of the line, five frigates and some smaller craft. The fleet was to have four months' stores set aside, but only one month's supplies were to be taken on board. To save funds, the committee limited the number of officers to be employed in fitting out to two lieutenants and a small number of men per ship. The purpose was to avoid paying seatime money to other officers, petty officers, and the majority of men. The result was that neither the commanders, nor the majority of crews were acquainted with each other until the ships were ready for sea.

The Captain of the Fleet, Otto Nordenskiöld, who had extensive experience in both the British and French

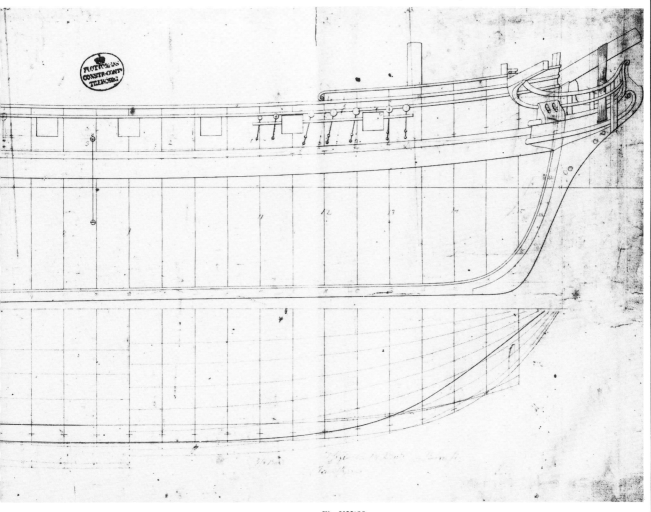

Fig VII/22.
Original sheer draft of the frigate Ulla Fersen
(Krigsarkivet, Stockholm).

fleets, suggested to Chapman that the new ships of the line could carry additional sails, as he believed that the additions of a fore topmast studdingsail, a fore topgallant studdingsail and a boom mizzen sail would provide additional speed. Chapman agreed. He was able to obtain 20,600 metres of sail cloth for 8869 riksdalers, for which purpose the committee grudgingly released funds on 28 May. He had two other problems to overcome. The first was the shortage of sailmakers, since the dockyard's own sailmakers had been mobilized for sea service. However, Chapman was able to get seven returned to the dockyard service. The second problem was the shortage of hemp for the rope walk to manufacture the necessary additional cordage. Chapman learnt of a ship loaded with hemp that had stranded on the island of Øland and sent a representative to Kalmar to bargain with the owners, but it is not known if there was any successful deal completed. To make matters even more difficult for Chapman, the committee prohibited the purchase of 'spot' parcels of hemp, but Chapman through his many years of experience and contacts was able to get 4470 kilos of hemp from Russian and Danish suppliers. The commission had reduced the daily rates of pay for carpenters and coopers, and as a result many had left the dockyard. Consequently, the shortage of coopers led to several ships going short of fresh water. Chapman had to overcome the shortages of coloured bunting for signal flags so he decided to use whatever cloth he could get locally and dye it. As a result, many of the signal flags were made of linen, but eventually he was able to obtain some woollen bunting from Lubeck.

Not only was Chapman deprived of skilled carpenters and sailmakers, but even boys between the ages of six and twelve, normally employed as messengers, and to ring the dockyard bells, were pressed into service on board the new ships. To overcome the shortages of men for the fleet, twenty percent of the crews of the ships of the line were taken from infantry regiments, and thirty percent of the crews of the heavy frigates were foot soldiers.

Eight

THE SWEDISH FLEETS
IN THE
1788–90 WAR

How did Chapman's new ships fare in the campaign against the Russian fleet? The Russian High Seas Fleet was commanded by the Scottish Admiral Greig and included many foreign officers in its senior ranks, such as the Danish Admiral Krus, the Dutch Admiral van Dessen, and the British captains Crown and Elphinstone. The Swedish High Seas Fleet, commanded by Gustaf III's brother, had also recruited foreign officers and surgeons, amongst whom were Captains Cox, Sydney Smith, and Sir Jahleel Brenton. The Chapman ships were suited to the confined waters of the Gulf of Finland because of their shallow draught and ease of handling. Although smaller than the Russian vessels, the 36-pounder guns of the Swedish vessels should have given them the advantage in the weight of broadsides.

When hostilities broke out between Russia and Turkey in 1787, Gustaf III believed the opportunity to settle affairs with Russia had now arrived, since he considered it unlikely that Russia would launch an attack on Sweden while at war with Turkey. Gustaf was unable under the terms of the Swedish constitution to declare war without the Riksdag's (parliament) authorization, so, in June 1788, to get around that problem he arranged for a party of Swedish soldiers dressed in Russian uniforms to attack a Finnish border post. In response, the Swedish forces counter-attacked and seized the nearby Russian Nyslott fortress. By this means the king brought about hostilities with Imperial Russia.

King Gustaf's war plans required the new High Seas Fleet to seek out and destroy the Russian naval forces; thereafter the Inshore Fleet, carrying the military forces, would cross the Gulf of Finland, land them as close as possible to St Petersburg — preferably at Oranienbaum — and take the Russian captial. Unfortunately Gustaf's plans had ignored the fact that the Russian navy was already fully mobilized. Indeed, before hostilities began, a part of the Russian fleet under its Dutch commander van Dessen was already under way in the Baltic, en route for the Mediterranean and Turkish waters. Duke Carl's fleet's instructions were to patrol the entrance to the Gulf of Finland, and both fleets met there shortly before the war-provoking incident had occurred. An earlier treaty between Sweden and Russia had stipulated that where ships of the two nations' navies met, no formal salutes would be exchanged. The king's orders required Duke Carl to insist on exchanging formal salutes should the Swedish fleet meet with Russian fleet. Should the Russian vessels refuse, Duke Carl was to open fire. The two fleets duly met at the entrance to the Gulf. However, the Russians complied with the duke's request; consequently van Dessen's squadron was able to proceed to Copenhagen, where the news of the Swedish attack quickly became known. The duke's Captain of the Fleet O H Nordenskjöld, had recommended an immediate attack when the two fleets met, but his advice was ignored. If an attack had been made, the Russian ships, being unprepared, would have surrendered. The duke's failure was to have unfortunate consequences.

On 7 July 1788, the Swedish fleet captured two Russian frigates off Reval (Estonia), the *Hector* and the *Jarislawitz* (which was to be recaptured by the Russians at Viborg in 1789). The main Russian fleet under Greig left Kronstadt on 9 July 1788 and met the Swedish fleet off the island of Hogland on 17 July (fig VIII/2). The two fleets joined battle and as a result of the engagement each navy lost a ship, Sweden the *Prince Gustaf* and Russia the *Vladislaff*, commanded by the Norwegian Captain Berg. The Russian casualties were about 600 men and the Swedish 200. The higher Russian casualties may have been the result of the Swedish action of directing fire primarily against the masts and rigging rather than at opponents' hulls. The Russian fleet retired to Reval where Admiral Greig died and the Swedish returned to Sveaborg. It was in a weak position because it had used all its ammunition for the 36-pounder guns for which there was no replacement stock held in the Sveaborg fortress. The fleet remained at Sveaborg until the autumn of 1788, when it returned to Karlskrona, bringing with it typhoid fever which was rife on board the captured

Russian ship *Vladislaff*. The epidemic was to spread through the Swedish fleet, and would kill about 8000 people in the Karlskrona area.

The Russian squadron which Duke Carl had failed to attack in June 1788 was now based in Copenhagen. As a result of the Danish–Russian alliance, Denmark entered the war, supplied the Russian squadron with information about Swedish fleet movements, and launched an attack on Sweden from Norway. The Russian squadron attacked the Swedish west coast fishing village of Råå, but the Swedish west coast squadron comprising the Chapman-designed 40-gun frigates *Bellona*, *Diana* and *Venus*, captured the 26-gun Russian frigate *Kildouin* in the autumn of 1788.

The Swedish fleet for the 1789 campaign consisted of twenty-one ships of the line, nine heavy and four light frigates including the new light frigate *Ulla Fersen* of 18 guns built to Chapman's design, and completed in that year. She was the last ship built in accordance with Chapman's and Trolle's original programme. Duke Carl was to remain commander-in-chief of the active fleet, but Admiral Wrangel was replaced by O H Nordenskiöld, now promoted to the rank of rear-admiral. The fleet made up its losses of men from disease, by the transfer of 3600 soldiers to the navy.

The fleet was ready for sea by the end of June. On 24 July, it met the Russian squadron based at Copenhagen off the island of Öland for another indecisive action. The reasons for the result was the failure of Rear-Admiral Lilliehorn, an officer who had not been to sea for twenty years, to follow orders. He was court-martialled and sentenced to death, but, after a period of imprisonment, was exiled.

In the Finnish skerries, Fleet Admiral Ehrensvärd's Inshore Fleet was defeated in the first battle of Svensksund (24 August 1789) by superior Russian forces commanded by two mercenaries, Prince Karl of Nassau-Siegen (who had been in French and Spanish service) and Giulio Litta, a Venetian who had served in the Maltese galley forces. Another Swedish loss was the capture of the frigate *Venus* in the Danish waters of the Oslofjord. She was taken into the Russian service, but some years later was transferred to the Neapolitan Navy.

The year 1789 ended with few Swedish successes. By the spring of 1790, the Karlskrona fitting-out committee, consisting of Chapman and Nordenskjöld, Munck and Toll, had been able to dock twenty ships for graving (bottom-cleaning and coating with a mixture of sulphur and tar which was held to provide anti-fouling protection); some ships also required caulking, and some were sheathed with copper. By the end of April 1790 the dockyard had completed the fitting out and repair of seven 70-gun ships, eighteen 60-gun ships, ten heavy frigates, five small frigates and sixteen miscellaneous craft.

The fleet mounted 2240 guns and was manned by about 18,000 men. When it left its southern base on 30 April, it was the largest fleet in the history of the Swedish Navy. The king gave the most unusual instructions to Nordenskjöld, requiring him to be responsible to the king that 'the commander-in-chief's [Duke Carl] orders are carried out in the same way as secretaries of state to the King of England are responsible to parliament.' Nordenskjöld protested to the king about this extraordinary and ambiguous order, but to no avail.

The objectives of the fleet were to prevent the Russian squadrons based at Kronstadt and Reval from uniting. Part of the fleet successfully attacked Baltichport and destroyed large quantities of stores. An attack on Reval failed, because Duke Carl rejected the advice of Nordenskjöld and delayed the operation by one day, thus losing the element of surprise. When the fleet eventually sailed into Reval on 13 May the Russian squadron was fully prepared to meet the intruders. The result was a Swedish withdrawal, during which the *Tapperheten* ran aground but was refloated by the jettisoning of her guns, and the *Riketsständer* (not a Chapman-designed ship) ran aground and was burnt by her crew. The *Prins Carl* was dismasted and forced to strike her colours.

The attack on Reval accomplished nothing and worse was to follow. After an unsuccessful engagement with the Russian fleet under the Danish-born Admiral Krus off Kronstadt on 3 June, the king and Duke Carl ordered the High Seas Fleet to enter the Finnish skerries to protect the flank of the Inshore Fleet. Nordenskjöld advised against this move, stressing the difficulties for the large ships in the confined waters. His warnings were ignored, however, and the fleet entered Viborg Bay. Immediately, the Russian squadrons from Reval and Kronstadt joined forces and blockaded the Swedes. Gustaf decided that the High Seas Fleet should attempt to break out at the earliest opportunity. On 3 July the wind was favourable, and the fleet weighed anchor. Two of the inshore frigates and the *Dristigheten* (fig VIII/4) led the fleet through the entrance, all guns blazing. The captain of the *Dristigheten*, a Colonel Puke, who had risen from the ranks, called on his men to give the Russians hell. The *Dristigheten*, followed by the *Rättvisan*, the *Adolph Fredrik*, the *Tapperheten*, the *Fädnernesland*, the *Försightighet*, the *Äran*, the *Wasa*, the *Fredrik Adolph*, the *Gustaf III*, the *Camilla*, the *Dygden*, the *Euredice*, the *Götha Lejon* and the *Vladislaff*, did succeed in clearing the inlet. The last ships to get underway were the *Enigheten* and a fireship intended to disorganize the Russians, but the fireship was badly handled and ran into the *Enigheten* and the *Zemire*, which caught fire and blew up. The smoke made visibility difficult and the *Hedvig Elisabet*, the *Charlotta*, the *Ömheten*, the *Finland*, the *Uppland* and the *Jarislawitz* ran aground and were captured by the enemy. Later

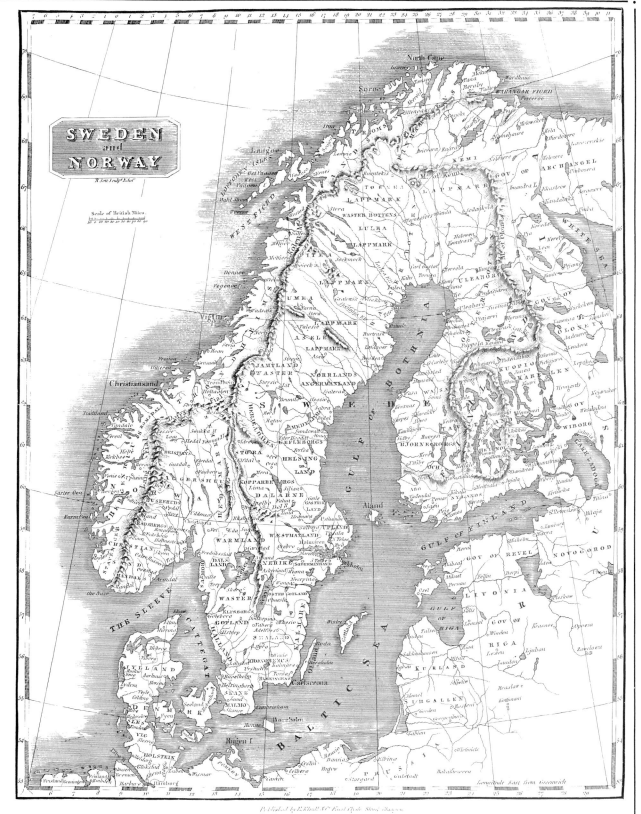

Fig VIII/1.
A contemporary map of the theatre of
operations during the 1788–90 Swedish–Russian War.
The map was published about 1809
(author).

L. J. Desprez

DEDIÉ A SON ALTESSE ROYALE
en memoire de la Journeé

Fig VIII/2.
A contemporary engraving by L J Desprez showing the flagship
Gustaf III *with Duke Carl on board being cheered by the fleet following the*
battle of Hogland, 17 July 1788
(author).

MONSEIGNEUR LE DUC DE SUDERMANIE,
du 17 Juillet 1788, par Son tres respectueux Serviteur
Louis Jean Desprez.

J.F. Martin Sc.

at sea the Russian gunfire dismasted the *Sophia Magdalena* and the *Rättvisan*. Both surrendered. This was the end of the campaign so far as the High Seas Fleet was concerned, but at least the bulk of the Inshore Fleet had escaped to Svensksund.

However, the losses at Viborg made the position of the Swedish Inshore Fleet and the land forces very precarious. Fearing the loss of Finland and probably, in consequence, his throne, King Gustaf forced the reluctant commanders of the Inshore Fleet to stand and fight at Svensksund. He made the Finnish-born C O Cronstedt flag captain since this officer was the only senior commander who supported the decision.

The Swedish force which took up position over a 5-kilometre front on 8 July comprised 275 vessels, about 440 heavy guns and 860 swivels, manned by 13,000–14,000 men. The Russian numbers were 274 ships and boats but with at least 850 heavy guns and 19,000 men it was in most respects a superior force. Therefore, despite worsening weather conditions, the Russians attacked on the morning of 9 July, advancing in three columns. During the deployment phase the Russians suffered disorganisation and some collisions due to the very varied sailing qualities of the mixed fleet, and a Swedish counter-attack took advantage of this. With insufficient sea-room the confusion in the Russian fleet increased, and after some attack and counter-attack a misunderstood signal caused the retreat of some Russian squadrons, which gradually turned into wholesale panic.

By late afternoon only the larger Russian vessels — frigates, schooners, and some chebecks — were still

Fig VIII/3.
A painting by Elias Martin of the Hemeenmää Oden,
captured in 1789 and re-taken at Svensksund in 1790
(Finnish National Board of Antiquities).

Fig VIII/4.
The Chapman-designed Dristigheten, *under the command of Johan Puke, leads the Swedish squadron after the*
unsuccessful attack on Reval, 13 May 1790. Oil painting by Jacob Hägg
(Sjöhistoriska Museum, Stockholm).

engaged, but although fighting valiantly they were caught in a Swedish cross-fire and most were sunk, burned or surrendered. The fleeing Russian small craft were harried right through the evening, and many foundered or were wrecked in the heavy weather, and the following morning the Swedes completed a resounding victory. When accounts were completed it appeared that for the loss of the Udenmää *Ingeborg*, three gun-sloops, one gun-yawl and a bomb vessel, 171 killed and 124 wounded, the Swedes had destroyed or captured fifty-three Russian vessels, including five frigates, and captured about 6000 men, while a further 3000 had been killed in battle or drowned. This was effectively the end of the war and the peace treaty was signed at Värälä shortly afterwards.

When Gustaf III drafted his despatch to the cabinet, his secretary suggested he ascribe the victory to God; Gustaf interrupted and said, 'Add also please, my gun-sloops.' The king, at least, believed that Chapman's special vessels had proved their worth.

As a result of the losses at Viborg and Reval, Rear-Admiral Chapman, as dockyard superintendent, in a memorandum dated 12 August 1790 stated that forty-nine boats were required to make good war losses. Owing to the shortage of carpenters in the dockyard — most having been sent to sea with the fleet — Chapman requested leave to have ten longboats, eighteen barges, twelve 8-oared, ten 6-oared and nine 4-oared boats built by private yards at Västervik, Norrköping, Kalmar and Stockholm, to be sent to Finland on com-

Fig VIII/5.
Patrick de Laval's diorama model
of the Swedish fleet's break-out
from Viborg, 3 July 1790
(Sjöhistoriska Museum, Stockholm).

pletion. Chapman stressed the necessity of boats for ships, especially when the ships are lying at anchor. In addition, Chapman stated he was prepared to defer the construction of the 4-oared boats, but considered the others essential. Chapman attached cost estimates for each type of boat to his memorandum, and asked for a quick decision because of the difficulties of obtaining oak for their construction, and the urgent needs of the fleet.

The treaty of Värälä of 14 August 1790 ended the war between Russian and Sweden. It also terminated Russian and Danish interference in Swedish internal affairs. Chapman's ships for the Inshore Fleet had shown their great value. His excellent and well-armed High Seas Fleet ships would likely have produced far better results if fully trained crews, experienced officers and petty officers had been available to man them. In addition, if the high command had been in the hands of an experienced officer such as Nordenskjöld instead of such a nonentity as Duke Carl, the results of the naval warfare would have been very different. The war losses proved that the best built ships cannot, without well-trained crews and above all, without courageous leadership, prevail against a well-led opponent. The end of the war brought about the laying up of the greater part of the surviving fleet and the paying-off of the crews.

The Chapman-designed ships which survived the 1788–90 war with Russia, were to participate with the Danish Navy in the neutrality patrols which lasted

Fig VIII/6.
Oil painting by J F Schoultz
depicting the Russian attack on the
Swedish line at the battle
of Svensksund, 9 July 1790
(Sjöhistoriska Museum, Stockholm).

Fig VIII/7.
In the same series as the previous painting, this view shows the Swedish counter-attack at Svensksund, 9 July 1790
(Sjöhistoriska Museum, Stockholm).

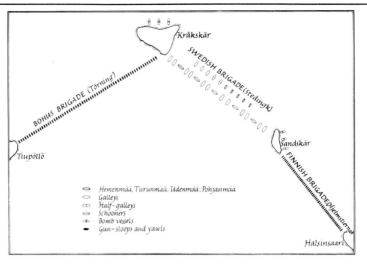

until the British attack on Copenhagen in 1801. On occasion thereafter, Swedish naval vessels sailed into the Mediterranean to protect Swedish merchant ships engaged in trade. The fates of the surviving Chapman constructed ships are as follows:

NAME	DATE LAUNCHED	DATE DISCARDED	NOTES	NAME	DATE LAUNCHED	DATE DISCARDED	NOTES
Ships of the Line				Large Frigates			
Fredrik Adolph	1774	1825	Broken up	*Bellona*	1782	1809	Wrecked at Öregrund
Adolph Fredrik	1775	1825	Broken up				
Gustaf III	1777	1825	Broken up	*Minerva*	1783	1789	Lost by internal explosion
Wasa	1778	1827	Broken up				
Fädnerslandet	1783	1864	Broken up				
Dygden	1784	1793	Lost by internal explosion	*Diana*	1783	1802	Broken up
				Fröja	1784	1834	Broken up
				Thetis	1784	1818	Broken up
Äran	1784	1874	Rebuilt as frigate 1839, sold 1874	*Camilla*	1784	1842	Broken up
				Galathe	1785	1854	Broken up
				Euredice	1785	1858	Broken up
Försiktigheten	1784	1825	Broken up	Small Frigate			
Dristigheten	1785	1869	Broken up	*Ulla Fersen*	1789	1807	Wrecked off Pomerania
Manligheten	1785	1864	Broken up				
Tapperheten	1785	1825	Sold to Colombia. In Portugese Navy 1848				

Note: One of the Chapman-built ships, the *Rättvisan*, which had been captured by the Russians, was some years later taken by the British Navy in Portuguese waters.

The average life of Chapman's ships of the line was 60 years, and for the large 40-gun frigates 42 years, which speaks well of the construction and the materials used. The non-existence of ship-worm in the Baltic must have contributed to the vessels' long lives; in addition Swedish ships were at sea usually for far shorter periods than British, French or Spanish vessels because of the Baltic's annual freeze-up, which can last up to four months.

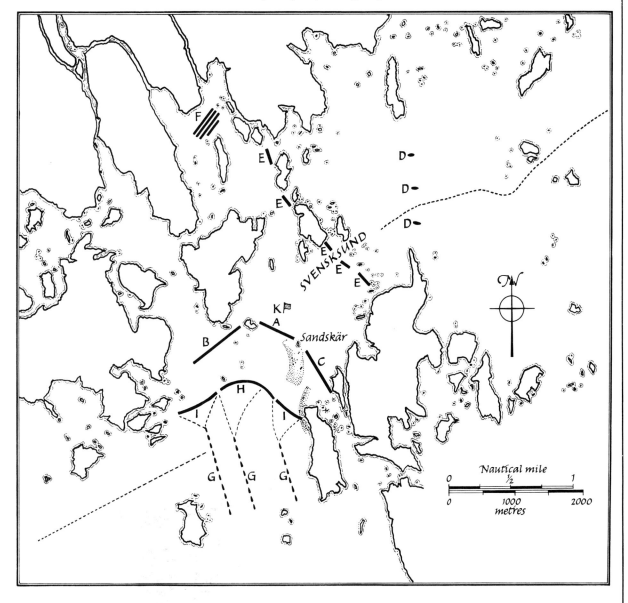

Fig VIII/9.
Battle of Svensksund, 9 July 1790

A. Swedish centre (commanded by Stedingk)
B. Swedish right (Törning)
C. Swedish left (Hjelmstierna)
D. Gun-boats in reserve
E. Fleet reserve (Cronstedt)
F. Swedish transports
G. Russian lines of attack
H. Russian centre during battle
I. Russian wings during battle
K. Gustaf III's yachts, including Amphion

Fig IX/1.
Karlskrona dockyard mast crane
designed under supervision of Chapman 1803
(Naval Museum, Karlskrona).

Nine

AFTERMATH OF THE RUSSIAN WAR

In spite of the peace treaty with Russia, Gustaf III planned to rebuild the navy and ordered Chapman to prepare alternative schemes for a fleet comparable in strength to those of Sweden's neighbours. Chapman was still admiral superintendent of the dockyard, but was now subject to some restrictions. In a memorandum dated 30 September 1790 (discovered in the Swedish National Archives in February 1987), he replied that he was willing to meet the king's wishes under certain conditions:

I respectfully ask to be relieved of other obligations. The reasons are that I am now seventy years of age and my hands are trembling so that I can scarcely prepare draft drawings to illustrate my ideas. I am afraid the trembling in my hands may increase. So that I may undertake the project undisturbed in accordance with the attachments A, B and C, I humbly ask to be relieved of some of the daily tasks.

Chapman proposed that the routine matters of the shipwrights and ordinance departments should be handled by the civilian staff: 'I will nonetheless take care of the more important matters at least once a week, so that Your Majesty's wishes will not suffer or be put aside. I can assure you that my time, abilities and strengths will be kept unsparingly for the service of Your Majesty and the state.'

Chapman proposed that a new fleet should comprise twenty-seven ships of the line instead of twenty-one, and carry 66, 74, 80, 90 and 110 guns. His recommendations for larger ships were the result of the 1788–90 war experiences, but he estimated that the proposed new ships would require one-third more personnel for manning than the vessels of that war. With his proposal Chapman submitted the table set out below, to show the allocation of personnel to the different action stations for each new type of ship of the line.

TYPES OF SHIPS

ACTION STATIONS					
	110 Guns	*94 Guns*	*80 Guns*	*74 Guns*	*66 Guns*
Top men	12	12	12	12	12
Musketeers	50	—	41	40	40
Forecastle, gangways	50	91	40	40	40
Aft	20	10	8	4	4
At the guns	56	—	63	56	56
Powder carriers	10	—	10	9	8
Seamen to trim sails	120	120	120	118	116
At the guns and as powder carriers					
Upper deck	160	126	158	148	138
Middle deck	208	191	—	—	—
Gun deck	240	210	209	181	181
In magazine and main hold	84	77	63	52	55
TOTAL	1010	837	722	658	595

The fire power of the new ships was to be increased by equipping them with 36-pounder guns as the main armament.

Chapman proposed extensions to the Karlskrona dockyard facilities, which he felt were necessary for the new fleet. The construction of the dockyard improvements was to be spread over a period of ten years, and included a stone mast-crane, which required 96 men at four capstans to lift a mast from a ship of the line. It was finally built in 1806 and still stands (fig IX/1 and 2). However, the economic conditions in Sweden after the war prevented implementation of most of Chapman's other proposals.

Early in 1791, Chapman sent the king his final quarterly report, dated 31 December 1790, on the state of the fleet. It states that twelve ships of the line, eight frigates, five despatch vessels and seven merchant vessels had been lost in the war, but contains no information about the losses of the Inshore Fleet in the two battles of Svensksund. Chapman gave full details of the repairs that the surviving units of the once great fleet required, but he complained of the lack of skilled personnel to carry out the repairs to the ships' rigging, and the shortage of funds which prevented the restoration of every component of the fleet. The French subsidies which had financed part of the fleet's original construction were no longer available — the revolution of 1789 had ended them.

Chapman was promoted to the rank of vice-admiral, with the pay rate appropriate to the rank, in December 1790. His letter of January 1791, acknowledging the promotion, addressed to the deputy minister Cronstedt, is couched in the flowery language of the period.

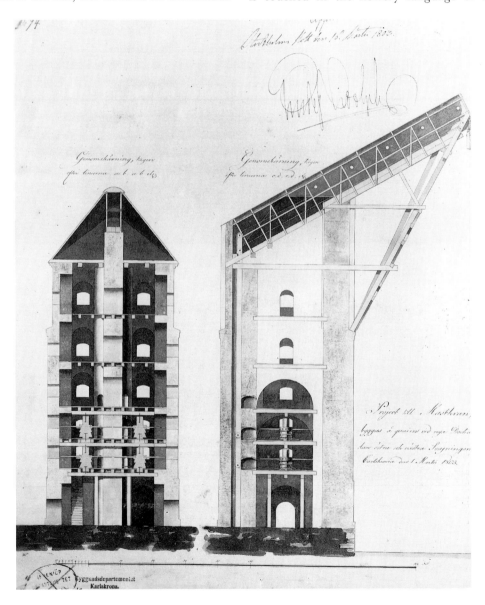

Fig IX/2.
Drawing of the Karlskrona dockyard mast crane
(Naval Museum, Karlskrona).

Chapman requests Cronstedt to convey to the king his most humble thanks for the promotion, which at his age was most unexpected. Perhaps Chapman emphasized unnecessarily his hard-headed Yorkshire heritage in the last sentence of the letter, where he states that the new salary of 3000 riksdalers was an even pleasanter gift to receive than the promotion in rank.

The Crown cancelled all shipbuilding activities, and instructed Chapman to reduce the dockyard's operations and costs in such a way that should new construction be authorized, it could begin without difficulty. These instructions and a new decision-making process caused Chapman problems. He wrote to the Crown on 6 January 1791, 'Sheldon is now over eighty years old; Neuendorff is in his seventies. Both are so sickly and seedy that they are unable to render any service.' He continued by saying that Sheldon could not carry out the duties and responsibilities demanded of one paid a salary of 600 riksdalers. Therefore, Chapman recommended generous treatment of his old enemy, placing him on a pension at full salary, and allowing him to keep his official residence until death. To replace Sheldon as chief shipwright in Karlskrona, Chapman proposed the Inshore Fleet's shipwright, Trygg, whom he considered sufficiently qualified to take on Sheldon's responsibilities — moreover, the new chief shipwright could carry out the duties at 200 riksdalers a year.

Chapman's friend and supporter, Ehrensvärd, had resigned from his position as fleet admiral after the first

Fig IX/3.
The drawing office in Chapman's house at Skärva, with the telescope
set up at a special window to allow him to watch
ships entering or leaving Karlskrona dockyard
(Naval Museum, Karlskrona).

battle of Svensksund, because the king had rejected Ehrensvärd's advice, which resulted in a Swedish defeat. In the latter's place, the monarch appointed one of his favourites, the army general, J C Toll, to have overall responsibility for the royal dockyard's operations. Toll, an unpopular figure, had scant knowledge of naval affairs or of dockyard management, and although Chapman retained the title of admiral superintendent, he no longer had the freedom of action to which he had been accustomed. He found it irksome to have to refer his decisions to an army general for final approval. Chapman's letter of 13 October 1791 to the deputy minister expresses his feelings about the change. He wrote:

I know very well that in the present situation everything is no longer my responsibility, and now is that of the general intendant, or whoever is responsible for the release of funds. Nonetheless, I show no indifference to such urgent matters as the state of the fleet.

The letter implies that Chapman had no alternative but to accept, reluctantly, the government changes in dockyard management. Chapman ended his letter with some general information about the construction of a building to be used by the Cadet Corps and repairs to the admiral's and chief shipwright's official residences.

King Gustaff III was assassinated at a masked ball given in Stockholm Opera House on 16 March 1792 by a member of a conspiracy of discontented noblemen.

Fig. IX/4.
Naval Corps of Constructors' uniform button 1793
(courtesy of Commodore (E) G Schoerner RSwN, ret).

Fig. IX/5.
A faint drawing of Chapman's
special inspection vessel for
Landskrona fortress
(Sjöhistoriska Museum, Stockholm).

The famous Swedish artist Sergel expressed the feelings of all intellectual and artistic circles, including no doubt those of Chapman, when he said, 'Our sun was drowned in blood'. Chapman, the creator of both the new Inshore, and High Seas Fleets, lost in Gustaf III a man who had been early to recognize, and support his genius. The new regency's interests in the humanities, arts, and sciences were to prove to be minimal.

RETIREMENT

Early in 1793, Chapman requested permission to retire from the office of dockyard superintendent, because he found the restrictions placed on his activities by the new control system burdensome. The appointment of Duke Carl as regent, a man who had often opposed

the introduction of Chapman's proposed changes, might have been another reason to leave the naval service. Chapman's request was granted. He was allowed to retire, and to retain his vice-admiral's pay, on the condition that he continued to prepare drafts and submit proposals as and when the Crown so requested. Chapman no doubt desired to spend the rest of his life trying to find solutions to the problems of ship design, and to publishing the results of his research. A man who had been active all his life was hardly one to sit back and willingly fade into oblivion. Cicero has described four reasons for the disadvantages of old age: 'the first it makes us unfit for work, the second it weakens our bodies, the third it takes away nearly all pleasures and fourth, death can occur at any

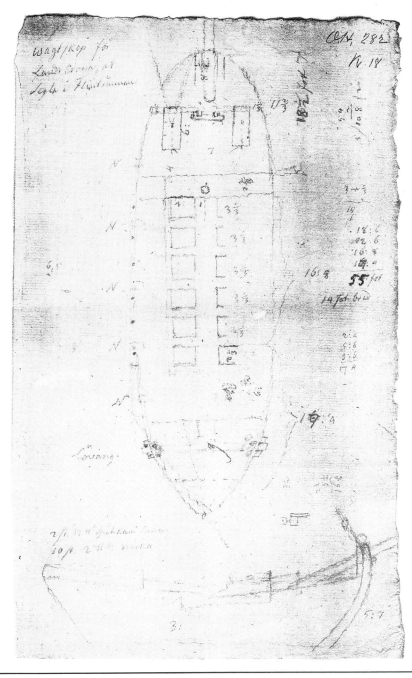

157

moment.' He suggested that the best and most reliable remedies against ageing were scientific studies, and the exercise of virtue. 'Where such activities have been followed in my life span', he continued, 'they will bring riches which can never be forgotten, not even towards life's end, the memories of a well-used lifetime and the memory of many honourable activities will provide the greatest pleasure in old age.' Chapman certainly possessed the memories of an active life, and he was to apply Cicero's remedies, and continue with his research, not only into the problems of the ship, but also to those of gunnery and rigging. Chapman's term as dockyard superintendent marked the end of the old shipbuilding methods in Sweden as far as the navy was concerned; in future its ships would be built by the

application of scientific principles and the use of mathematics. Furthermore the constructor would be totally responsible for the vessel's ability to meet the requirements for armament, storage space, endurance, and good sailing qualities. The old methods which had brought about such disasters as the loss of the *Wasa* in 1628, were now to begin to disappear.

On retirement, Chapman moved to his country mansion at Skärva where the end of the upper room facing Karlskrona is constructed like the stern of an eighteenth century ship, with a drawing board placed directly below the replica's stern windows. To the right of the stern windows, there is a small aperture for a telescope through which Chapman could observe the movements of vessels in and out of the Royal Dockyard

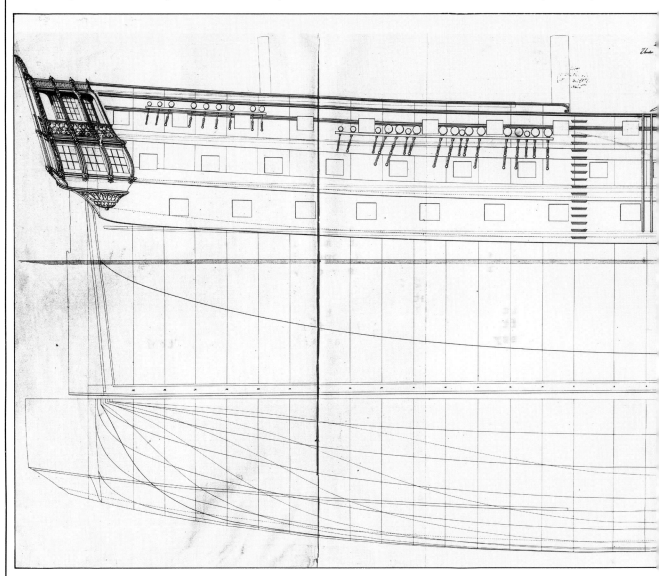

(fig IX/3). This second career as a consultant, constructor, and researcher was to continue for sixteen years.

One of Chapman's first activities on retirement, at the government's request, concerned the reform of the corps of naval constructors. A corps with military ranks had existed when Chapman was active in the Inshore Fleet. Its members wore the naval officer's uniform of 1784, consisting of a top hat with white and gold plume, blue jacket, gold epaulettes, brass buttons, black facings and cuffs, blue breeches, blue and gold cummerbund, white stockings, black boots, and white shirt; a curved sword completed the dress. Sheldon, as chief shipwright, had held the rank of lieutenant-colonel in the corps. In 1793, Chapman recommended the establishment of a new corps of naval constructors for each fleet to replace the existing organization, and this was accepted. One of the changes was the introduction of a new uniform similar to the army's pattern, with a crimson jacket. An unusual item of the new uniform of corps of naval constructors, was the button which carried the formula for the calculation of metacentric height — thus $\dfrac{\int \frac{2}{3} y^3 dx}{P}$. The formula in simple terms was the equivalent of

$$\frac{\text{Load waterline inertia factor}}{\text{Volume of displacement}}$$

This unusual button (fig IX/4) lasted only some eight or nine years; it was then replaced with a plain button bearing an anchor. At the same time, the naval

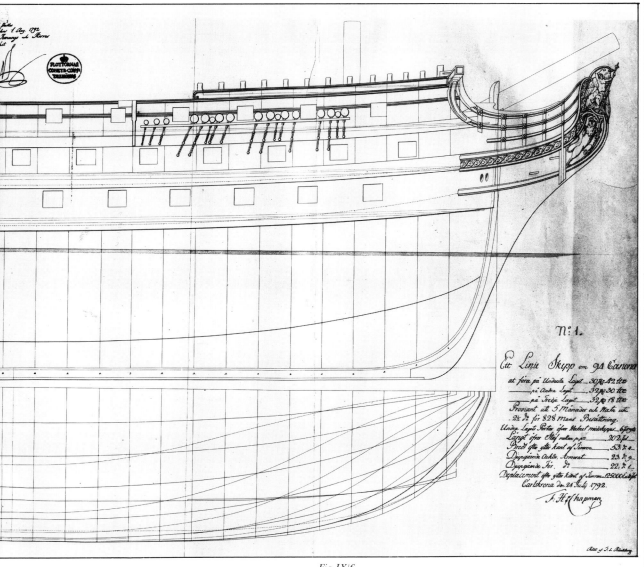

Fig IX/6.
Profile and lines of proposed 94-gun ship dated July 1792, to be
armed with thirty 42-pounders (lower gun deck),
thirty-two 30-pounders (middle deck), and thirty-two 18-pounders (upper
deck); to carry 5 months stores (crew 828).
Dimensions were: length overall 202 feet, max beam 53 feet,
draught aft (full load) 23 feet, draught forward (full load) 22 feet
(Krigsarkivet, Stockholm).

style of uniform was restored. In 1804, Chapman and his pupil Nycop drew up the training programme for candidates to the Naval Corps of Constructors. This was to consist of two stages of training: the first, instruction in general subjects including mathematics, mechanics, physics, and shipbuilding; the second stage to comprise practical work in the royal dockyards. The final qualifying examination included English and French, and general naval topics such as gunnery, rigging and naval tactics. Chapman's *Tractat* (*Treatise on Shipbuilding*) was one of the recommended text books for the course, but because text books covering all parts of the course were unavailable, the teaching staff had to write those necessary. All the courses were free of charge, except for language instruction for which the students had to pay.

Chapman was ordered by the Prince Regent Carl, in a letter dated 13 March 1793, to draw up courses for naval offficer cadets. The regent required courses to include the study of ship's drawings and rigging plans, and furthermore, insisted the cadets acquired a thorough knowledge of ship construction, which he considered to be of great importance. The letter closed with these complimentary words: 'We cannot consider anyone more suitable to complete this task than you, with your great experience and knowledge'. Chapman probably appreciated these words coming from one who had so often opposed his new ideas. Chapman published his programme for the naval cadets' training at the military college in 1795. The programme con-

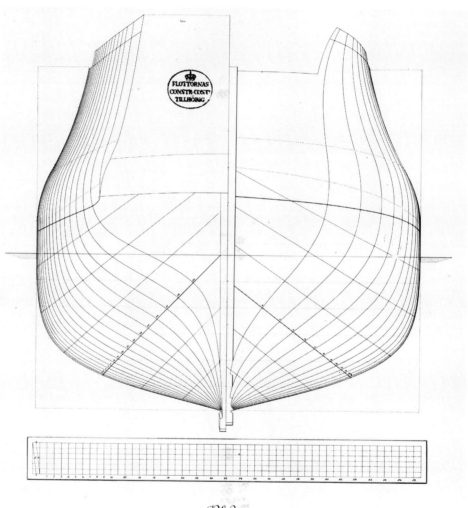

Fig IX/7.
Body plan of proposed 94-gun ship
(Krigsarkivet, Stockholm).

sisted of some twenty parts, the preface of which outlined Sweden's geographical situation, and gave the reasons for the separate Inshore, and High Seas Fleets. Chapman's syllabus was applicable only to cadets bound for service in the High Seas Fleet, as the Inshore Fleet, still a separate force under the army, had some of its training facilities at Sveaborg, Finland. The more important sections of the training programme can be summarized as follows:

Section 1

The cadets were to acquire a thorough knowledge of ship construction and be able to calculate a vessel's displacement, centre of gravity and metacentric height. The cadets were to be able to estimate the weights of guns, gun carriages, shot, stores, and water. This part of the course directed the students to be aware that when shot was used up in an action, the centre of gravity would be moved up higher, and the stiffness modules would also change.

The students were recommended to study Chapman's *Tractat* for this part of the course.

Section 2

Explains the purpose of ballast. A well-designed ship according to Chapman will only need a very small amount of ballast.

Section 3

The text deals with the action stations for a ship of the

Fig IX/8.
Sail plan for proposed 94-gun ship
(Krigsarkivet, Stockholm).

line's 658-member crew, both those to serve at the guns and to work the ship.

Upper deck: Each gun will require 9 men and 1 boy, while 1 senior lieutenant, 1 junior lieutenant and 2 petty officers will be responsible for every ten guns.
Quarterdeck: Each gun will need 7 men and 1 boy; 4 commissioned officers and 7 petty officers will be responsible for the armament on this deck.
Forecastle: 7 men and 1 boy will serve at each gun; 2 commissioned officers and 3 petty officers will exercise command over these guns.
Gun deck: 13 men and 1 boy will man each gun.
Magazine: 16 men will be stationed in the magazine.
Orlop deck and cockpit: 4 barber-surgeons and 1 priest will be stationed on this deck to attend the wounded.

To work the ship during an action, 59 men were to be stationed aft, 13 by the fore mast, 13 by the main mast, and 13 on the gangway.

Note: The total complement of 658 was the number of personnel required for the Swedish 74-gun ship. The allocation of personnel shown above differs from those of the Chapman 1790 proposal.

Section 9
The section covers the calculations of provisions, water, and fuel and refers to the ration lists for crews for each day of the week, drawn up by af Trolle on 20 October 1782. The daily allowance of fresh water per man was to be 3.4 litres. The crew's rations included bread, peas, porridge, salted herring, and meat and a 16-centilitre ration of akvavit per man on Mondays, Wednesdays, and Saturdays. On Sundays, Thursdays,

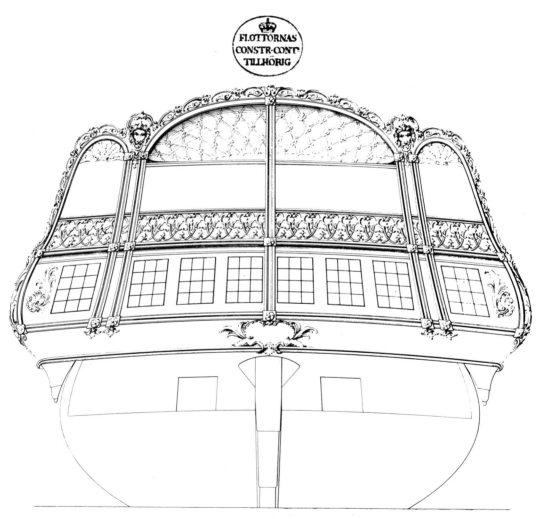

Fig IX/9.
Stern of proposed 94-gun ship
(Krigsarkivet, Stockholm).

and Fridays, the ration was doubled, half to be drunk at breakfast to which a certain amount of onion juice was to be added.

No akvavit was issued on Tuesdays for which the author has found no reason: nor has any reason been found for the extra allowance of akvavit on Sundays, Thursdays, and Fridays. In the seventeenth century, a gallon of beer per man per day was issued for the crew to neutralize the high salt content of the diet, but Chapman has not included any issue of beer in his ration list.

Section 16

The course sets out the information which the cadets should have to enable them to examine the draughts of different types of ships. It includes information on the theory of shipbuilding. To design a ship on the basis of theory:

> First determine the number of guns that there are to be on each deck, the height of each battery above the water, the period for which it shall be provisioned, the total tonnage of the vessel, and all that belongs thereto. The hull should be designed in such a way that the total sail area shall have a certain relationship to the area of the midship section, and the distance between metacentre, and centre of gravity be such that the heeling moment of the sails together with the total weight of the crew on the leeside at the guns shall give the ship a pre-determined angle of heel.

The section also describes the methods to be used to calculate a vessel's length between the perpendiculars, displacement, and the metacentre of a 74-gun ship.

Section 17

This section concerns the methods to calculate sail areas and spars lengths.

Section 18

This part of the course covers fitting out, and loading methods.

Section 19

The section sets out the procedures for determining a ship's stiffness.

Section 20

The section outlines the procedures for carrying out trials with a ship under sail.

RENEWED WORK FOR THE NAVY

In 1793, the Crown again commanded Chapman to produce a plan for the renewal of the fleet, and to design special service vessels. In a letter dated 16 August 1793, the Crown requested Chapman to design a small vessel suitable for the interception of ships entering the Flintrännan section of the Sound, which was to be a tender to the Landskrona fortress. Chapman sketched his ideas in a rough draft shown in fig IX/5. The proposed craft was to have the following dimensions and armament:

Length	55 feet (16.34 metres)
Beam	14 feet (4.16 metres)
Draught	5½ feet (1.63 metres)

Armament
Ten swivel guns
Two 12-pounder guns, mounted on the forecastle.

The vessel was to be cutter-rigged and could be rowed. All the lines of the draft have a jagged nature, which is a clear indication of the trembling in Chapman's hands about which he so often complains in both his private, and official correspondence. The vessel, named *Dragon*, was built at Karlskrona.

In 1797, the new king, Gustaf IV, instructed Chapman to 'prepare drafts of those ships of the line which are most useful to the state, to plan the fleet's future composition, and present a scheme for the implementation of any proposed new construction together with cost estimates'. In reply, Chapman prepared and presented a detailed document approximately 1.5 metres long and 60cm wide to provide not only the information required by the Crown, but also to show the estimated service lives of the existing ships of the line. The document provided details of the quantities and prices of the materials needed to construct the new ships. Chapman's plan, which covered the years 1799 to 1834, included estimates of costs for ships, the costs of new facilities necessary to support the proposed fleet, and suggestions that the new fleet should consist of no less than eighteen 74-gun ships and three 94-gun ships. He stressed in the text the importance of heavier armament for the new ships of the line, which he considered should compensate for a lack in numbers. The 74-gun ships were to have twenty-eight 36-pounder guns on the upper deck, and sixteen 12-pounders on the forecastle and quarterdeck. Chapman maintained that the fleet ought to be stronger than that of the weakest power in the area, and should consist of three divisions of seven ships each; the leader of each division should be a 94-gun vessel (fig IX/6), armed with thirty 42-pounder guns on the gun deck, thirty-two 30-pounder guns on the middle deck and thirty-two 18-pounder guns on the upper deck. No guns were to be placed on the forecastle. Chapman, in his presentation, examined the efficiency of the 80-gun ship, maintaining that in a fleet of 74s, 80-gun ships provided little extra fire power, but he held that not only did the 94-gun ships have the greater advantages in fire power over the 80-gun ships, but where the fleet should comprise only 74- and 94-gun ships, the operating and maintenance costs would be less.

Chapman proposed that if the Crown wanted to have a fleet of twenty-one ships of the line in a high state of readiness at all times, the number of vessels ought to be increased to twenty-three, because refits would take vessels out of service from time to time. He pointed out when he prepared his submission that only eleven ships of the line were serviceable. He recommended that one new ship be completed annually from 1799 if, by 1812, the fleet was to consist of twenty-three ships of the line, of which twenty-one were to be in a complete state of readiness, and that the service life of ships of the line would be about fifty years. He omitted the construction of frigates to be used for convoy duty and other small craft from his proposals, as an additional appropriation of funds would be necessary for these. The document provided details of the costs of equipment required each year from 1798 to 1834 for the proposed new ships of the line, including the costs of hemp, sailcloth and bunting, timber, anchors, iron ballast, guns, shot, powder, and labour. Chapman quoted prices for copper sheets, but the text does not indicate if the hulls of the proposed new ships were to be copper-sheathed. Chapman's schedule quotes prices for both German and Swedish oak — he mentions that German prices were over 100 percent higher than the Swedish, and, recommends that whenever possible Swedish oak should be bought. The estimates show that the highest prices quoted were for

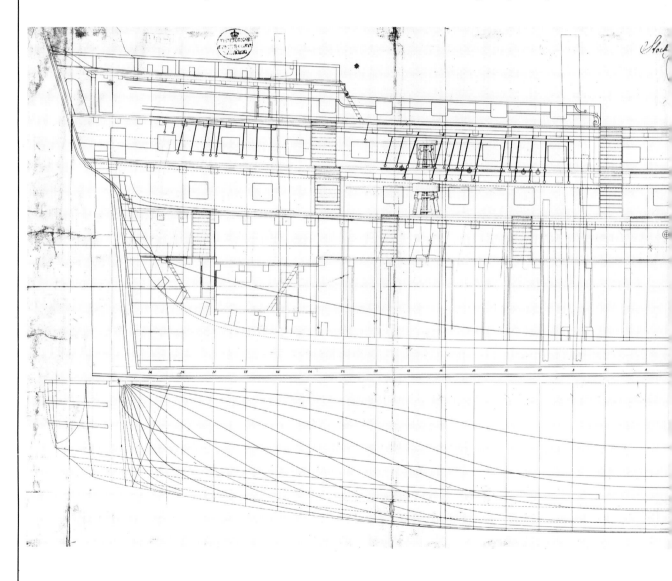

timber for yards. Chapman proposed that the masts for new construction be built of heavy pine, and the lower sections made from several pieces of timber coaked together. Chapman, having worked in British shipyards, was familiar with the methods of constructing 'made-masts' as described in Steel's *Elements of Mastmaking, Sailmaking, and Rigging*. The estimates include prices for coal, which is probably charcoal as Sweden has no fossil fuel resources. The plan shows the cost estimates spread over several years for the completion of dry-docks, slips, a storage building for rigging and yards, a powder magazine, barracks, bridges, a bakery, and repairs to the old mast crane. Chapman advised against the use of old guns as ballast because they took much time and effort to move: iron

weights, he said, were preferable. Finally, Chapman stressed the importance of hiring good, experienced constructors with the ability to direct and supervise carpenters.

Chapman had now come to the conclusion that the traditional massive figureheads were a hindrance to good sailing qualities, expensive to carve, and out-of-date. In his letter of explanation to the Crown dated 24 February 1797, he proposed a simple bust-type figure for the 94 (fig IX/6):

As this form of bow and type of figurehead for a ship of the line makes it ride better and rise easier over the waves, then a figurehead such as a simple warrior's head which is smaller, and for the connoisseur, more attractive than

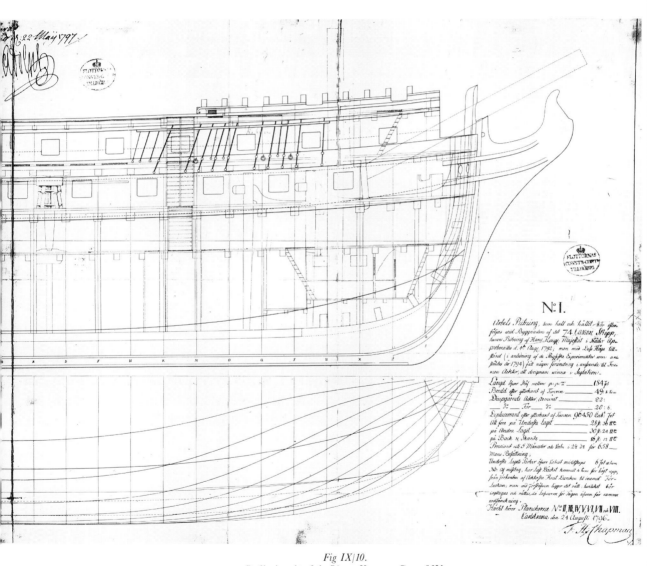

Fig IX/10.
Profile draught of the 74-gun Konung Gustaf IV,
dated 24 August 1796
(Krigsarkivet, Stockholm).

those hither-to used, gives the ship a smarter appearance. In addition, as this type of figurehead is smaller and above the water, the waves will not be able to twist off the false stem which in the past has often happened. For this reason, I would submit in all humility that all ships of the line, frigates, and smaller vessels to be built in the future, should have the same type of bows and figureheads.

Chapman's plan proposed that the new ships be roofed over when laid up in the dry-docks. The roofs were to reach out over the wales, and the fore and aft guns on the gun deck were to be placed amidship to prevent hogging. 'Ventilation holes' were to be made in the bow and in the transom, and the lower gun ports were to be left slightly open to ensure the passage of air throughout the hull. Chapman proposed that at certain intervals shown on the schedule, each vessel should be brought to a state of readiness for sea duty, which was similar to the procedure already in force in the Inshore Fleet stationed at Sveaborg. Chapman credits the origin of his proposed storage methods to Field-Marshal Augustin Ehrensvärd, who had suggested similar methods for the Inshore Fleet some thirty years earlier. Chapman included no estimates for the maintenance or repair of the old ships. He wrote, 'Annual maintenance costs of the old fleet cannot definitely be determined. It is impossible to know when repairs are carried out what the costs will be — sometimes twice as much as estimated and sometimes much less.'

Chapman's proposals were approved by Gustaf IV, but as only half the annual appropriations for the plan were available due to the state of Sweden's finances, only minor parts were ever implemented. The Crown appointed a committee, which included the army's General Toll, to determine how much of Chapman's plans could be carried out with the funds available. Chapman, in a letter of 6 June 1797 addressed to a colleague, wrote that the committee made the following decisions:

1. No 94-gun ship was to be laid down.
2. One 74-gun ship was to be built in the covered shed, for which a new slipway was to be laid down. The ship was to be ready for sea trials by the year 1800.
3. One of the older ships of the line should be placed in one of the two completed docks, and two or three ships moved into the basin.
4. The three incomplete docks were to be finished, and vessels should be built there.
5. Double docks should be built so that the whole fleet could lie there.

Chapman opposed the committee's last proposal. He states that Admiral O H Nordenskjöld, who was a committee member, could accomplish nothing as the other members would not bind themselves to any work

plan. 'I should be indifferent to the outcome but to prevent them from going ahead as lunatics, I am preparing another plan to fit the available funds — whether it is accepted or not, I have done what I could to prevent the kingdom from being without any fleet.'

One 74-gun ship the *Konung Gustaf IV* (fig IX/10) was laid down in Karlskrona in 1798 and was launched and completed in 1799. She embodied the experiences of the 1788–90 war, and had the following dimensions, armament, and complement.

Length	165 feet (49.00 metres)
Beam	36 feet (16.69 metres)
Draught	19.8 feet (5.88 metres)
Displacement	2720 tons
Complement	695 men

Armament
Twenty-eight 36-pounder guns on the gun deck
Thirty 24-pounder guns on the upper deck
Sixteen 12-pounder guns on the forecastle and quarter-deck

After Gustaf IV was deposed in 1809, the ship's name was changed to *Gustaf den Store* (Gustaf the Great) and, in 1825, to *Försiktigheten;* she was to have a life of seventy-six years. This ship was to show an important change in Swedish naval ship construction policy because the stipulation that all ships of the line must have shallow draughts to enable them to pass through the Drogden Channel in the Sound, was now abandoned in favour of larger vessels with greater fire power. A fully rigged model of the *Gustaf IV* with all sails set which was intended for instructional purposes is in the Swedish Maritime Museum. In the same year that the *Gustaf IV* was launched, Chapman set down his opinions about the decorations of ships' sterns and the provisions of figureheads. He wrote that since repairs to figureheads and highly-decorated sterns damaged in naval actions or heavy seas were both expensive and difficult to complete, the ornaments of sterns ought to be limited to mouldings and pilasters. As mentioned earlier, he maintained that the massive figureheads which were placed on the stems of ships of the line and frigates did not add to a vessel's sailing qualities; in fact they often diminished them. Chapman's memorandum on the topic contained the following:

A ship's stern should have three features:
1. A beautiful outline.
2. A fine structure, so that the stern shall boast a smooth and an unrestrained appearance.
3. All mouldings ought to have proper proportions and suitable profiles so that all expensive carving can be avoided.

4. There should be nothing on the middle of the taffrail nor on the gallery which requires significant costs and time to make.

The authorities accepted Chapman's recommendations, and to simplify the decorations of ships' sterns, the practice of transferring the decorations of discarded vessels to replace damaged carvings on vessels retained in service was continued. For example the bust from the figurehead of the ship of the line *Dygden*, burnt in 1793, was placed on the stem of the ex-Russian ship *Vladislaff*. Another example of change was in the instance of the frigate *af Chapman* completed in 1803, where a simple bust of af Chapman replaced the usual massive figurehead, but it in turn, was later removed in favour of a shield bearing Chapman's coat of arms.

This period was one of retrenchment because of the war's costs, Swedish poverty, and the lack of French subsidies, and Chapman must have often felt frustrated to see so little of his carefully prepared plans for the renewal of the High Seas Fleet implemented.

Ten

THE YEARS OF
NEW HORIZONS
1792–1808

Retirement from the navy, and relief from the dockyard superintendent's responsibilities gave Chapman time for research, experiments, the writing of technical papers, and to act as a consultant. He was to prepare plans for the renewal of the High Seas Fleet when the Crown made its requests, which included drafts for new types of special service vessels for the Inshore Fleet which have been described in Chapter III. Almost none of the new types of warships which Chapman designed for either of the two fleets was ever built, because of lack of available funds.

In addition the Crown was to call upon Chapman to provide advice on a variety of topics, including procedures to carry out sea trials. Individuals, and the Swedish East India company, were to request him to design vessels suitable for particular trades or services. He was to continue to be active in his search to improve the qualities of the sailing ship as he now had both time and opportunity to carry out experiments which he believed could prove his theories. He developed a complex geometrical method of estimating a ship hull's resistance from its lines plan and sought proof of his theories in a series of experiments. He built a water tank about 100ft (30m) long. Two poles, A and B, and two shorter ones, C and D, were fixed in the tank. Two copper pulleys were attached to each of the two poles, through which lines were run to support the weights (as shown in fig X/1). The model under test was attached fore and aft to the ropes E and G. Their purpose was to hold the model on a straight course. Two red markers L and K about 74ft (22m) apart were attached to the rope. The observers were to make notes of the times when the markers passed the point L. The models or shapes used were about 28ins (70cm) in length. The models were ballasted with weights depending upon the shape of the model, which weighed from about 5.4 to 12 kilos. The results of Chapman's experiments (shown in fig X/2) suggested that the position for minimum resistance of the greatest area depended upon the velocity. At this period of the eighteenth century, the separtion of frictional resistance

from direct resistance had not been made.

One of the shipbuilder's major problems was to design a vessel which would sail well to windward, but it was no easy problem to solve because of the inherent limitations of the square rig and the full hull shapes of the period. Chapman wanted to give the ship as high a speed as possible and a maximum righting moment for stability and to reach these ideals he combined a full waterline coefficient with fine body sections. In addition, he recommended the use of the curves of sectional axes as the measure of resistance rather than a diagonal line.

In the summer of 1794, Chapman received a state grant to continue his experiments. He had a wooden tank about 68ft (19.4m) long 15ft wide (4.5m) and 4ft deep (1.2m) built in the grounds of Skärva, his country residence. The tank was filled with water to a depth of about 3ft (90cm) and different models or shapes, of lengths varying between 6ft (1.8m) and 8ft (2.4 m) were pulled along the tank by a system of weighted silken cords rove over metal discs and steel axles. Some sixty-six shapes or models, some fitted with rudders to make control easier, were tested, each carrying different weights and, at different speeds. Each shape was tested four times with first one end ahead, and then the other, so that a good average was obtained. The speed at which the various shapes were drawn through the water was of the order of 5 feet per second, but the difficulty with these experiments was that only primitive instruments were available to measure speed and resistance. Chapman had the idea of dividing total resistance between friction and wave-making resistance, but at that time, the laws of equivalent speeds were unknown, and consequently he could not arrive at any conclusions of practical use.

Chapman also tried to determine bow and stern resistance. He believed the bow and stern met with the resistance of two forces, namely the physical or cohesion force, and a mechanical or compressive force. He believed that the stern's resistance was caused by the water's binding force, so he divided a vessel's bottom

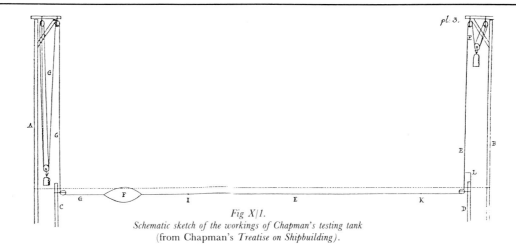

Fig X/1.
Schematic sketch of the workings of Chapman's testing tank
(from Chapman's *Treatise on Shipbuilding*).

Weight of the bodies		N°. 1 27 pounds	N°. 2 27 pounds		N°. 3 27 pounds		N°. 4 22 pounds		N°. 5 19 1/4 pounds		N°. 6 16 3/4 pounds		N°. 7 12 pounds	
Form of the bodies		A A	B	C	D	E	F	G	H	I	O	P	R	P
Moving weights	Retarding weights	Time the bodies have been describing the space of 74 feet, in seconds													
		Seconds A	Seconds B	C	Seconds D	E	Seconds F	G	Seconds H	I	Seconds O	P	Seconds R	P
3/4 the weight of the body	1/2 the weight of the body	25 1/2	26 1/4	24 3/4	27 3/4	26 1/2	25 3/4	25 1/2	27 1/4	24 1/4	30	29 3/4	45	29 1/2
The weight of the body	1/2 the weight of the body	14	14	14 1/2	14 1/2	16 1/2	13 3/4	13 3/4	15	16	24 1/2	24 1/4	38	24
1 1/2 weight of the body	1/2 the weight of the body	11	10 1/2	11 1/2	10 1/2	13 1/2	11	11	10 1/4	11 1/2	12 1/2	17 1/2	30 3/4	19 1/4
37 pounds in all	12 lb. and 1/3 in all	12 1/2	lost		11	14	10 3/4	11	10	11 1/4	12	16	—	—

The bodies N°. 1. has its greatest breadth at the middle, and its two extremities formed by parabolic lines.

    N°. 2. has its greatest breadth at 2/7 of its length from the point B; the two extremities are also parabolic.

    N°. 3. has its greatest breadth 3/7 of the length from the point D; the two extremities still parabolic.

    N°. 4. has its greatest breadth at the middle; the extremity F parabolic, the other G conic.

    N°. 5. has its greatest breadth 2/7 of the length from the point H; the extremity H parabolic, the other I conic.

    N°. 6. has its greatest breadth 2/7 of the length from O; the two extremities conic.

    N°. 7. wholly conic, having the greatest breadth equal to that of the other bodies, and its length twice and an half the breadth.

Fig X/2.
Table of results of experiments with testing tank
(from Chapman's *Treatise on Shipbuilding*,
by courtesy of the Royal Swedish
Academy of Engineering Sciences).

into a series of triangles and rhomboids. He then calculated the resistance for each surface with consideration for their area and angles of incidence. The sum of all these resistances Chapman reduced to the resistance of a single plane perpendicular to the direction of motion, the so-called 'resistance plane'. He found the activity difficult although he was a master at solving such problems with diagrams, and he discovered the stern's shape of his models played an important part, and the resistance was at a minimum when the sides of the stern formed an angle of 13° 17′ with the mean line. As a result of this discovery, Chapman developed his relaxation method of construction.

The relaxation method consisted of making the stern's diagonals rectilinear to the stern post and this form was to be maintained as far as possible. These diagonals should make an angle of 13° 17′ towards the mean line. He laid down the following rules for the plotting of a diagonal in the stern. The diagonal in the body plan should have an angle of 27° 19′ towards the vertical, and its extension towards the mean line was to be at an angle of 13° 17′ but Chapman held that since a hull will distort slightly on launching, this angle was to be indicated on the draft as 13° 51′ so that in reality when the vessel was afloat, it would have the desired angle of 13° 17′. Chapman's relaxation method was based upon his resistance experiments with prismatic shapes in still water, but its application to real ships brought about several difficulties. As the fullness

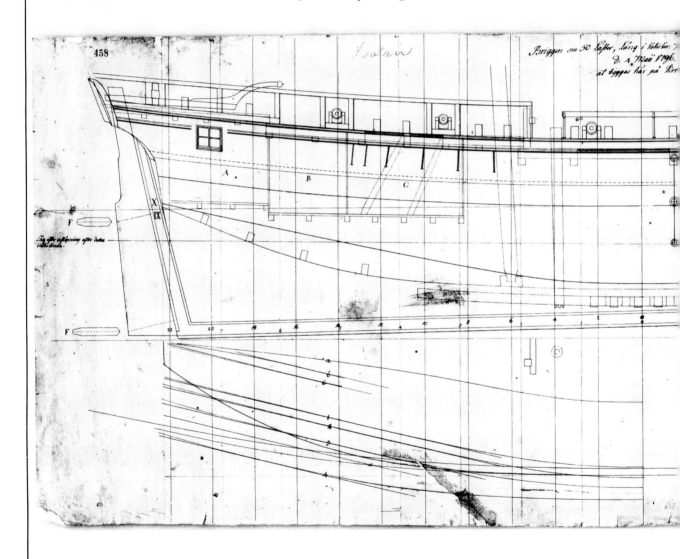

of the stern was more or less fixed by the shape of the diagonal, and as the displacement was already determined, the choice of a proportionate midships section was important to prevent the bow from being too full.

Chapman discussed his relaxation theories when he presented a paper entitled 'Physical Achievements' to the Royal Academy of Sciences in 1795. Eventually he was able to test his theory in two ships constructed in accordance with the relaxation method. These were the brig *Svalan*, 10 guns, built in 1797 (fig X/3) and the frigate *af Chapman*, 40 guns, completed in 1803. Both vessels were built by the Royal Dockyard Karlskrona, and Chapman was to supervise their sea trials.

Chapman had drawn up the following procedures for testing ships in 1797:

When a vessel has been rigged and is lying at the quay, all sails should be hoisted one after another and bent on to determine that they will sit well when sailing close-hauled. Some ballast ought to be placed amidships so that it is easily accessible when needed to be moved forward or aft, to alter the vessel's trim. A vessel's initial trim shall be established when its anchors are hanging at the cat head.

If a vessel is both to sail and handle well, those in charge should note when sailing close-hauled in a fresh topsail breeze if it carries any weather-helm, or if the rudder has to be kept a little to weather. Two methods may give a vessel these properties. For the first, the trim

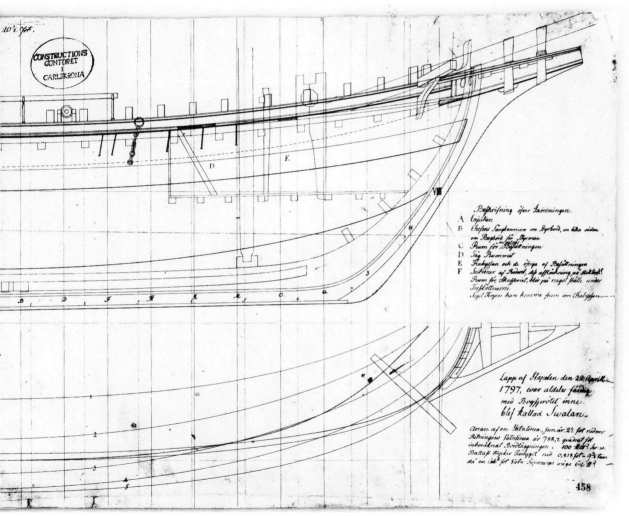

Fig X/3.
Brig Svalan, *sheer and waterline draft*
(Krigsarkivet, Stockholm).

of the ship can be altered. If the bow is pressed down the weather-helm will increase; or if the stern is lowered in the water, the weather-helm will be decreased. The second method is by adjusting the sails. If the sail area is reduced forward, or increased aft, weather-helm will be increased; when the sail area is increased forward, and reduced aft, the amount of weather-helm will be less; and where all the sails' common centre of gravity is forward, but reduced aft, the amount of weather-helm will be less. There are no other ways to increase or decrease weather-helm except by these two methods.

If a ship is to sail well, it must be in such a way that the water makes as little resistance to its movement as possible. As good sailing depends partly upon the vessel's form, and partly upon its draught, trials of vessels of the usual shape ought to be made trimmed by the bow or by the stern, until the trim is reached that will give the greatest speed. For each trim, the sail area shall be increased or reduced fore or aft to give the vessel some moderate weather-helm when sailing close-hauled.

The increase or decrease in sail fore or aft may take place in two ways: firstly, by increasing or lessening the rake of the masts and shrouds; or secondly, by putting on, or taking in the head sails or aft sails. Because the first method cannot be carried out while underway, the second method will have to be used. For example, where a vessel is not sufficiently weatherly when sailing close-hauled in a topsail breeze with all three topsails, topgallants and others set, first furl the fore topgallant sail, second reef the jib, third move the ballast aft of the

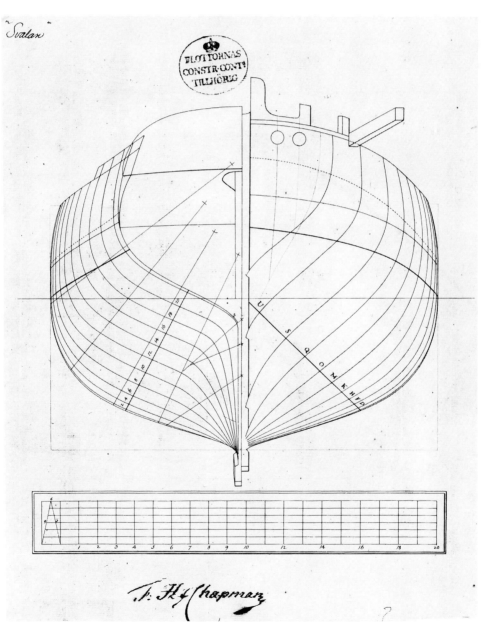

Fig X/4.
Brig Svalan, *body plan*
(Krigsarkivet, Stockholm).

mizzen, fourth take one or two reefs in the fore topsail, partly to get the vessel to lie hard on the rudder, and so heavily that the ship becomes too weatherly. When the vessel has become sufficiently weatherly, note the draught fore and aft and also which sails were used; then determine their total area, and the position of their common centre of gravity forward of the vessel's centre of gravity. The purpose of this is to be able to change the rake of the masts so that the centre of gravity normally obtained when sailing close-hauled, may be the same as that of the sails used in the trials. After making calculations, a suitable anchorage should be found where the rake of the masts can be adjusted.

When trials are to be conducted with ships of new construction, and where the stern is built in accordance with the relaxation lines principle, the draught ought to be in accordance with the waterline shown on the plans. Consequently it is only necessary to increase or reduce the sail areas fore or aft to obtain the desired weather-helm. To determine whether the direction of the relax-ation line is correct, trials should be carried out with two variations from the design differences in draught fore and aft, 1) with one-third less, 2) with one-third more than the line shown on the draft. For example, where the waterline shown on the draft is for 15 inches of trim [by the stern], the difference between the draughts of the stern and bow, then will be in the first case 10 inches and, in the latter instance 20 inches. When sailing with each of these differences in draught, the sail areas shall, as before, be increased or decreased forward or aft until

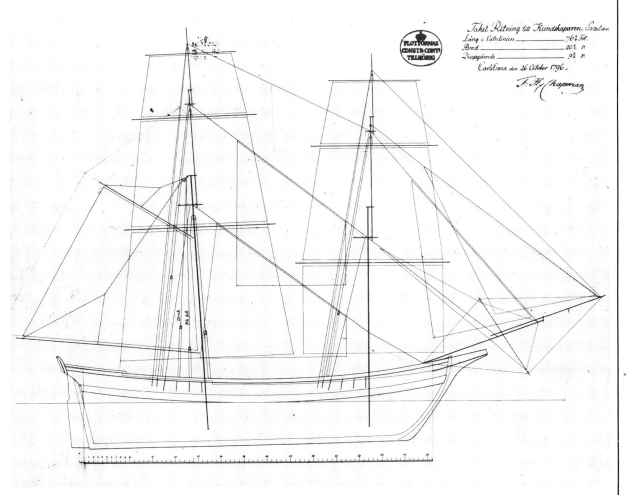

Fig X/5.
Brig Svalan, *sail plan*
(Krigsarkivet, Stockholm).

the vessel in both instances gets the desired weather-helm. Trials with three different trims will show which trim the vessel ought to have, to get the maximum good sailing qualities.

When Chapman wrote the above procedures, he was yet to carry out the trials with the brig *Svalan*. However, on 15 February 1798, he wrote to his assistant Bogeman stating that he was preparing drawings for nine frigates to carry 44 guns and three brigs to carry 8 to 12 guns. 'All these will be in accordance with the new theory as a result of my experiments. The brig *Svalan* built in accordance with these has met my expectations.' In the same letter Chapman refers to his own state of health:

I am keeping well, no illness except a little lassitude

having regard to my age — the trembling of my hands is such that I cannot hold a compass in my hands, I cannot use knife, fork and spoon or take a glass to my mouth. I must rely on others for help, only when I press my hands hard against a table, can I draw and write in pencil.

The frigate *af Chapman* (fig X/6) completed in 1803 in accordance with Chapman's relaxation theories had the following dimensions and armament:
The frigate *af Chapman*'s trials under the direction of Chapman, now eighty-two years old, began on 14 August 1803 and lasted until the middle of September. The frigate had a complement of 250 men, was provisioned for six months, and carried a full load of shot. The crew's water allowance for drinking and

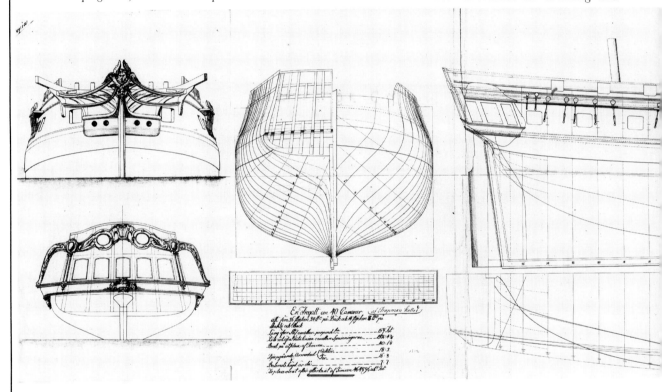

Length	154 feet (45.74 metres)
Beam	39 feet (11.58 metres)
Draught	18 feet (5.35 metres)
Complement	330

Armament
Twenty-six 24-pounder guns
Two 12-pounder guns
Twelve 8-pounder guns

cooking was to be $3\frac{1}{2}$ litres per man per day. The frigate's draught was 5.4 m (18ft 4ins) aft and 4.8 m (16ft 8ins) forward. The height of the gun ports above the water was 2.25m (7ft 5$\frac{1}{2}$ins), and the rakes of the masts at the commencement of the trials were: fore mast 1°, main mast 3° 50′, mizzen 8°. After the initial trials, the frigate returned to an anchorage at Marvin where, after making calculations, the rakes of the masts were changed as follows: fore mast to 0.5°, main mast to 3°, mizzen to 6° 35′.

The commander, L Fischerström reported that the frigate was very stiff, and sailed well when close-hauled with little leeway in fresh topsail breeze, making about $6\frac{3}{4}$ knots, she went about in four to five minutes, and her best speed was 10 knots. He stated that large lumps had formed on the hull from the mixture of sulphur and tar applied as anti-fouling to the vessel's bottom, and in his opinion these had prevented the frigate from sailing as well as had been anticipated. He pointed out that the frigate was able to carry more sail than any other frigate in the fleet and was able to keep all gun

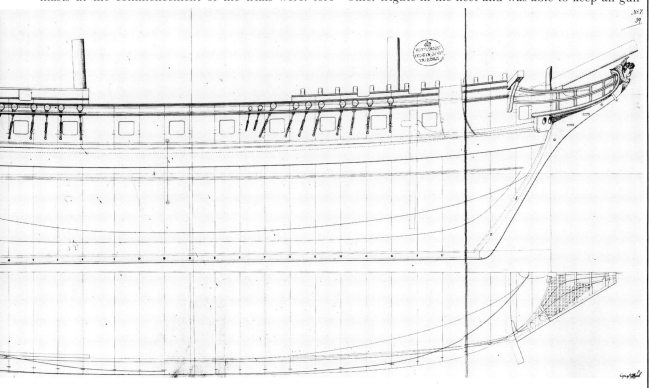

Fig X/6.
Frigate af Chapman, *sheer draft,*
body plan, bow and stern views
(Krigsarkivet, Stockholm).

ports open in topsail breeze. In the commander's opinion, if the frigate had been sheathed with copper and provided with about 90–135 kilos more ballast 'she would have sailed extraordinary well'. Chapman did not consider that the trials' results met with his expectations of the relaxation method. He wrote:

That the application of the relaxation line system does not contribute more to better sailing can be concluded from the following. The relaxation line has been used in a new 40-gun frigate, which should have had the greatest possible effect to reduce the water's cohesive power aft. I directed the trials, held in the Baltic during the summer of 1803, and I had the trials conducted in an ordinary steady topgallant breeze and smooth sea, close-hauled

but not closer to the wind than 7–6½ points, and at a speed of 9 knots; I gave the frigate more or less trim by the stern. I had a certain amount of ballast placed amidships. There was continuous logging of the vessel's behaviour, and she made greater speed when floating at the waterline shown on the draft than when it had more or less trim by the stern, which confirms the correctness of the theory, but in a heavy sea, there was a difference in speed. If the frigate had been copper-sheathed, the difference would have been greater. However, in all circumstances, the conclusions should be drawn that the advantage obtained by the use of the relaxation lines is of little importance to good sailing qualities. Furthermore, its application to ship construction can be discontinued. Nevertheless a method to calculate the water's effect to

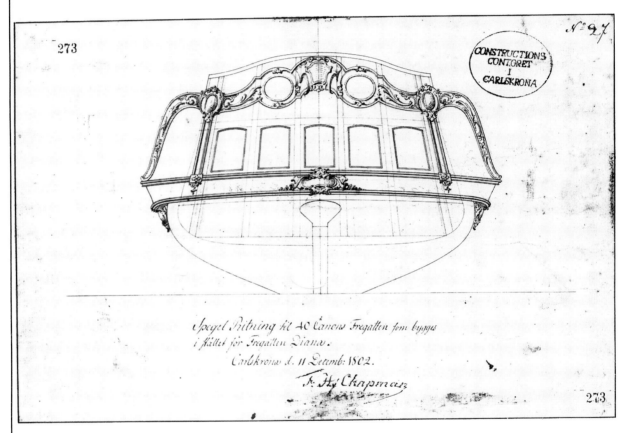

Fig X/8.
Frigate af Chapman, *stern decoration drawing*
(Krigsarkivet, Stockholm).

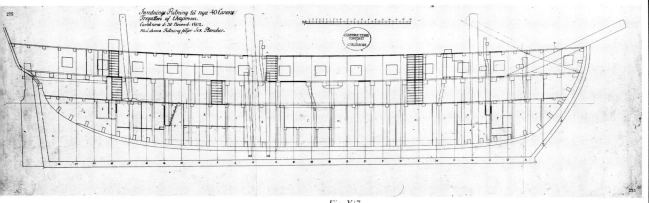

Fig X/7.
Frigate af Chapman, *internal profile*
(Krigsarkivet, Stockholm).

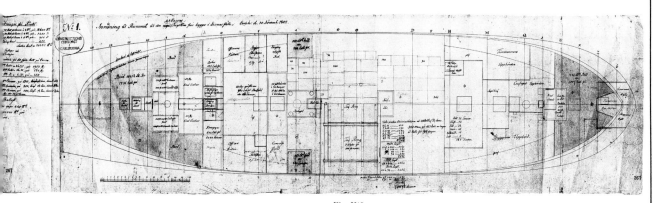

Fig X/9.
Frigate af Chapman, *plan of orlop and hold*
(Krigsarkivet, Stockholm).

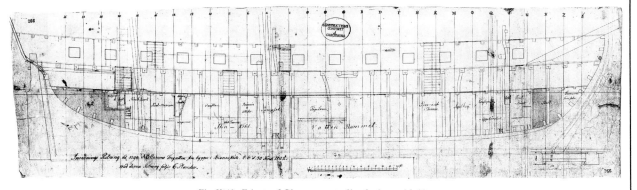

Fig X/10. Frigate af Chapman, *profile of orlop and hold spaces*
(Krigsarkivet, Stockholm).

hinder a vessel's forward movement will always remain permanent and it can be ignored in the design of ships of the line.

Chapman in his paper 'The theory of the size and form of the ships of the line' published in 1806 again discussed the reasons for the failure of his relaxation design method. He stated that in the application of the relaxation lines to the stern, he had been forced to increase the width of the forward section of the frigate because he could not reduce its displacement. The result was that the centre of gravity of the 'water hole' (displacement) was one foot further forward, which hindered the ship's ability to go about. Chapman continued that, as the construction of ships of the line in accordance with his relaxation method would be difficult, he recommended instead the use of the simpler parabola method. The navy accepted his recommendation, and all major wooden vessels continued to be built in accordance with Chapman's parabola method. The frigate *af Chapman*, in the opinions of her commanders, became a good sailer after more adjustments had been made to the rigging. Apparently certain types of racing yachts built in the United States of America, imported into Scandinavia in the early 1900s, are said to have had Chapman's relaxation lines incorporated into their hull designs. Chapman, as mentioned earlier, was pleased with the results obtained by the brig *Svalan*, built after the relaxation system, so perhaps his system could provide some advantages for small craft.

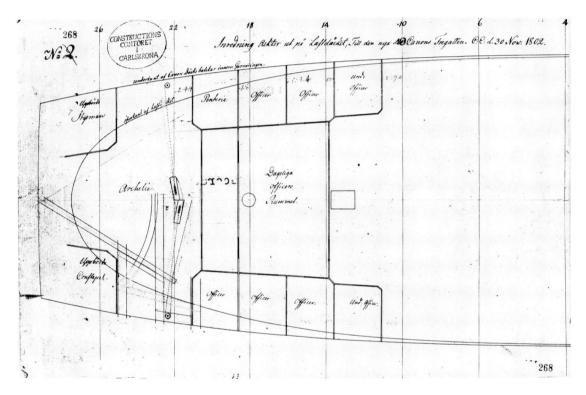

Fig X/11.
Frigate af Chapman, *officers' cabins*
and tiller flat
(Krigsarkivet, Stockholm).

During this period, Chapman wrote a paper which he never published, about ships' rudders. The title of his paper was 'The problems of ships' rudders and rudder lines'. (In 1921, according to a publication of Göteborg's Maritime Museum this paper was in possession of Thore Thelander, P.Eng. Unfortunately its present whereabouts are unknown.) By the laws of mechanics, the rudder with the greatest effect to turn a ship quickly should have an angle of 55 degrees where no consideration is given to the effects of the line of flow. However, practice shows that the best angle is 35 degrees. Chapman advanced a theory in which he maintained the helm angle should be 39 degrees, from which he deducted between 3 and 4 degrees because the direction of flow was not parallel with the keel, and obtained a coincidence with what practice has shown to be correct. Chapman's reasons for not publishing this paper are unknown. Perhaps he had no funds to carry out the practical experiments to prove or disprove his theory.

In 1798, Chapman made some experiments to determine the strength of tarred cordage and, through Admiral C O Cronstedt, obtained a Crown grant to conduct comparative trials of rope spun with 36 strands used for ships' anchor cables and shrouds laid in the current way, and rope laid in accordance with Chapman's ideas. The trials were made with about 5½ metres of each type of rope. The standard cordage broke after being subject to about 5.4 kilos stress weight, whereas rope spun with 180 strands in accordance with

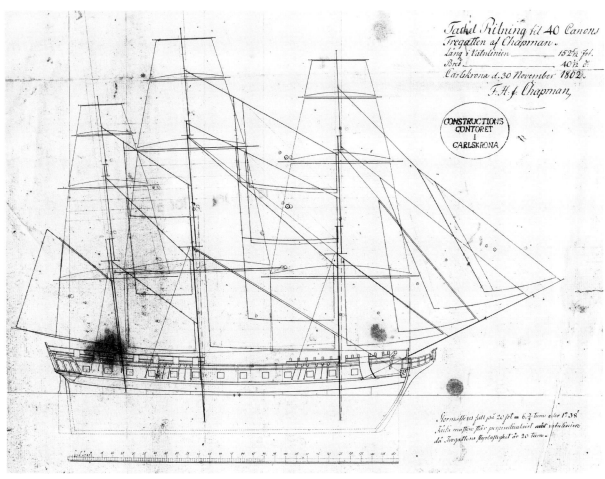

Fig X/12.
Frigate af Chapman, *sail plan*
(Krigsarkivet, Stockholm).

Chapman's method broke when subjected to 8.1 kilos stress weight. In the same year, Chapman designed a machine for the Karlskrona dockyard to spin rope so that all strands would be equally stretched (fig X/13). The machine was built and did produce much stronger cordage, but as it was entirely made of wood it did not perform as well as the inventor had expected. A technician some thirty years later wrote that the principal fault with Chapman's machine was the yarn not passing through a cylinder made of iron, or other metal before spinning began. 'Had the machine contained metal parts instead of wood', according to the technician, 'it could have been possible to have spun as good rope as the machines imported from Britain in 1834.'

Chapman was to continue to receive requests for advice about designs of vessels needed for special purposes, or particular trades. In December 1797, the Crown asked Chapman to submit proposals for naval craft suitable to intercept shipping operating between Denmark and Norway, and which could be employed in Göteborg skerries. He submitted proposals for two different types of 36-gun frigate (fig X/14). He proposed these vessels be copper-sheathed and huckert-rigged which in his opinion, should lessen rolling and pitching, and be more practical for service in the west coast skerries. Chapman's design provided for seven or eight pairs of sweeps, which he held to be very necessary for handling in the confined waters of the skerries. In addition he recommended that only decked vessels be stationed on the west coast because the western skerries were more open to the sea than those of the Gulf of Finland. Because it would take time to build the new vessels, Chapman suggested that two of the larger frigates should be temporarily stationed on the west coast, and he added that since their stay would be short, copper-sheathing for service on the west coast would not be necessary. None of the frigates proposed for west coast service was ever built owing to lack of funds.

The Crown continued to request Chapman to prepare drafts for different types of vessels for both the Inshore and High Seas Fleets during his life's remaining years. When the Crown requested drafts for new decked gun-sloops early in 1802, Chapman replied in his letter of 21 March 1802, that he would be glad to complete the requested drafts, but the Crown must wait until the autumn because,

> I am fully engaged at work on a theory about the correct form of ships of the line — their proper form and size — I would likely lose the concepts on which I am working if I should now be interrupted. When one is eighty years old one does not have the memory of one's earlier years — there are great differences between one's memory when one is seventy, and when one is eighty — half the drawings are completed.

Chapman submitted drafts to the Crown for two types of gun-sloops for use in the Sound, Kattegat, and the Göteborg skerries on 5 September 1802. The first type (fig X/15) was to be armed with one 24-pounder gun in the bow and stern, four 6-pounder carronades and four 2-pounder swivel guns; the second vessel, similar to the Pojänmää of the Inshore Fleet, was to be armed with four 12-pounder carronades on each side and two 24-pounder long guns in the bow and stern. On 22 September 1802, the Crown informed Chapman that it had sent both his proposals to a committee of the High Seas Fleet for review, and as a result of the committee's recommendations, the Crown decided to build only the first gun-sloop.

Chapman maintained a keen interest in the welfare of the High Seas Fleet; and he was horrified to learn of a proposal in 1802 to reduce Sweden's sea defences to a few frigates and the Inshore Fleet. On 11 October 1802 he wrote to Admiral C O Cronstedt, the following:

> That the Navy shall consist of the Inshore Fleet and a few frigates, I consider ridiculous. If we should be at war with Denmark, she will send some ships of the line and frigates into the Baltic to prevent all trade and communications with Germany and Russia. The Inshore Fleet and a few frigates cannot prevent this. Denmark will station ships of the line in the Kattegat and Sound to cruise continuously between Denmark and Norway. All Swedish merchant vessels trading to the Mediterranean will be taken by Danish warships. Our foreign trade will be given a hammer blow, none of our products will be able to be shipped out — fisheries will cease — there will be shortages of salt — home trade will decline — there will be no income for the state from taxes or customs duties, and the state's ability to maintain either an army or navy will be very limited. If Denmark attacks us, there are no reprisals possible — any invasion of Denmark will be impossible — the only countermeasure is to attack Norway — the Inshore Fleet cannot prevent the enemy landing in Sweden at a hundred different places — the result could be our capture of Norway, and the loss of Sweden.
>
> An experienced seaman in heavy weather in a leaking vessel under jury rig and facing a lee shore does not run straight for the beach to save life; he tries, by carrying a greater press of sail and the hope of a favourable wind, to avoid disaster.
>
> Sweden has at all times been a sea power because of her position and history.

Admiral Cronstedt's reply is not known, but Sweden did continue to maintain a reduced High Seas Fleet.

In addition to preparing drafts and proposals for the two fleets, Chapman was to give advice to various individuals concerning the types of merchant vessels suitable for specific purposes. In a letter to Count G Wetterstedt dated 7 July 1796 about a vessel suitable for trade on Lake Mälar — a large body of water stretching some 117 kilometres west of Stockholm — Chapman wrote:

> The vessel's hull must be sharp at both ends to be able to sail well and be able to bear away. It must not be built longer in proportion to the beam, since it would then turn more slowly, which is not ideal for confined waters. In addition, the bottom must not be too flat, where that part of the cargo of wheat is to be stowed so that when the vessel is heeling and tacking it will not get wet. Leeboards are not often used in Sweden, but this vessel should be fitted with these so that her leeway will not be too great. The vessel should be built of pine and I

recommend that you should have the vessel built at Gävle where there is a good shipwright who can follow drawings.

It is not known whether Chapman provided the drafts for Wetterstedt's vessel or if it was ever built.

A certain baron who was a shipowner asked Chapman in a letter dated 16 February 1798 to prepare draughts for a vessel suitable to sail on Lake Väner and to be able to pass through the locks to Göteborg. In his letter of 8 March 1798 Chapman made the following proposal:

> If this vessel is to sail on Lake Väner, pass through the locks on route for Göteborg, have a draught of 7 feet, be

Fig X/13.
Rope spinning machine designed by Chapman
for the Karlskrona dockyard
(Naval Museum, Karlskrona).

able to carry 500lbs (225 kilos) of iron, 500 tons of wheat, three alna-long (1.8 m) firewood, sawn lumber and barrels, it must be able to withstand the storms in Väner's short seas, be easily handled in the lake's eddies and be rigged as a tjalk with two masts. I would add to it, leeboards between the forward and aft hatches, a larger long hatch between the two masts and, one aft of the main mast, both to have high coamings. The vessel should be similar to a Hartloper Galliot (Dutch Hoy) — in other words, ought to have a rounded stern. It should carry topsails on both masts in light winds (see drawings). If the vessel is built with high freeboard so that it can be loaded 10–12 inches deeper, such a vessel ought to be able to sail to all places in the Baltic and North Sea. As soon as I have finished my drafts for frigates, I will complete the drafts for this vessel and send them to you.

The Baron also requested Chapman to design a larger vessel for service on Lake Väner to be capable of carrying about 400 kilos of iron and between 40–50 sawn logs. Chapman replied that he had to consider the matter further before he could prepare a draft of a suitable vessel. No records show if Chapman completed the drafts for this special craft.

In 1806 the Swedish East India Company commissioned Chapman to prepare drafts for a new ship suitable for the Göteborg–Canton trade. Chapman prepared the hull and sail plans for a vessel of about 350 lasts (or 840 tons) which he presented to the directors of the company in January 1807 (fig X/16). The new East Indiaman was to have the following dimensions:

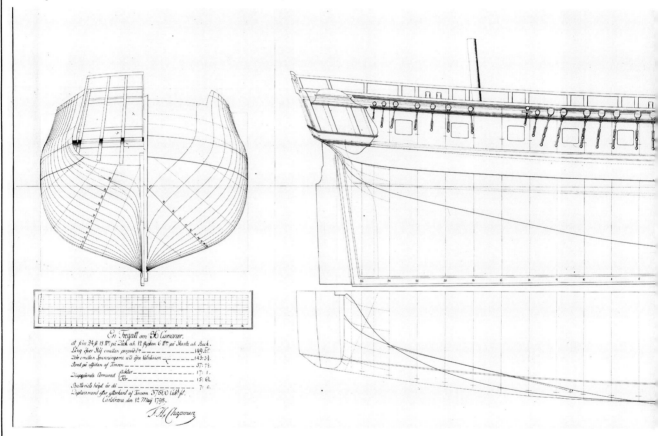

Length	139½ feet (41.43 metres)
Beam	38 feet (11.29 metres)
Draught, full load	20½ feet (6.09 metres) aft
	15⅚ feet (4.70 metres) forward

The tumblehome was to be only 2½ feet (75cm), whereas Chapman's earlier East Indiamen had been given a tumblehome of 3½ feet (105cm). The heights between decks were to vary between 6½ feet (1.90 metres) and 6¾ feet (1.02 metres).

The drafts show that the bow describes an elegant curve up to the figurehead which was to be a simple shield, in some ways anticipating the coming clipper ship. The stern remains spacious — no doubt the all-powerful supercargoes were reluctant to give up any of their comforts — but the customary elaborate decorations of the stern galleries, bow, and bulwarks have only been included to round off or complete the lines. This part of the proposed design would have no doubt met with the desires of the company's directors who wished to be as economical as possible with all expenditures owing to the company's financial difficulties. Chapman must have been aware of the company's situation, and consequently he designed a vessel to comply with its economic needs.

The original lines plan (fig X/16) shows in black the vessel's waterline when fully loaded, with the centre of gravity and metacentre positions shown by two small red circles. The hull was pierced for twenty guns on the upper deck, although the hulls of the other Swedish

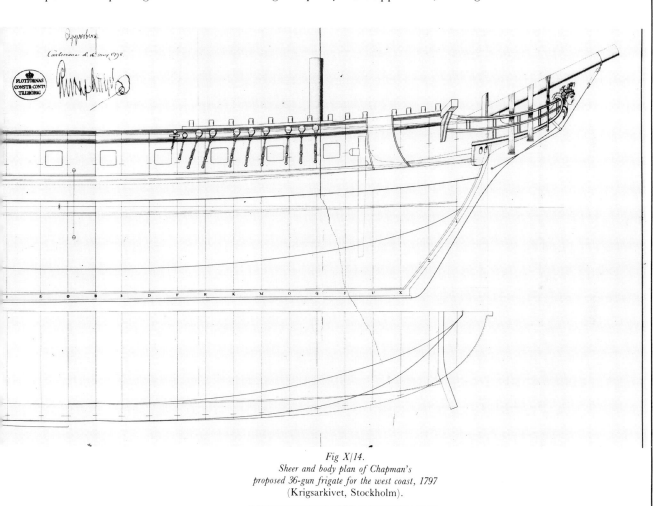

Fig X/14.
Sheer and body plan of Chapman's
proposed 36-gun frigate for the west coast, 1797
(Krigsarkivet, Stockholm).

East Indiaman designed by Chapman, were pierced for twenty-two to twenty-eight guns — actually large numbers of guns were never carried, some of the gun ports simply serving to provide ventilation in the hot climates.

Chapman's sail plan (fig X/18) for the ship bears the following note:

Suppose the ship's centre of gravity is 1.5 feet below the waterline. The sail moment from that centre is 96,000 and the displacement = 58,000, then 96,000/ 58,800 = 1632. As a result it can be assumed as a constant rule for merchant vessels, that the eight sails' moment from the vessel's centre of gravity shall be sixteen times the ship's displacement.

The sail plan shows that, besides the courses, the vessel was to carry the following canvas: flying jib, jib, fore topgallant, fore topsail, main topgallant, main topsail, mizzen topgallant, mizzen topsail and mizzen sail. The plan omits the fore sail, main sail and any stay sails. The plan shows no royals, but it was unusual for Scandinavian ships to wear royals in the eighteenth and early nineteenth centuries in northern waters.

Chapman provided the company's board with a plan (fig X/17) to illustrate the best stowage of cargo for the return voyage from Canton to Göteborg. Chapman required the lower deck to be caulked and the partitions shown on the plan to be set up only after the ship's arrival at Canton. The plan shows the principal cargo to be stowed was tea packed in chests,

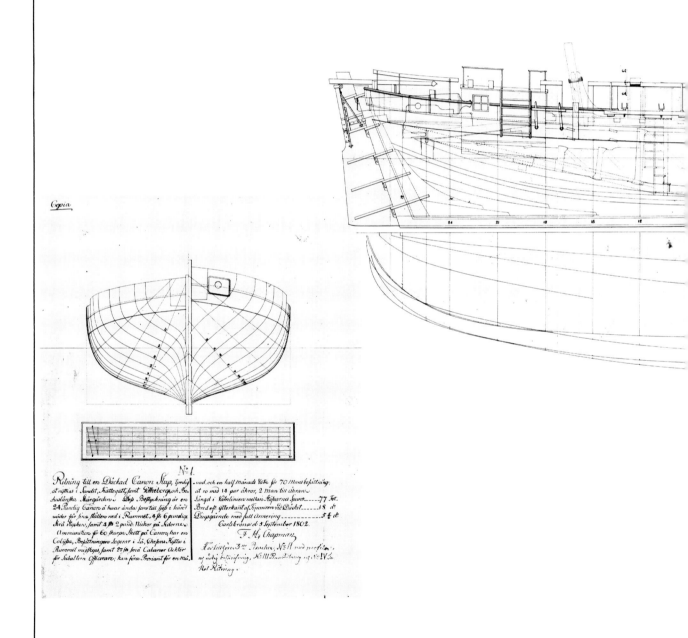

1017 of which were to be stowed ahead of, and 600 aft of the main mast, and 140 chests of green tea were to be stowed in the stern. The draft shows in detail the storage of water casks, akvavit barrels, other stores and firewood. Chapman's draft indicates the centre of gravity with the letter 'A', and also the metacentre. He added the following notes on the plan:

The space B, or forepeak, will contain the sail locker, coal, charcoal, pitch, tar barrels, boatswain's and carpenter's stores etc, and salted provisions for the cabins. Access to these is through companion ways in the second and third decks forward of the fore mast. The quantities of water and provisions are in accordance with the Royal Navy's ration lists. When all the cargo had been stored in accordance with this draft, the vessel will keep its equilibrium at about the centre of gravity 'A'. Now remember, as regards the daily consumption of water, when two casks' contents are consumed aft of the main mast, the contents of three forward of the main mast ought to be used at the same time.

A pantry for the saloon can be placed between the second and third decks ahead of the cabins located forward of the great cabin. The master's and third mate's quarters will be on the poop.

Twenty-three-lispun (about 25kg each) weights are to be kept in the cable locker. These are to be moved fore, or aft to give the ship its proper trim.

Karlskrona 29 January 1807
22 February FHC

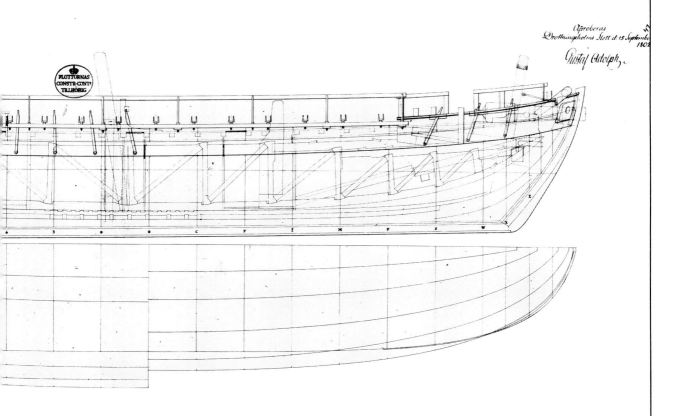

Fig X/15.
Sheer, lines and body plan of proposed decked gun-sloop No 1 for use in the
Sound, Kattegat and Göteborg skerries, dated September 1802
(contemporary copy). Dimensions were: length at waterline 77 feet
(23.46 metres), maximum beam 18 feet (5.48 metres), draught fully armed
5⅚ feet (1.83 metres). Armament: one 24-pounder at bow and stern,
four 6-pounders, four 2-pounder swivel guns, 60 shots for each gun.
Commander's quarters amidships, Junior officers aft in 23 small cabins.
To carry one month's stores and 15 days' water for crew of 70.
Vessel to be rowed by 14 pairs of oars, 2 men to each oar
(Krigsarkivet, Stockholm).

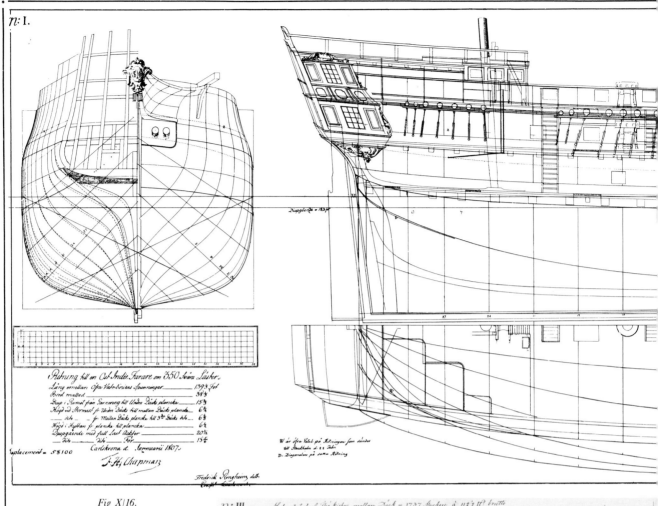

Fig X/16.
Proposed East Indiaman,
sheer, half-breadth and body plan
(Göteborg Maritime Museum).

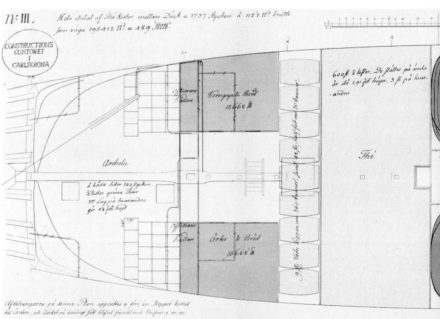

Fig X/17.
Proposed East Indiaman, cargo stowage plan
(Göteborg Maritime Museum).

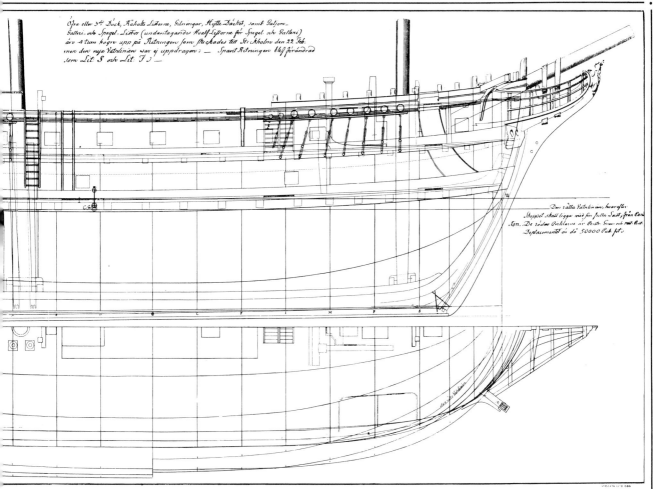

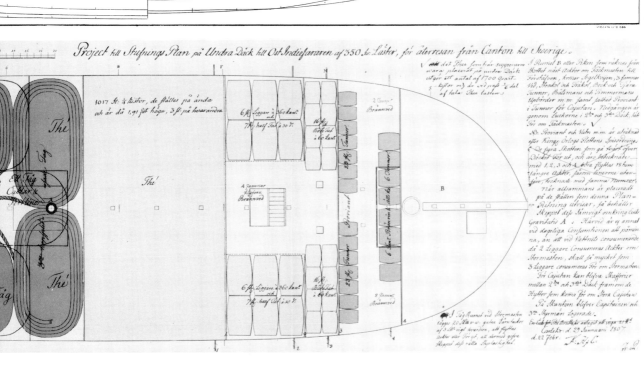

Chapman's initials on the drafts show the trembling in his hands, of which he complained for several years.

The Swedish East India Company built no new ship in accordance with Chapman's drafts; its profits from the sales of the tea, porcelain and other products imported from Canton, were insufficient to finance a new vessel. The company ceased to send its own ships to the Far East after 1804, the last returning to Göteborg in the first quarter of 1806. One ship, the *Hoppet* (The Hope) was sent to Britain towards the end of 1808 with a cargo of iron bars, where it was intended she should join a British convoy sailing to Bengal, but the shift in Swedish politics in March 1809, which resulted in the deposing of Gustaf IV, caused the cancellation of the voyage and *Hoppet* returned to

Göteborg, which resulted in a heavy loss to the company. Nevertheless, the company had sufficient goods on hand which it was able to sell at comfortable profits over the next four years and in 1813 it was dissolved.

Chapman was able, in spite of the Napoleonic wars, to keep in touch with the developments in shipbuilding outside Scandinavia. In a letter to a shipowner dated 1 March 1804, he discusses the use of iron hanging knees in place of those made of pine. A shipowner had written to Chapman to ask his advice about replacing pine knees with iron knees in the construction of a 90 lasts (215 tons) brig. Would the iron knees last longer than pine knees and would there be any economic advantage? Chapman in his reply states that he had

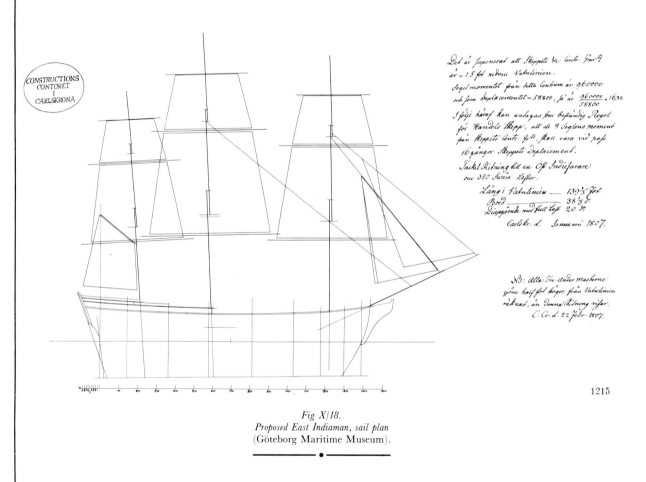

1215

Fig X/18.
Proposed East Indiaman, sail plan
(Göteborg Maritime Museum).

always been ready to use oak or iron knees in ships of his construction. He would have preferred to have used iron knees in his major naval construction programme had iron knees been available. Probably the Swedish iron industry of the day, although able to produce bar iron, was unable to make sufficient iron knees for the ten ships of the line, and the ten frigates of the 1780 programme within the time frame for its completion. In 1805, Chapman wrote a report in which he examined the replacement of oak knees with iron hanging knees, and expressed some concern that weight problems could occur. However, he was likely to have been aware from his close connections with the Swedish East India Company, that the British East India Company's chief surveyor, Gabriel Snodgrass, had begun to use iron knees in the British ships from the 1770s.

Chapman maintained a keen interest in the development of the sailing merchant vessel for the rest of his life. He was busy on new studies to improve merchant ship design at the time of his death in 1808, but because of the increased trembling in his hands, he could only write his proposals and calculations on slates, and although these still exist, it is very difficult to read either his writing or to follow his calculations. Chapman used his last years to the full in his search for the perfect sailing vessel.

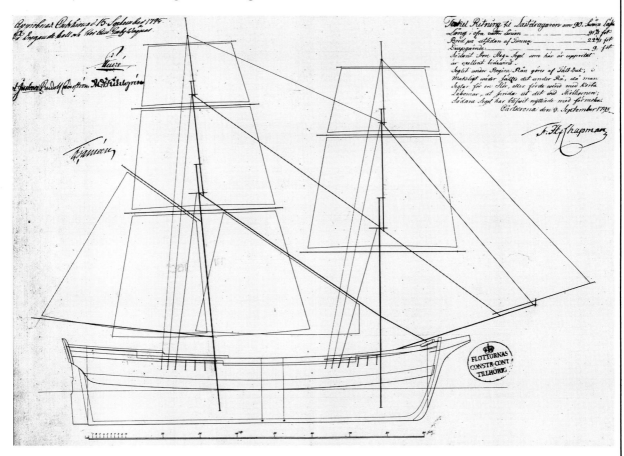

Fig X/20.
Sail plan of merchant vessel of 90 lasts
(Krigsarkivet, Stockholm).

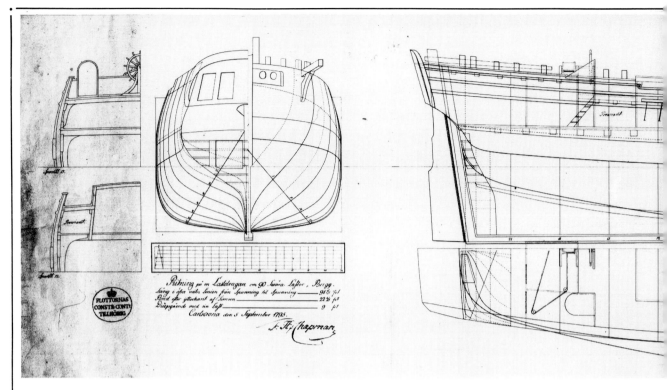

Fig. X/19.
Sheer and body plan of merchant vessel of 90 lasts
(Krigsarkivet, Stockholm).

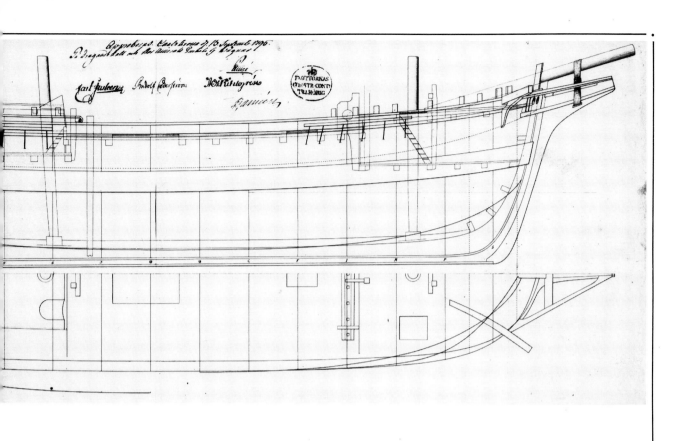

Fig XI/1.
Fredrik Henrik af Chapman,
painting by L Pasch, 1778, which depicts
Chapman wearing his working jacket
(National Museum, Stockholm).

Eleven
CHAPMAN THE MAN

There is surprisingly little information on what Chapman was like as a person, on his interests outside shipbuilding, or on the opinions of his friends and colleagues. One possible source of such information is his own memoirs of the years 1720–98, dictated by Chapman about a year before his death, to which his adopted son Lieutenant-Colonel G A af Chapman added a few notes. The memoirs list Chapman's accomplishments for almost each year from 1720 to 1798, but unfortunately shed little light on the naval architect's character. Chapman gives details of his ancestry and particulars of his father's career in the British and Swedish navies. His official correspondence, comprising reports, submissions and the like, show him to have been, especially in his Stockholm and early Karlskrona years, an individual holding strong views, convinced that these were correct. The diaries of G J Ehrensvärd and Admiral Tersmeden's memoirs reveal something of Chapman's character, but as Tersmeden and Chapman had opposing opinions on most matters, including style of living, the former's opinions of the naval architect were seldom complimentary.

Chapman's contemporaries describe him as a fairly tall, heavily built man with an attractive face, which is confirmed by the portrait by L Pasch (fig XI/1). He is described as a vivacious individual, who on occasion could be irritable and impetuous, but his anger was usually short lived. Chapman's company was instructive and pleasant, even for the ladies, whose company he enjoyed, even in old age. In spite of one indiscretion, he lived a moderate life by eighteenth century standards. He was a man who liked to be seen and heard. He never suffered from an inferiority complex; in fact he held himself in high esteem, and he liked to show himself off as someone important and remarkable. Chapman always kept a sharp look-out with regard to his own interests, particularly the economic ones. His reactions on promotion to vice-admiral, referred to earlier, prove his interest in adequate emoluments in return for his work and responsibilities. Although Chapman was determined to be the leading light at all times, nonetheless he engaged able assistants such

as Bogeman, Ringheim and his brother William Chapman. The latter was to complete many of the drafts of ships for which his elder brother was the designer. Although Chapman was tardy with recognition of his associates' work, he had some concerns for their welfare. In a letter to Bogeman dated 15 February 1798, Chapman wrote, 'I am sorry to hear that you are plagued with troublesome headaches and are still taking medicine for the tiresome cough. You cannot now have many happy times, which makes me sorry.' Chapman then describes his own health problems particularly the trembling in his hand and adds that even leeches had not eased his difficulties.

Chapman had an immense capacity for work up to the very end of his life, when he was working on improvements to the hulls for merchant vessels. Every day he rose early (in summer at 4am) and worked for sixteen hours each day, although on reaching the age of eighty, he did reduce his working day to fourteen hours. When living in Karlskrona he made a habit of following a custom of many inhabitants of Blekinge county, which was to sit quietly for an hour or so at dusk before lighting the lamps, to contemplate the events of the passing day. Chapman was always busy on one or other of his projects, but would make himself free to talk to whoever came to visit. He had a gift of being able to leave his work, even if in the midst of complicated calculations, talk to the visitor, and then continue with the calculations at the precise point where he had left off, as if he had never been disturbed.

He had an open and friendly manner towards both his equals and his subordinates, and was always willing to share his knowledge. He could express himself easily, clearly, and where necessary, forcibly. He demanded much of his staff and he never considered that anyone could ever get tired from hard work. Nonetheless he was sometimes prepared to show consideration to his staff. For example, a young officer of the Constructor Corps — one of his best draftsman who, from the early morning to evening, was expected to stand at the drafting table — was bold enough to ask for one day's leave. Chapman became angry and threatened the young officer with arrest. The young officer replied, 'Thank you, Admiral. I would certainly prefer to sit in the guard house, than have to stand day after day at the draughting table — I need the rest'. 'Oh no', replied Chapman, 'I did not intend to be so unkind — come with me to Skärva and we can amuse ourselves in the countryside.'

Chapman kept up the interest in the arts which he had probably acquired during his years in France, and in Stockholm when the great school of Swedish artists — Hall, Pilo, Roslin, Rehn, Sergel and Krafft — flourished. He was probably acquainted with all of these leading artists through his friendship with Sergel. He was politically astute, having formed friendships with the Ehrensvärds, father and son, af Trolle, and others close to Gustaf III, such as the brothers Scheffer.

He received some distinguished visitors at Karlskrona both during his time as dockyard superintendent and in his retirement years. F de Miranda, the South American hero, wrote in a letter dated 14 December 1787 about his visit to Chapman in Karlskrona:

Baron von Stedingk came to fetch me, and we went on our naval tour, first to Rear-Admiral Chapman's house. He is responsible for the naval construction activity. He received me very kindly and spoke to me in English as he did not understand French. He asked pardon that an illness prevented him from accompanying us on our tour. He gave orders to his Adjutant-Lieutenant Sjöstierna to accompany us.

The British Captain (later Admiral) Sidney Smith, who had served with some distinction in the Swedish Inshore Fleet in the 1788–1790 war, seems from correspondence held in the Swedish National Archives to have met Chapman but no actual records of their meeting have been found. According to Barrow, Smith's biographer, most of his records of his service with Swedish fleets were lost in a fire. In a letter dated 8 November 1790, Smith asked Chapman to find employment for his Swedish servant described as 'an excellent and indefatigable man — fit for employment as a courier or as a porter at the gate'. The letter continues:

Deliver my boat and its belongings to the mate of the

Fig XI/2.
Chapman's house at Skärva, front view
(Naval Museum, Karlskrona).

brig *Disa* as a small reward for saving me and my crew on board the yacht *Aurora* when she was sunk by the Russian line of battle ships at the passage at Viborg. Should the boat be out of repair, may I beg you to give it so much as will set him afloat without any expense to him which he could not afford.

Smith wrote to Chapman again from London and in his letter dated 23 April 1792 asked Chapman to receive his friends Bootle and Parkinson who were to tour Northern Europe. 'They will be highly gratified to see your ingenious and masterly work together with the naval establishment of the ports and docks.' There seem to be no record of any meeting between Chapman and the two Britons.

The French Duke of Angoulême, who arrived in Karlskrona from the Continent with other members of the French Royal Family in 1807, requested Gustaf IV to arrange for a visit to Chapman. Palmquist, a court official, wrote to Chapman on 9 June 1807 to ask for leave for the Duke of Angoulême's visit. 'Your wide knowledge and great qualities have awakened in this prince the same admiration which fills all others who have got to know about your famous name. He will visit you at 3pm, if it will not bother the Admiral too much.'

Chapman believed in living comfortably, and during his service as admiral superintendent of the dockyard built what he called a 'simple farm labourer's cottage' a few kilometres from Karlskrona. He used both dockyard labour and materials to construct a 24-room house with clock tower (fig XI/2). His use of dockyard labour and materials was not without precedent; his predecessor, Admiral Tersmeden, had used both to construct a summer house on his property. The king had agreed to the cost of Tersmeden's house being absorbed by the Crown, and granted permission for the construction of Chapman's house, which still stands, carefully maintained by the Wachtmeister family. It has yet to be declared a national heritage building. It contains a few of Chapman's original furnishings, a portrait of Bellman, his collection of Chinese water colours illustrating different types of Chinese river craft (including a floating brothel), and paintings by unknown and lesser-known artists, probably bought by Chapman to fill up wall space. The house contains several spittoons from Chapman's time (at that period it was a common belief that saliva was harmful, and should not be allowed to accumulate in the mouth). The famous Swedish tiled stoves, installed in Chapman's time still heat the rooms. Chapman maintained an open house at Skärva for friends, relations and other visitors, and is reported to have been a genial host.

Chapman was honoured by the Swedish government during his lifetime; not only was he enobled, but in 1799 he received the Grand Cross of the Vasa Order from King Gustaf IV. Chapman, then in his eightieth year, wrote in a letter to a court official about the award after a visit of Gustaf IV to Karlskrona:

> I wrote and thanked him [Gustaf IV] but I forgot to thank him personally when we met. When I was driving back to Skärva, the reflection of the order in the window of the carriage reminded me of the big mistake I had made. So if I am alive when he comes again, I dare not show myself. So it is when one grows old — one forgets things — I am ashamed and will never be happy again.

The Crown decided in 1793 to erect a monument to Chapman in the model room of the Model and Hiring Hall building (fig XI/5) in the Karlskrona dockyard. C A Ehrensvärd wrote to Duke Carl about the monument:

With most humble respect, your Royal Highness has ordered in recognition of Admiral Chapman that a medallion of him should be placed in the model room. I have already written to Professor Sergel about it, and asked if it would not be possible in such a large medallion to sculpture the inscription outside of the medallion. Sergel has replied that it can be done, and if your Highness agrees, he will take on the work.

The medallion was completed in Italy in accordance with Sergel's design. The stone on which the medallion, carved in white marble, is mounted bears the following inscription:

FREDR: HENRIK AF CHAPMAN Knight Grand Cross

Fig XI/3.
Chapman's house at Skärva, rear view
(Naval Museum, Karlskrona).

of the Vasa Order, Knight of the Order of the Sword. His genius and patriotism, working for King Gustaf III's aims, gave Sweden new fleets built after improved methods. As in accordance with the King's orders the work has continued. Carl, Duke of Södermanland, Sweden's Grand Admiral, has dedicated this portrait of the creator to hereafter.

The monument also consists of a wooden carving representing on its right, a mountain range and immediately below it a sphinx. The idea originated in an old Greek myth which relates that a sphinx sat on a mountain in Thessaly requiring passers-by to answer a riddle. Those that failed to give the correct answer were thrown down the mountain-side, but should the passer-by give the correct answer the sphinx would be cast down. Here the monument is intended to show that Chapman has solved the riddles of shipbuilding, and therefore the sphinx has been thrown down from the mountain tops. Sergel's monument was dedicated in Chapman's presence on 10 May 1800. Admiral Adam Wachtmeister, the dockyard commander, made the dedication speech to which Chapman's reply was short. Afterwards the party returned to the admiral's house for dinner, when the guests proposed many toasts to Chapmam throughout the evening.

The Royal Academy of Sciences informed Chapman in a letter dated 5 January 1808 that because of his great knowledge of ship construction, his important services, and the recently filed papers, a medal had been struck in his honour. The medal shows on the one side a planked-up hull, and on the other Chapman's

Fig XI/4.
Chapman's house at Skärva, the drawing office
(Naval Museum, Karlskrona).

effigy. The motto inscribed on the medal is *Faman feret per orbera* (His fame shall spread all over the world).

Chapman's election to honourary membership of the Royal Society of Naval Sciences was delayed until 1798 when he was seventy-seven years old. He became the forty-second member of that society, which was founded in 1771. It seems probable that the delay in bestowing the honour may have been due to the opposition by some of Chapman's old opponents, Admirals Falkengren and Tersmeden, who had earlier prevented his election. The citation reads as follows: 'The Society has decided to call Vice-Admiral Fredrik Henrik af Chapman to be an honourary member after taking into consideration his remarkable gifts, and the results of his works. He is the first to have this honourable distinction.' Chapman replied, 'The honour which the Royal Society of Naval Science has given me when it called me to honourary membership, is a highly complimentary proof of its confidence and kindness. I therefore venture to ask the Colonel to assure the Society of my keenly sensitive gratitude and my unlimited esteem.' The Royal Academy of Military Sciences and the Academy of Painters and Sculptors had already elected Chapman to their membership in 1774.

The British Society for the Improvement of Naval Architecture elected Chapman an honourary member in 1791, an indication that even in those rather restricted circles, there was some appreciation of theoretical naval architecture. Chapman's *Mercatoria* would have been known to the British Society, and possibly something of his *Treatise on Shipbuilding* which, although not available in English, had already been translated into French. Unfortunately the British Society's life was short; it was dissolved in or about 1800.

Chapman tried to establish relations with the British Admiralty through a certain Henry Pierrepont, a British diplomat understood to have been stationed in Copenhagen. Henry Pierrepont in a letter to Chapman, dated Malmö 22 January 1807, refers to a model of a vessel of a new type of construction, and plans which were to be sent to the British Admiralty. Pierrepont wrote:

> Your son was so good to deliver to me a model of a vessel upon a new construction of your own invention, together with plans which accompanied it, requesting it be forwarded to the Board of Admiralty. Grenville, First Lord, returns his thanks for this most ingenious and useful invention which upon inspection has met with the most perfect approbation of all whose professional knowledge render them competent to give an opinion upon subject of this nature.

Unfortunately, neither the British nor Swedish records held in national archives seem to contain any informa-

tion about the nature of the invention which Chapman sent to the British Admiralty.

Chapman maintained good health, except for the trembling in his hands, to the year of his death. He was able to bend down and 'bite his heels even when he was eighty-seven years old'. He even survived living in eighteenth century Stockholm which, after Paris, had the highest death rate of any major city in Europe, the result of insanitary conditions and the lack of pure water. The city's shallow wells produced brackish water, so its citizens had difficulty in quenching their thirsts. In the summer of 1808, severe dysentery ravaged Karlskrona's citizens and one day in August of the same year, Chapman stopped working, put his working papers and study in order, and sent for a priest. Chapman, who had not been a church-goer and had often ridiculed the clergy, spoke for some time alone with the priest. A few days later, on 19 August 1808, he died. He was buried at Angerums churchyard because he had sold Skärva, including its contents and a burial vault in 1806.

To conclude, Chapman devoted his whole life and genius to two ends: the improvement of the sailing ship by the application of mathematics and physics, and the establishment of effective naval forces. His illustrated book *Architectura Navalis Mercatoria* is one of the finest works ever produced on shipbuilding, and with all the technical information it contained, must have been of extraordinary importance to contemporary shipbuilders, the majority of whom were unaware of the most basic elements of shipbuilding. Chapman's *Treatise* provided the contemporary shipbuilders with clear and concise definitions of basic concepts, and demonstrated the practical application of the earlier developed theories. His parabolic method of construction made it possible to determine the characteristics of a vessel on the drawing board, which had previously only been discovered by experience, and practical experiments. Chapman was the first in northern Europe to introduce prefabrication methods to the shipbuilding yard, and the construction of twenty warships in record time is an indication of his exceptional organizational abilities. The many papers that Chapman presented to learned societies throughout his long career, are witnesses of his many interests and abilities in the shipbuilding field. He proved his intellectual honesty by reporting to the Royal Academy of Sciences the failure of his relaxation method of construction, on which he had pinned so much hope. He was forced to be an egotist and had to use every means and opportunities to advance the new shipbuilding techniques in which he so firmly believed, when faced with ignorant and unscrupulous individuals opposed to any change in their primitive and empirical ship construction methods. Chapman had the acumen to cultivate and make friends with those close to the centre of power — Gustaf III. Those friends realized

that Chapman's genius was to the benefit of Sweden
and therefore gave him their full support. He also had
the good fortune to gain the confidence of a monarch
interested in learning and the arts, who recognized
genius and organizational ability, and was prepared
to give his whole-hearted support to an individual with
such qualities.

Chapman, a genius, was one of the leading lights of
the Gustavian age.

Fig XI/5.
*T Sergel's monument to Chapman
erected in the dockyard museum
and hiring hall, Karlskrona*
(Naval Museum, Karlskrona).

Fig A/6.
Chapman's proposed 'sea fortress' to defend iced-in warships
(by courtesy of the Royal Swedish Society of Naval Science)

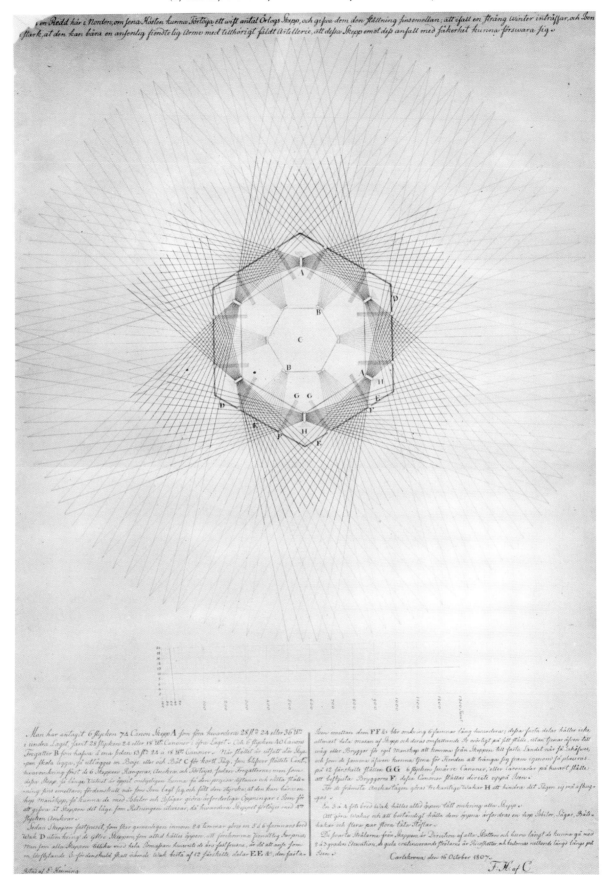

Appendix 1
PERSONALITIES

The following are notes on the more important personalities referred to in the text.

ARTISTS

Martin, Elias, 1739–1818
Painter and engraver, one of Sweden's leading landscape painters. Lived years 1768–80 and 1788–91 in Britain. Accompanied Chapman to Finland 1763. Member of the British Royal Academy.

Pasch, Lorens, 1733–1805
Portrait painter; painted Gustaf III, Gustaf IV, and Fredrik Henrik af Chapman amongst many others.

Rehn, Jean Erik, 1717–93
Architect, engraver, designer of faience, silver and furniture. Designed several rooms for the royal palaces in Stockholm and Drottningholm. Professor at the Royal Academy of Arts. Acquainted with Chapman. Involved in design of royal yachts and barges.

Sergel, Johan T, 1740–1814
Sculptor and sketcher; studied in France and Italy, specialized in portrait sculpture. Designed plaque for Chapman memorial at Karlskrona dockyard and sculpted the bronze statue of Gustaf III, unveiled in 1808. Friend of Chapman.

NAVAL AND MILITARY OFFICERS

Cederström, Olof R, Admiral, 1764–1833
As a young officer soon showed outstanding qualities in seamanship and naval actions; commanded the raiding force of frigates which successfully attacked Baltischport and destroyed Russian naval and military stores. Promoted to flag rank in 1801, commanded forces sent to protect merchant vessels operating in the Mediterranean, served there for 20 months to reduce Tripolitan pirates, commanded force blockading Prussian ports in 1806. Commanded force protecting Southern Sweden from French and Danish naval forces in 1808. C-in-c High Seas Fleet 1814. C-in-c of both fleets when separate Inshore Fleet abolished in 1823.

Cronstedt, Carl Olof, Vice-Admiral, 1756–1820
Born in Finland. Entered army 1768. Transferred to Inshore Fleet 1774; in British Navy 1776–79. Served in the neutrality patrols 1779–82. Returns to Inshore Fleet, chief-of-staff to C A Ehrensvärd 1789. Chief-of-staff to Gustaf III at battle of Svensksund 1790. Disgraced 1801 and sent to Sveaborg. Surrendered Sveaborg fortress, and major part of Inshore Fleet to Russia in 1808. Died in Finland 1820.

Ehrensvärd, Augustin, Field-Marshal, 1710–72
Originally an artillery officer, planned the defence of Finland and the Sveaborg fortress. Commander-in-chief of Swedish forces in war with Prussia 1759–62. Originator of the separate Inshore Fleet, engaged Chapman to design vessels for the same. Commander-in-chief, Finland 1769–71.

Fig A/1. Admiral Carl August Ehrensvärd, 1784: drawing by T Sergel (National Museum, Stockholm).

Ehrensvärd, Carl August, Admiral, 1745–1800
Son of Augustin Ehrensvärd, trained for the Inshore Fleet, an intellectual, travelled extensively on the Continent — France and Italy. Participated in the naval operations in war against Prussia. Appointed fleet admiral 1784 after death of af Trolle. C-in-c both fleets based in Karlskrona 1789, C-in-c Inshore Fleet at first battle of Svensksund; as a result of the defeat dismissed, and returned to Karlskrona, and resigned. Friend and supporter of Chapman.

Falkengren, Kristoffer, Admiral, 1722–89
Held commission as lieutenant in French Navy for three years. Commanded the French 30-gun frigate *Volage* in seven-hour battle with a British 70-gun ship of the line *Stirling Castle* 1745. He was taken prisoner of war and brought to Gibraltar. The French king awarded Falkengren a gold sword for his services. Translated P Hoste's book on rules for manoeuvres at sea, commanded cadet school in Karlskrona. Opposed creation of the Inshore Fleet, last President of independent Board of Admiralty 1776. Opposed Chapman's shipbuilding reforms.

Lilliehorn, Per, Rear-Admiral, 1729–98
Served in French Navy, for political reasons promoted to flag rank, commanded a division of the High Seas Fleet. Utterly incompetent, failed at battle of Öland in 1790, sentenced to death, but sentence reduced to exile.

Nordenankar, Johann, Vice-Admiral, 1722–1804
Served several years in the British and Maltese fleets. Considered a very capable navigator; wrote the first text book in Swedish on navigation, subsequently wrote a book on hydrography — earlier, responsible for the naval training of Prince Carl.

Nordenskjöld, Otto Henrik, Admiral, 1747–1832
Born in Finland, served in British, and French navies. 1788 chief-of-staff to c-in-c High Seas Fleet, Prince Carl. Highly competent naval officer but hamstrung by Prince Carl's inability to make decisions. Retired in 1798 and took up farming.

Tersmeden, Carl, Admiral, 1715–97
Served in Netherlands and British navies. He was responsible for the Swedish adoption of the British style of rigging in place of the Dutch; supported Gustaf III's revolt when c-in-c Stockholm naval base, and then appointed admiral superintendent Karlskrona dockyard. He objected to Chapman's sail plans for the Inshore Fleet's new vessels, and vigorously supported the Sheldons against Chapman's new ideas. Gustaf III encouraged Tersmeden to retire. Tersmeden kept extensive diaries which are good sources for information on Swedish eighteenth century life.

Toll, Johann, General, 1743–1817
Gustaf III's faithful counsellor at time of 1772 revolution, carried out reforms in the army in preparation for the 1788–90 war with Russia, later exercised control over the Karlskrona dockyard, fell in disgrace with Gustaf IV. Governor of Skåne 1801–1809. Tried to prevent Gustaf IV from involving Sweden in the Napoleonic wars without success. Following Napoleon's invasion of Swedish Pomerania, he was able to arrange for return of the defeated army to Sweden.

Fig A/2. General Admiral Henrik af Trolle: oil painting by Per Kraft (National Museum, Stockholm).

Af Trolle, Henrik, General-Admiral, 1730–84
Began career in High Seas Fleet but transferred to Inshore Fleet during war with Prussia, 1773. C-in-c Inshore Fleet, and promoted to major-general; 1780 appointed c-in-c both fleets with rank of general-admiral and was based in Karlskrona. The most intelligent, and active c-in-c of peacetime fleets, friend and supporter of Chapman.

Wachtmeister, Clas A, Admiral, 1755–1828
Division chief in Prince Carl's 1788 fleet, captured at battle of Hogland when the *Prins Gustaf* dismasted and forced to surrender. C-in-c Karlskrona 1799, refused to obey orders to join Danish fleet in 1801. Dismissed the service but reinstated in 1802.

Wrangel, Anton J, Admiral, 1724–99
Had nominal command of High Seas Fleet under Prince Carl. Held senior command Karlskrona 1790–92, chairman of committee for naval administration 1797–99.

THE POLITICIANS

Carlsson, Johann G, von, 1743–1801
Deputy minister of war responsible for national defence from 1783. President Åbo Court of Appeal 1792. Ornithologist.

Creutz, Gustaf P, 1731–85

Poet, diplomat; minister Paris 1766–83. Friend of Gustaf III — as a result of the 1772 revolution was able to keep the king well informed of French policies 1783–84. President of the Privy Council during the king's visit to Italy 1784.

Ehrensvärd, Gustaf J, 1746–83

Diplomat and courtier, cousin of C A Ehrensvärd. His diaries give detailed account of life at Gustaf III's court and describe Chapman's, and af Trolle's fleet rebuilding negotiations.

Scheffer, Carl Fredrik, 1715–86

Minister to France 1743–52. Strong supporter of Gustaf III. Became counsellor to Gustaf III, and was active in putting through many of the monarch's social reforms.

Scheffer, Ulrik, 1716–99

Brother of C F, minister to France 1752–64, Counsellor and later Minister of External Affairs. One of Gustaff III's most able ministers. Scheffer recognised Chapman's genius during the latter's stay in France and arranged for the latter's first Crown appointment — he retired in 1783.

Sparre, Carl, 1728–92

Privy Counsellor (1775) and governor of Stockholm from 1773. He co-operated with Gustaf III to improve Stockholm's appearance with an extensive construction programme. He became minister responsible for the defence forces.

THE ROYAL FAMILY

Adolph Fredrik (1710–71), King 1743–71

As a result of Sweden's 1741 defeats, Russia forced Sweden to accept the Prince Bishop of Lubeck as heir to the throne. He attempted to increase the monarchy's powers but could not defeat the all-powerful estates and their secret committee. It was a period of struggle between the Hat party supported by French monies and the Caps supported by British, Danish, and Russian bribes.

Gustaf III (1746–92), King 1771–92

An enigmatic character, charming, open and natural, domineering, undependable, intriguing, imaginative, liberal and dramatic. He was much influenced by French culture as a result of a visit to France where he met the *philosophes*, and amongst others, Rousseau, Quesnay, and d'Alembert. He learnt to speak French and some Italian. He could often express himself better in French than Swedish. He had objections to two things: tobacco and German. Gustaf loved the theatre, and encouraged all the arts. He was much concerned with justice for the individual. He abolished torture,

Fig A/3. Gustaf III by L Pasch, 1780 (National Museum, Stockholm).

revised the criminal code, and improved the lot of illegitimate children. Gustaf was determined to end Russian, Danish, and Prussian interference in Swedish internal affairs. He gained the support of the middle classes and farmers against the nobility to this end. He was determined to increase the power of the monarchy and, for this reason he brought about the 1772 revolution.

Gustaf IV (1778–1837), King 1792–1809

He was an unfortunate individual, nervous, lacking in self confidence, and insisting on the rigidities of protocol. He was suspicious and gave way to outbursts of rage. He was opposed to the philosophies of the Enlightenment, and had no interest in the arts. His mental weakness may have been inherited from his grandfather, Christian VII of Denmark. In foreign affairs, he involved Sweden in the Napoleonic wars on the side of Britain. As a result of an agreement between Napoleon and the Russian Czar Alexander, Russia attacked Sweden and seized Finland in 1808. Gustaf IV was deposed and exiled in 1809 as a result of the defeat.

Carl XIII (1748–1818), King 1809–18

Brother of Gustaf III, held the title of Duke of Södermanland. He lacked the intelligence of his brother, and although he had been trained as a naval officer, he was indecisive at crucial moments. He had no interest in the arts, his interests lay in freemasonry, and other fraternal organizations. He was Regent during Gustaf IV's minority.

Appendix 2
CHAPMAN'S DESCRIPTION OF A BRITISH
50-GUN SHIP'S CONSTRUCTION AND LAUNCH

Directions

Proposals for Building of a Ship of 50 Guns

First for Shifting the Body the length of the floors to be about 12 ins. on each side longer then the Breaking of the Bearing of the Ship, the first futtok to have at least 6 feet Shift above the floor Heads, the second futtoks to reach the Orlope Clamps, the Third futtoks to reach the gundeck Clamps, the fourth futtok if can be conveniently gott to reach the up:r Deck port Cell, be sure to gett them to run up that comes in the upper Deck ports, and all they fourth futtoks that makes a Side of a gundeck port to be fourth futtok and toptimber in one If can be gott, and be sure the Side of any timber that makes a port to be Square wood Clear of Sapp, and put as many four futtok and Toptimbers in one as you Can gett in the weak of your fore and main Channels.

To frame your Stern frame together Cross all the Heights and flights of your Transoms on Your Sternpost, moult and coke your false post to the main post as High as the lower Edge of the Deck Transom, then lay your moult on the Post and Sett of all the Heights and flights of the Transoms on the Sternpost, then block the Sternpost in the most convenient place for Your work, Blocking the lower part up untill the wing transom drops perp: in it's place. keep all The Transoms to their proper flights, and Horn your wing Transom from the midle line of Your post, Level & Shore him to the head of the post, Level the others and Horn them by the fashion piece mould and Shore them one from the other, Then get your fashion pieces on and prick the ends of the transoms up into them, and fasting the pieces by putting Treenails Through the fashion piece into the end of every Transom, cutt of the end of the Sternpost by your moult allowing about 6 int. longer for Tenanting into the Keel

Then lay Your Blocks and let their declivity be ⅝ inch to one foot and hang 3 ins. in the length of the Keel, allowing your Ship to Drop afore and aft when she comes in the water, Let the foremost block be 3 foot 6 ins. High, or according to the declivity you intend the launching ways, for the Keel to go clear of the afterpart of the Ship, the distance of the blocks one from another about 6 foot Except the fore and after part of the Ship, and there to be closer together to prevent the fore and after body from Setling, allow the Splitting blocks to be 11 or 12 ins. thick and to be as clear from Knotts as posible, and a Cap of 5 or 6 ins. thick according to the thicknes of the false Keel, The remainder part to be of any roff thick pieces, then provide your Keel of as many pieces as you are directed in the Establishment, and let the fore and after piece be as big as you can get it the up and down way, the foremost End of the foremost piece for the better Boxing or Scarphing and Shorting your Stem, and likewise help making part of the gripe, the after part of the after piece of Keel makes So much of the Deadwood as you leave it to big, the Scarphs to be about three times the breadth of the Keel, and bolted with 8 bolts agreable to the Establishment, then provide Slides to be the Height of the upper part of the Blocks, and to be cleated at the Side of the Ship and fasted at the blocks to Slide the Keel on the blocks, and to make Stage for getting the floor timbers a cross, then Slide the Keel on the blocks and bolt all the Scarphs and take out the Rabbits, then Sett the Keel Straight on the blocks, and let them be Wedged on boath Sides of the Keel on every Block with a Treenail Drove into the Block, Then gett up the Stern frame, and Stem, minding to have a perp:t line, and the height of all the Decks and Ribbands and their names Rest on the Stem and post, then set your Stem and stern post to their Rake, by the rake and level made agreeable to the Declivety of the up:r Edge of the Keel, and level them by a line made fast at the midle line about 20 feet, more or Less, up on the Stem & post, and caried about forty or fifty feet from the Stem & post on the midle line of the Keel, then on the line let fall a point Iron and Sett the Stem and post until the point Iron fall on the midle line of the Keel, and the perp: lines Rest on the Stem & post answers with your rake and Levels, and the wing Transom booms from the midle line, then Shore them Securely and Nog all the Shores — Then set of all the Stations of the Timbers on the up:r Edge of the Keel, and gett the Dead wood on the Keel, the midship piece to be about 8 in:s thick and over hang the Keel 1½ inch on each side, for the better letting down the floor timbers and letting in the heels of the half timber and long Timbers, then gett on the fore and after pieces of Dead wood, The Height agreable to the fulness or cleeness of the Body, the midship pieces ownly to treenail into the Keel, and forward and aft to bolt through the Keel and Stem & post and into oneanother, then Square up all the Stations of the timbers on the Dead wood, and Raise the midle line in on the Dead wood. Then lett your floor timbers down all fore and aft, Leaveing full as much hole Timber in the Throught of the floor timbers as the timber is Sided, then gett your ribbon along all fore and aft at the floor Sir mark and Shored, Then gett a Levell in on the floor and lay it on the floor, Keeping the bottom of the Levell well with the moulding Side of the floor timber, and set the floor timber that way it Requires, untill the midle line of the Levell is well with the midline of the body, then Nail that floor timber ~~the the~~ and the same with all the rest, then your floor is Horn'd, Then proceed to level your floors, by fixing your level on the Riseing line or Level line which is always Rast on your floor timber, then Set your shore until that line is Level, then nail and nog all the Shores, and the floor is Lvel'd & horn'd; Then gett a line on the Dead wood afore and abaft for the Heels of the Cant Timbers, Either to sinck in Scores for the Heels of the long timbers or to have a Rabbit taken out of the Dead wood, which you shall think proper, then Sett of the Heels of the Cant Timbers and Square them up from the up:r Edge of the Keel, Then put all your frames together as near their Rooms as your Ship will admit of, ~~from~~ for all above 20 guns, frame onely the 1:st 2:d 3:d & 4:th futtocks, and from 20 guns downward the whole frame, and in every Shift Drive 3 Treenails very Thaught through the frames, when the frames are together Cant them on their Bagg, keeping their Setts on untill they are hove & tied in their place, then chock the frames before you gett them up, then proceed to gett them up, first getting a Ribbond about a foot from the Side of the Keel, for the Heels of the first futtocks to Lodge on Slightly Shored, for getting them up in their places there is 3 ways 1:st with a Ridge rope from the foremost Sheerhead to the after Sheerhead, with Travlers reaving fore and aft on the Ridge rope, to make the takles fast to Hoist up the frames 2:d by the oposite Standards Securely guided, 3:d with the Shears you hoist the

Stem with

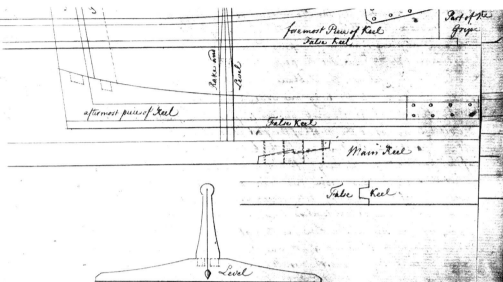

foremost Piece of Keel
False Keel
Part of the Gripe

Rake and Level

aftermost piece of Keel

False Keel

Main Keel

False Keel

Level

Item with, beginning the foremost frame first, then move them to the Next and so on
with all the rest, keeping them on the aft side of the frame untile all is hoisted, then
take them down out of the way, as you Hoist the frames Crofspaul and litely Shore
them, then gett the first Second and Third futtock Ribband about at their respective
Sirmarks, and Lett the Harpins reach two Square frames, and Horn all the cant frames
and the two Square frames by the Harpin mouls, then Horn the midships frame,
first lay a levele on your floor, the midle line of the levele with the midle line
of the body, then Train a cord a Thwart the Body at the upper part of the Joint of
the frame, and another between that and the floor, then make fast a line att the
midle of the cord and bring it down to the moulding side of the floor timber, and if
the midle line answers with that up and down line you are shure the Joint of the
frame is straight, then Horn and Sett the, frame to the Rake and Levele,
by Setting the frame untile that up and down Line answers with the Rake and Kiel
and the two lines a thwart and the level are out of winding, then nail all the ribbands,
and the rest of the frames Horn by their proper Roome and Space, then properly Shore
all the frames at the first Second and Third futtock ribbands, then Levele the
frames by a point Iron Dropping from the midle of the crofspaul, and Jett the
frames until it falls into the midle line of the body, then nail and Nog all the
Shores; then proceed to gett up all the Toptimbers. Either by a Ram clog and rip
them over the third futtok Ribband with a takle to the opposite Standard, the
Standard being Securely guided, or by making a Stage on the main breadth crofs-
spauls, and point their Heels to their places and hoist them up to their ribbond, do,
or by a Pomptin fixt between two frames upon the Second futtok ribband,
with a Takle at the head and that Serves two frames, by Dropping of it first for
one frame and then for the other, then Shift it between the two next, and so on
untile they are all Hoisted, then crofspaul them to their proper Breadth, and

get a point Iron over the middle of the crospaul and Set them over one way
or the other untill it Drops in the middle line of the body, then fastning the
Top timbers to the Side of the fourth futtocks with Three Treenails then make the
Stern Stage and gett up the Starn timbers minding when you lay them down that
you Consider the falling in and the Round aft of the Stern, and let them stand
flatt on the wing Transom, Keeping them to their proper Breadth at the height of the
top timber breadth, and Set the perps. lines Rast on the Stern timber to the Rake and
Levele, Then Nail all the Ribbans, and gett up the false Rails of the Stern, and all the
Rails and Harpins to the body and Nail Them, taking care they come clear of the main
wale, then Sett of all the Ports and gallery Doors and paint them on the Ribbans, and if
the ribbans are not at the heigth of the port cels, it would be proper to get a line fore and
aft and paint it on the timbers, for the better Casting the Timbers and making the Sides
of the ports, then fill the body with timber making the Sides of the ports faire, and let the
timbers keepe an equal room and space and Stand one over another, and to crofs the
rooms as litle as pofsible, Then proceed for the Knighthead Timbers and Haws Pieces,
minding the Knighthead timbers leeves room for the Bowspritt to go between them, and
to be left as bigg as the Bowe is through from the Head down to the beak head and
to rake forward between a perpr. and the rake of the Stem, the Hawsepieces to be in
Three or four Pieces and the moulding sides of them to look to the opofite fashion put
the Boxing to reach the upr. Deck brest hook, and down to the upr. Edge of the gundeck
Spirketing, the upr. part of the holes to be about 6 in. under the upr. Deck breast hook
and to point to the Bitts and to Drops forward below a level one Inch in a foot
and the Boxing to be above and below the Hawse holes without board 5 or 6 in.
at least, to Stand Caulk Then Chock the Heels of the Knighthead Timbers and
Hawse pieces, Leaveing a hole at the most convenient side for a brow, to run in
the gundeck beams, Keelson pieces, Riders, Steps, Breasthooks, Crutches, Bittpins
&c. then crofs chock the floor, and put in the fillings in the weak of the Keelson
and Dubb out the floor and gett the Keelson in and scarph him, and let the
Scarphs reach Three floor timbers, and let down 8 nails into every crofs Chock minding
the Scarphs of the Keelson are Shifted Clear of the Scarphs of the Keel, leeve the
Keelson unbolted as long as you can, and before you boult the Keelson Search
the Keel very Strictly Weather it be decayd or no Then Dub the Ship down to the
proper scantling from the Tops. Breadth ribband down to the Keel on the outside,
then go in the inside and Dubb from the same Heigth all down to the proper Scant
ling Chocking all the frame as you come down, and if the Ship is not wanted
Let her Stand for the Timbers to Season, then let the filling be put in as High as
the floor Sir mark and caulk Inside and out, then begin planking the bottom,
leiving out the garbord Strake and one or two more in case the Keel should require
to be Shifted, and let the plank have 9 feet Shift, or the Shift to be ¼ of the
length of the plank, and to have Three Strakes between, before one Butt come
over another, and plank the Bottom out as far as the first futtock head, and
Bieldge Shore the Ship where the floor Ribband was, and another Teer of Shores
where the first futtock Ribband was then work the main wales Shifting the
Butts clear of The gundeck Ports (Sett of the wale from the Heigth of Breadth down
by a gage made to the breadth of the wale) and work them anchor Stock fashion
then work the thick Stuff under the wale as Directed in the Establishment, and

Shore the wale

Shore the wale, and fasting pieces of Elm to the lower part of the wale at the
head of the Shores to keep the Shores from spauling the Edge of the wale, and then
Treenails that comes in the weak of the Elm, Drive out and put through the Elm
for fasting them, Then planck down untill you meet the other plank, putting a
Teer of Shores at the 2d futtock Sirmark, Then begin about the Orlope clamp
first getting a Brase level athwart at the Heigth of the Orlope Beams in mid
Ships, then fasting a Line at the Heigth of the Orlope on the Stem and carry it
and make it fast at the Heigth on the Post, and let the line hang untill it
Touches the upper Edge of the Brase, and put some Iron rings on the fore and
after part of the line to make it hang nearer a fair Sweep, without rings it
would be to Streight afore and abaft, Then gett lines athwart at every 6 or 6 feet
distance, and let them touch the Ram line and look them out of winding with
the Edge of the Brase, and there make Spotts, and if you have any round to
the Beams you must Sett the round Down, by taking the breadth of the Ships
at the Spotts on the Side, and as much as the Beam Rounds in them Breadths it
must be sett down from them Spotts on the Side and that is the Heigth of the orlope
beams at the Side, Let the orlope Clamps be about 1 foot 2 ins or 1 ft 3 ins broad,
and the Schaphs to be wrought plain with a piece in the middle about 6 ins long an 1
thick, the Scarphs to be 3 ft 6 ins long and the other thik stiff to hook up between
Scarphs 1 in, Sett of the Orlope Beams either on the Side or by a long Staff Scarp
together and the beam Spacess on them, and put it on the middle line att the Heigth
of the Clamps on Slight gallases with hole deal battens, and horn the Beams to the
Side to the middle line, Setting of the foremost beam from the aft side of the Rabbit of
the Stem, then gett the Beams in and let them down about 2 ins into the Clamps
then work the Lodging Knees 2 or 2½ ins below the orlop Beams, and Sided agreeab
to the Establishment and to lay flush on the clamps, and let them be on the aft
side of the beam from afore to X and the fore side of the Beam from abaft to X
the bolts to be belayd with Rings & forelocks, Then work one Strake above the
Beams Prickt down to the Lodging Knees and to be about 12 or 13 ins above the
beam, and then to leave an opening about 9 ins for air, and a piece about 9 ins broad let
in between the opening home to the Timbers, the up & down way for to support the But
then work the Binding Strakes at the Joint of the Timbers, and the Strake next the limb
boards agreable to the Establishment, then Sett of the gundeck by getting a Brase athwart
the Ship in X at the Depth in Hold, from the Strake next the limber boards, and look
lines out of winding and Sett the Round of the Beams down as Directed by the orl
then work the Clamps about 1 ft 5 ins, or 1 ft 6 ins broad and Scarph under the gund
poarts, for the better Shifting the Butts of the Spirketing between the ports, the scarp
to be about 3 ft 6 ins long, plane with a piece cut out of the middle about 6 ins long
and 1 thick, and whork up between the Scarphs 1 in for a hook, then work th
stiff between the clamps and the opening, then Sett of the beams as directed
the orlope, and gett them up in their places, and let them down about 2 ins,
work the hanging and lodging Knees, the hanging knees on the fore side
the lodging Knees on the aft side of the beams afore X and abaft X the
reverse, and to be below the beams 1 inch, and bolted as directed in the Establish
and leave the Remains of the thickness of the Beam for an opening between the
Knees and the Clamp, belay the lodging and hanging Knees with rings and for
then work the Deck breast hook and waterways, then sett of the gundeck ports to
the Joint of the

the Joint of the frames, and trim their sides Square athwartships except the fore and
after port, and them Square from the side, and Sett of the port cels from the Deck,
and let them out Levele, it would be proper to allow the upper Cels bigger than directed
ed in the Establishment for better hanging the ports and driving the port hooks, then
Sett of the Channel wales and work them with Three plank strakes, Sett the Heights of
at every 5 or 6 feet distance with a gadge from the upr Edge of the main wale,
Keeping the Edge of the gadge perpr and the side of the rake and level, then gett a
large line fore and aft on the side of them Spotts, and look the line fair by placing yourself as near level with the line as you kan, when that line is fair
line it on the side, and get a gage Sett to the Breadth of the Channel wale, and keep the
Edge of the gage perpend: and the side of the Rake & level, by fixing a piece of wood at as many feet
down from the top of the gage as is Necessary in the middle line, and as many feet as that is
down on the gage So many ins or ½ ins that piece must be from the side of the gage or according to the declivity the ship has, Square the middle line out on the piece and when
your plumbline falls well with the middle line and the End of the piece the gage is perpr and
to rake and Level, Sett of the whale in that manner all fore & aft, and line the lower
Edge, then divide the wale into 3 equal parts, and strike them lines in, and shift the
buts clear of the ports, when the channel wale is wrought, Shett in between the
Channel wale and the main wale, then sett of the upr Deck, it would be proper to sett
3 or 4 men on the Stern beginning with the counter timbers and Helm port transom
&c. for Setting of the upper Deck fix a base level a Thwart at the Height of yr Deck
in ⊗ and if the middle line of the Deck is parallel to the Gundeck, mark a Staff at
the height, and fix it on the gundeck Beams at the middle of the Beam, and get lines
across at that height and look them out of winding with the Base, and make Spotts
on the side, and Set the round of the beams down as directed before, then allow the Knees
to lay about 1 inch below the Beam, and the Scantling of the Knees as Directed by the
Establishment, and that gives the upr Edge of the Clamps, the Lower Edge is given by
the port cels, work the clamps in one strake, Shifting the Scarphs between the ports
the Scarphs to be about 3ft 6ins or 4 feet long or as the Timber falls out to place the
Butt on the timber, to be a plain Scarph with a piece in the middle 6ins long & 1½ ins
thick, work the upper Edge of the Klamps according to the round of the beam, the lower edge
Square from the side, and take the clamp up in the weak of the Ports between a level and
a Square, and arch at the corners, and beard the Clamps about ⅓ from the lower edge
leaving between the ports a Semicircle of about 1ft 6ins for the guns to house against,
then work the upr strake of Spirketing anchorstock fashion, and Shift the Butts
clear of the Scarphs of the gundeck Clamps, then shutt in between the Clamps and
Spirketing, leaving an opening of ½ at the Edge of the Plank and within a foot
of the sides of the ports, either work the Staff from one side of the port or the other, or work
up and down Pieces of about 12 ins broad at the sides of the ports, it's a support to the
Clamps butt then the fore and aft Pieces don't fastin to so many timbers put two
bolts Trough Every cele at the upr Edge of the Spirketing, and a bolt in each butt
of the Spirketing Through the side, then cut the Beams and prepare for getting
them up, first getting a ribband fore and aft at the height of the lower edge of
the Beams at the middle of the Beams, Suported by Bumpskins, to lodge the
beams on for you must take the beams in two because of the Tumbling in of
the side, Beard the beam about 12 or 13 ins from the End and take it up at
the end about 1in, when the beams are let down and the Scarphs bolted, gett a

Ribband

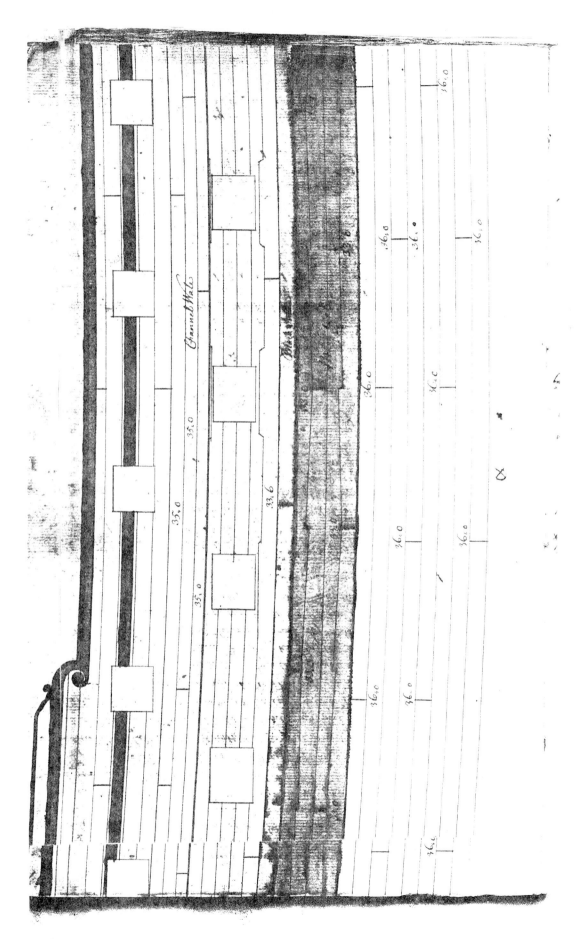

Ribband and nail on the Top of The beams, and Shore the beams to the proper Height
in the midle, it would be proper if hands could be spared from other work to work
the foot wailing and Search the Keel wether it be decayed and bolt the Keelson
if not, and fay the Riders Steps Crutches & Breasthooks and Pittpins and
Transom Knees &c. Let the uppr. Deck Lodging Knees be belayd with rings and
forelocks, the in and out bolts of the hanging knees to be Clench'd, the fore and aft
bolts of the hanging Knees to be Cutt ½ inch Short, Exept the inner bolt and that
belayd with ring and forelock, let the Lodging Knees be 1 inch below the upper Edge
of the beams for air, and to hook into the beam and to lay flush on the clamp
take a Calfs tongue out under the Knee at the upper Edge of the Klamps Let
the ~~lodging Knees~~ Let the lower end of the knee Lapp on the Spirketing about
5 or 6 in: the other arm and bolts agreable to the Establishment, take care
to cast the Knees Clear of the ports, and Ring & Eye bolts Lett the upper Deck
have Three teire of Carlings on each Side Exept the fore and aft part of the Ship
and there to leave out one Teire on account of the narrowing of the Shipp
the aft part of the Deck as far forward as the gunroom to have no Carlings nor
Ledges But a furr Beam between every two beams for the better convenience
for the Gunner putting his Spunge Staffs and Ladles &c. the other part of
the Deck to be furr Carlings and ledges as far forward as the aft part of the
forecastle, and then to be Oak Carlings and ledges, the Deck to have long
comings of Oak from the fore hatch to the beam before the mizon mast
and two binding Strakes on each Side of 4 inch plank, lett Down into the
Beams all fore and aft and work out from the Side, and all under the forecastle
of oak plank and the rest of the Deck to be 3 inch prussia Deal Clear of Sapp
and the comings and binding Strakes be bolted with one bolt in each Beam agreeable to the Establishment the Strakes of the Deck not be wrought above 9 ½
broad, the Gundeck to be all East country oak, and to have two binding Strakes
bolted agreable to the Establishment all the Rest of the Deck to be nail'd on
each Beam and Trunnel'd into each Ledge the Strakes to be about 10 in: broad
the Orlop to be laid with Inch oak Board, and the Ledges to be let Down
2 ins below the Beams exept at the fore and after platform, and the platt-
forms to be layd with Inch Deal the Quarterdeck forecastle and round
house to have no Carlings nor Ledges and be laid with prussia Deal, the
Quarterdeck to have long Comings in the wake of the Ladder way and gratings and
to work out about 2 Strakes of oak from the Side and the forecastle about 2
Strakes besides they waterways, and the round house to have no Oak plank but
the waterways lay the upper Deck, and Sett of the upper deck ports from the
Joint of the frames, and the Heigth from the deck and put out the port sells and put
the timbers over the ports, then work the Sheer Strake and Shutt in between that and
the Channel wale plank up above the forecastle and quarterdeck clamps in
outboard taking care that the Seams are Clear of the Railes, then Sett of the
Quarterdeck and forecastle Clamps in the Same manner as the other decks
and work them in one Strake with a plain Scarph with a piece in the midle
about 6 ins long and 1 ½ inch broad Shifting the Scarphs clear of the ports Then
work the upper deck Spirketting anchorstock fashion Shifting these Butts clear
of the ports, work the String anchorstock fashion, in those deep waisted ships
giving it good Shift abaft the aftermost Drift and before the foremost drift
　　　　　　　　　　　　　　　　　　　then work

Then work the quick work between the Clamps and Spirketting in the same manner as below, let the quick under the quarterdeck and waist be wrought with Deal and no openings in the wake of the cabbins abaft, under the fore castle to be wrought with oak plank Shett in close then gett the Beams a Cross Setting them of the same as the other Decks then Knee the Decks placing the Hanging Knees of the forecastle against the fore side of the Beam and the hanging knees of the Quarter Deck on the aft side of the Beam, where the upper Deck ports will admit of it, then ley the Decks and work the Strakes not more then 9½ or 10 in. broad then sett of the quarter deck ports in the Same manner as the upper deck ports and put out the ceils and the timbers over them then work up without board as high as the Drifts, it would be proper for some of the people to begin with the Knees of the head, Proceed to sett of the round house Clamps, the same manner as the other Deck Clamps, and work them in one Strake with a plain Scarph, with a piece in the midle about 5 in: long and 1 in: thick Shift the Scarphs clear of the quarter deck ports, when the Clamps are wrought, work the Quarter deck Spirketting in two Strakes anchorstock fashion, then Sheet in between the Clamps and Spirketting and sett of the Beams as Directed before, and the beam with one hanging and one Lodging knee, the Hanging Knees and transom knees in the great cabbin to be Iron, then work up to the plan shires, and go on with the finishing work agreable to your fancy, Then begin about the Launching ways their declivity to be 1½ inch to a foot If the Depth of water wile admitt of it and if the water is not Deep you must make the declivity accordingly, the length of the Buildge ways to reach forward to be able to fix a Driver on the fore most End of each Buildge way, and to go under the lower Checke of the Head, the after end to be about 12 ft afore the after part of the post, the outside of the Buildge ways to ⅖ of the Extream breadth and the Hipp to round up about 3 in: in the length of the Buildge ways, the Buildge ways to be properly secured with chocks & Spriggs at the Ends of them and a planck Prickt up to the Bottom and Trunnailed through each Shore and to have 3 Spurrs and a Driver afore, and 4 Spurrs aft, with a long thick piece of fire fayed down between the Chocks and the Spurrs and bolted through all and belayd with Ring and foreloks, Numbu all the blocks and when you have Splitt out all the Blocks Exept the 5 or 6 foremost ones then Cutt down all the whale Shores except about 10 of a Side clear aft under the wale taking care they Stand against the Ship, then cut away the after Shores, first keeping people ready when the Ship Starts to Cutt away the Rest, mind in bolting the Spurrs that the bolts are above the light Draught of water, and number all the blocks for the better giving orders what blocks to Splitt out.—

Appendix 3

CHAPMAN'S DRAWINGS OF FRENCH VESSELS HELD BY THE SWEDISH NATIONAL MARITIME MUSEUM

Name and Description	SSM no
Frigate *La Belle Poule* Profile, plan and transverse section	Ör 24501
Merchant vessel 75 tons Profile and plan	Ör 1457–1–2 & 3
La Bienfaisant, 64 guns Body plan	Ör 2442
La Palmie, 74 guns Body plan	Ör 2439
St Michel Line drawing	Ör 2441
Le Soleille Royal Construction drawing	Ör 2435
Le Superbe Line drawing	Ör 2445
Ville de Paris, 104 guns Profile and plan	Ör 2437–1 & 2

Appendix 4

CHAPMAN AND THE DANUBE

The Austrian Hof Kammer Archiv (Wien No 883) has Chapman's letter, written in French, dated 12 December 1766 offering advice in ship design for the Danube River (see translation below).

The Austrian Archives hold three memoranda dealing with Chapman's requests. The Minister of Commerce's memorandum of 22 January 1767 asks the Minister of Finance to collect the data from the waterways department, and send them to Sweden through the Secret Chancery. The waterways department, in its reply, stresses that Chapman is a foreigner, and that the information he requests concerns military affairs; in addition the standard map shows few of the necessary details, and a larger one to show all small islands and fortified banks would have to be specially made. It would take much time and cost much money.

No records are available of any reply to Chapman's enquiry. Chapman's associate Erik Åhsberg went to Vienna to design and supervise construction of frigates and other craft for the Imperial Government. Åhsberg's river frigate, built for both oars and sails, is a close relative to Chapman's Inshore Fleet frigates. The Austrian Military Museum — naval section Vienna, has a model of Åhsberg's river frigate (see fig A/4) which it found 25 years ago at the Korneuburg shipyard.

I am grateful to Dr and Mrs Erich Gabriel of the Military Museum Vienna for the translation of the Austrian documents written in eighteenth century German script which no one in Canada or Sweden could read.

The following English translation of Chapman's letter has kindly been provided by the Directorate of History, Department of National Defence, Ottawa:

Notice was recently given in the Gazette that the Royal Imperial Chamber of Commerce in Vienna wants to obtain some information on the best way to build ships that would be suitable for navigation on the Danube, especially ships that would be shaped and designed in such a way as to be easily capable of moving up the river under sail, even against the current, and with a view to

Fig A/4.
Model of Austrian Danube frigate built at Klosterneuburg yard in about 1768. The builder was Erik Åhsberg who was probably associated with F H af Chapman during his service as chief constructor of the Inshore Fleet. This contemporary model has no decks which were omitted to show the construction (Heeresgeschichtlichen Museum, Vienna).

decreasing the costs, which are constantly the price of all commodities carried by such ships.

In order that a suitable solution may be found to this problem, information is required about certain related circumstances, and it is necessary that all conditions be established as accurately as possible beforehand.

One thing that would considerably assist in this matter, and which is even essential, is to have a sketch prepared, or a sort of plan, by hand only if desired, which would show how the ships presently in service on the river are most usually built, along with a description of one of the best of these ships, and also, if there are several kinds and various sizes, indicating the measurements of such ships — length at the waterline from one end to the other, beam height at the centre from the keel to the top, draught when loaded, the location of the deck and the height of the strake, along with a drawing of the interior layout (cabins, compartments, bulkheads, holds) and also how they are fitted out or arranged in relation to the configuration of the masts and sails, and whether leeboards are used.

It is necessary that all these things be known in order not to move too far away from established custom since this would mean an inconvenience to the members of the crew who must handle the ships and who usually work only by routine. It would also be necessary to have some knowledge of the area and of customs; in other words, if there is little water or if the water is shallow, the ships would have to be flat; whether the river is narrow and there is not enough space for a ship to make a long tack; whether the river is fast and how much distance it covers in one minute; whether the water is usually calm or whether there are tides and swells, which must be the case in places where the river is very wide; whether it is customary to send these ships over long distances on the river, and whether the large ones are preferably used to sail the farthest; whether there are any bridges to be passed and the masts should be so designed that they can be lowered; whether it is customary to arm these ships in wartime and to have them ready to defend themselves by means of artillery, in which case it would be desirable to know the number and the calibre of the guns; whether it is customary to have certain facilities on these ships for the convenience either of the crew or of the passengers; whether the ships are covered with decks or are usually open; whether they move under sail only or whether oars are sometimes used as well, and also whether at times they are towed by horses along the edges of the river, and whether at times the unloaded, very light ships are allowed to drift, and whether the goods usually loaded on the ships are either very heavy in relation to their volume or take up a lot of volume without being heavy. It is assumed that the people are familiar with rigging and well accustomed to handling the sails, and that it is intended to reduce the size of the crew as much as possible.

If there are any basic and generally known defects in these ships, it would be necessary to be so informed in order to think about them and correct them.

If it is deemed desirable to send me this information, I shall assume responsibility for preparing plans for similar ships as I see fit and I shall do my best to succeed. If I am not lucky enough to succeed and my plans are not approved, nothing will have been lost; it will only mean that I have gone to a little trouble to no avail.

Stockholm, 12 December 1766
Fred H Chapman

Appendix 5

SUMMARY OF F H af CHAPMAN'S CALCULATIONS OF HYDROSTATIC PARTICULARS FOR 70-GUN SHIPS

by Lieutenant Commander (E) Eric Bramwell Msc, P.Eng, RCN

Chapman prepared the calculations for a 70-gun ship of the line in Stockholm in April 1767, and had these sent to Karlskrona dockyard. It has neither been possible to determine for which ship the calculations were made, nor if the Karlskrona shipwrights were able to use them.

The originals form part of the Chapman archives held by the Swedish National Maritime Museum, Stockholm, which has given permission for their reproduction.

This summary describes Chapman's method of calculation of the hydrostatic particulars of a 70-gun ship thought to be of his design, built in 1767 for the Swedish Navy. The original worksheets are reproduced below. Apparently produced for Chapman's own information, the worksheets are not labelled in detail and the intent of some of the calculations is not obvious at first glance. Examination reveals a methodical derivation of the hydrostatic particulars of the under-water hull form and an early example of what is now known as the 'displacement sheet'. The characteristics of the hull which have been calculated are:

a. displacement volume (using two methods);

b. location of centre of buoyancy;

c. location of the centre of flotation; and

d. location of the metacentric height above the load waterline.

The calculations consist primarily of integration using the numerical method of Simpson's Rule. This is an approximate method of integration based on the mathematics of the expression for a parabola. It is therefore sometimes called the parabolic method. The Simpson's method was a new idea in Chapman's time; he, in fact, studied under Simpson during his education in England. The method is well-suited to the integration of complex shapes such as a ship hull. A complete explanation of the Simpson's method of numerical integration can be found in several modern texts of naval architecture, for example, *Principles of Naval Architecture*, edited by Comstock, or *Basic Ship Theory* by Rawson and Tupper.

The first three sheets are a calculation of the volume of the hull below the waterline to determine the displacement volume. A description of the calculation follows.

The hull is measured at nine waterlines numbered from top (load waterline) to bottom and divided into twenty-nine stations from stern to stem. It is assumed that the nomenclature used for identifying the frame stations is the same as that used in the *Mercatoria*. That is, beginning at midships, using numbers to identify stations aft and letters to identify stations forward, thus:

30 27 ...12963   ⊕   C F I M ... W Z
After perp   (midships)   Forward perp

This nomenclature is just visible to the left of the column entries on sheet four.

The distance from centreline to the outer edge of the hull (half-breadth) is measured at each frame station. These are multiplied by the appropriate Simpson's multiplier using the series 1–4–2–4–2–4–1. The products are then summed. The sum is then multiplied by the common interval divided by three to obtain the area of half of each waterline. The common interval was determined through examination of the multiplier at the bottom of columns 1 to 9 of sheets 1 to 3. The Simpson's method calculates area as the sum of the functions of the ordinates (half-breadths) multiplied by the common interval divided by 3. Calculating in reverse, one obtains the common interval of 5.76 feet. This is confirmed by the notation at the upper right of sheets 5 and 6 (my numbering) of 5.76 which is used in the calculations on these sheets.

The area of each half-waterline is calculated in columns 1 to 9. It is of interest to note that a correction has been applied to the area of each waterline at the fore and aft stations. The foremost ordinate has been multiplied by 2 at each waterline and the aftmost ordinate has been multiplied by a factor which decreases with each lower waterline, starting with 2.5 at waterline 1 to 1.2 at waterline 8. The ordinate of the aftmost station at waterline 9 is zero, therefore, no correction is required. The correction for the foremost station appears to have not been rigorously applied since, at waterlines 8 and 9, the end correction is taken as 1, although multiplication by 2 would give 1.2 and 0.94 respectively. This discrepancy is, however, only a small percentage of the total areas calculated.

Sheet 3 applies the Simpson's method to the calculated areas (refer to the second and third columns at the top centre of the sheet). The common interval in the vertical direction is 2.1 feet (distance between waterlines) which when divided by 3 gives the 0.7 multiplier. This is multiplied by the sum of the functions of area (refer to third column top centre) to give the volume of displacement for the half-breadth of the ship (ie, half the total displacement volume).

Chapman has added two correction factors to this calculated half-displacement to obtain the final figure. The calculation sheets do not indicate clearly the source of these corrections. The half-displacement volume calculated is 39,710 cubic feet, giving a total displacement of 79,420 cubic feet. Values for one-quarter, one-half and the three-quarters displacement are also given.

Also on sheet 3 are shown the calculations for the centre of buoyancy of the underwater hull with respect to the load waterline. The third column at the top centre of the sheet lists the functions of volume which are multiplied by the lever arms (vertical distance) measured from each waterline to the load waterline (note the columns headed 0, 1, 2, 3, 4, 5, 6, 7, 8). The products are summed, the sum divided by the sum of the functions of volume to give 3.32. This is then multiplied by 2.1 feet, the common interval between waterlines, to give 6.972 feet. This resultant is the centre of buoyancy measured from the waterline, an ususual practice as the centre of buoyancy is now measured above the keel and labelled KB.

Although not clear, it appears that the remaining calculations on sheet 3 give the draughts at the 1/4, 1/2 and 3/4 displacement conditions.

On sheet 4 is a calculation of the displacement volume obtained through integration of the cross-sectional areas at each station rather than by integration of the areas of each waterplane as shown in sheets 1, 2, and 3. This double calculation corresponds to the now traditional 'displacement sheet calculation' wherein displacement volume is calculated using the two methods, checking that both results are the same. The columns marked U, U, F, Z and B correspond to the bottom five rows of the centre column on sheet 4 and give the half-breadth cross-sectional areas of the last five stations of the hull. The calculations for the remaining frame stations are not in these sheets of calculations. This method is 79,223 cubic feet vice the 79,420 cubic feet calculated on sheet 3.

The longitudinal centre of buoyancy is obtained by operating on the column of functions of volume by the lever arms measured with respect to the aftermost

[Handwritten manuscript of naval displacement calculations — columns of figures headed 7:e, 8:e, 9:e, with sub-totals and hand notes, including "Köl ... = 9,8,73", "Cent. gra. neder wah. l. = 6,97.", "9927,50 = ¼ Deplac.", "19855,00 = ½ Deplac.", "29782,50 = ¾ Deplac.", "Deplac. = 6661,36", "½ Deplac. är 6,67 neder uti wah. l.", and further columns of figures.]

hela Deplacementet på utsidan af
Timran jämt Köl & Stäf: 79450 Cubik fot

Ritningar på 74 Canons Skeppet som
Skickades till Carls Crona i aprill månad
år 1767

station. The sum is 14.4 which multiplied by 5.76 (the longitudinal common interval) gives 82.944 feet from aft. Since midships is 80.64 feet from aft, then the difference obtained is 82.944 −80.64 = 2.30 feet forward of midships, which is the longitudinal centre of buoyancy.

One should note that the symbol $(\sim)$ appears to mean 'midships', now denoted by the symbol $(\otimes)$.

A correction of 0.24 feet has been subtracted from the calculated LCB (longitudinal centre of buoyancy) giving 2.04 feet. The reason for the correction is not clear from the worksheets.

Sheet 5 shows calculations for the longitudinal centre of flotation (LCF) of the waterplane measured at the design waterline (column 1 of sheet 1; note that only every second frame station ordinate has been used to reduce the amount of calculation necessary. As described for sheet 4 the functions of area are multiplied by lever arms with the after station as base. The resultant LCF is 1.21 feet forward of midships frame.

Sheet 6 shows the calculation of the metacentre of the hull with respect to the waterline.

The half-breadth ordinates (top left column) are cubed (column 2) and operated on with Simpson's multipliers. The functions of the transverse moment of inertia (I_T) are summed (column 4) and the sum

5

5,05	1	5,05	0	
14,80	4	59,20	1	59,20
18,43	2	36,86	2	73,72
20,52	4	82,08	3	246,24
21,73	2	43,46	4	173,84
22,58	4	90,32	5	451,60
23,03	2	46,06	6	276,36
23,24	4	92,96	7	650,72
23,27	2	46,54	8	372,32
23,12	4	92,48	9	832,32
22,73	2	44,86	10	448,60
21,93	4	87,72	11	964,92
20,21	2	40,42	12	485,04
15,82	4	63,28	13	822,64
5,93	1	5,93	14	83,02
		837,22		5940,54

837,22) 5940,54 (7,095
5860,54
80000
75 3498
465020

7,095 × 11,52 = 14190, 35475, 7095 = 107844 0; − 7095 = 81,73 +4

5,76 / 11,52

8772 / 8772 / 964,92

4042 / 8084 / 485,04

63,28 / 18984 / 822,64

5,93 / 14 / 83,02

81,85
80,64
1,21 = Centr: grav: of disp: vol: aft of Spacial (2)

6

Simpson's Rule

Half Breadths y	y^3		
5,05.	128,79.	1.	128,79
14,80.	3241,79.	4.	12967,16
18,43.	6570,73.	2.	13141,46
20,52.	8640,36.	4.	34561,44
21,73.	10260,75.	2.	20521,50
22,58.	11512,56.	4.	46050,24
23,03.	12214,67.	2.	24429,34
23,24.	12551,87.	4.	50207,48
23,27.	12600,54.	2.	25201,08
23,12.	12358,43.	4.	49433,72
22,73.	11743,52.	2.	23487,04
21,93.	10546,68.	4.	42186,72
20,21.	8254,65.	2.	16509,30
15,82.	3959,31.	4.	15837,24
5,93.	208,53	1.	208,53
			374871,04

5,76 / 11,52 / 3,84

374871,04 × 3,84 → 2/3 common interval (h)   h = 5.7

149948416
29989683 2
112461312
1439504,7936
521,321
257,58
1440283,70 = y^3dx = I = Moment of Inertia of Waterplane $\frac{I}{2}$

End Corrections: 2,5 × 208,53 … 104265 / 41706 / 521,325

128,79 × 2 = 257,58

$\nabla/_2$ = 39600) 480094,60 = $\frac{1}{3}y^3dx$ (12,123 = $\frac{\frac{2}{3}y^3dx}{p}$ (BM)
396
840
792
489
396
934
792
1426

6,97

∇ = 79200

Metac: of vol: = 5,15

BM = $\frac{I}{\nabla}$

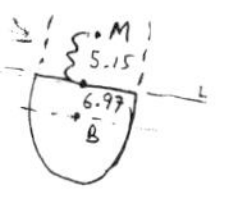

multiplied by 2/3 × the common interval or 2/3 × 5.76 = 3.84 as shown. The product has end corrections applied (as on sheet 1) and that total is divided by 3 to give the transverse moment of inertia of the half-breadth waterplane ($I_T/2$). This is divided by half the displacement volume ($\nabla/2$) giving the metacentric height above the centre of buoyancy or

$$BM = \frac{I_T}{\nabla}$$ a commonly used expression, even today

For this hull BM = 12.123 feet.

From this subtracted the distance of B below the waterline (6.97 feet) calculated at sheet 3. The difference, 5.15 feet is shown as the metacentre's height above the waterline.

The hull is probably similar to the frigate of Plate I of the *Mercatoria*, the details of which are:

LBP 164 feet (note that feet are Swedish feet of 29.7cm).
Moulded Breadth $42\frac{1}{2}$ feet.
Draught on the plan 22 feet 8 inches.
Draught Laden 23 feet 11 inches.
Burthen 532 heavy lasts.
Area Midship frame 713 square feet.
Area Load Waterline 5691 square feet.
Displacement 78,090 cubic feet.

Derivation of length of frigate from sheet of calculations is,

$$\frac{h}{3} = 1.92 \text{ feet} .. h = 3 \times 1.92 \therefore LBP = 28 \times 5.76$$
$$= 5.76 \text{ feet} \qquad = 161.28 \text{ feet}$$

which is similar to Plate I.

Note that sheet 5 shows midships as 80.64 feet, therefore waterline length is 2 × 80.64 feet = 161.28 feet. Just as another check as confirmation.

Block Coefficient CB is approximately 0.56 =
$$\frac{\nabla}{L \times B \times T} = \frac{79,450}{161.23 \times 46.54 \times 18.9}$$

Chapman, through systematic study of the distribution of the displacements in different ships (ie, the frame sections and their placing according to size along the length of ship), attempted to find a mathematical reason for this. He divided the area of each frame by the vessel's maximum beam at the so-called midship frame ('noll spant') and placed the quotients obtained as ordinators at each frame in any axis system with the waterline as axis of abscissa and joined these points with a line — the so-called 'frame line'. From this he found that the frame-line of a well-built vessel (ie, with a good shape of the underwater body) was most closely constant with a parabola, having its vertex at the vessel's greatest cross-section — the midship section. Chapman then drew up a formula. His method made it possible to determine beforehand the underwater body's centre of buoyancy and the area of frames at each end of the ship. The parabola method was to be of fundamental importance and, with certain modifications, was used in the present century.

SOURCES

Dingertz, S, *Svensk Skeppsbyggeri* (Stockholm, 1963)
Johnson, J, *Teknisk Tidskrift* (Stockholm 1909)
(Commodore (E) Gunnar Schoerner RSwN (Ret.) has kindly revised the text and provided the explanatory drawing.)

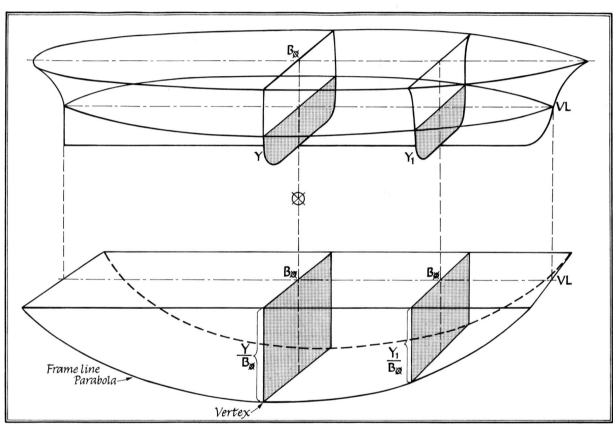

Fig A/5. Chapman's parabolic method of design.

Appendix 7

WASA: TABLE OF OBSERVATIONS, 15 AUGUST 1779

Translation of records for manoeuvres logged at 13.45 on 6 August 1779 (see Chapter Four).

HEADINGS

1. Day and Date	6 August
2a. Time forenoon	—
2b. Time afternoon	1.45
3a. Ship's speed, knots	4
3b. Ship's speed, fathoms	6
4. Course	North by west then south-east by south
5. Deviation in points	$\frac{1}{4}$
6. Wind	North-east by east
7. Wind force	Fresh topsail breeze
8. Weather	Clear
9. Sea conditions	Moderate
10. Sail hoisted	3 topsails, jibs and staysails
11. Rudder's position to windward or to lee in degrees	$\frac{3}{4}$ to lee
12. Heel in degrees	$3\frac{1}{2}$
13. Roll in degrees	2–5
14. Period of roll in seconds	3
15. Ship's pitching in degrees	1 to 2
16. Ship's leeway in degrees	$\frac{1}{2}$ to 1
17. Time taken to go about through the wind [lack]	Went about, came up into the wind in $2\frac{1}{2}$ minutes
18. Time taken to go about before the wind [wear]	

222

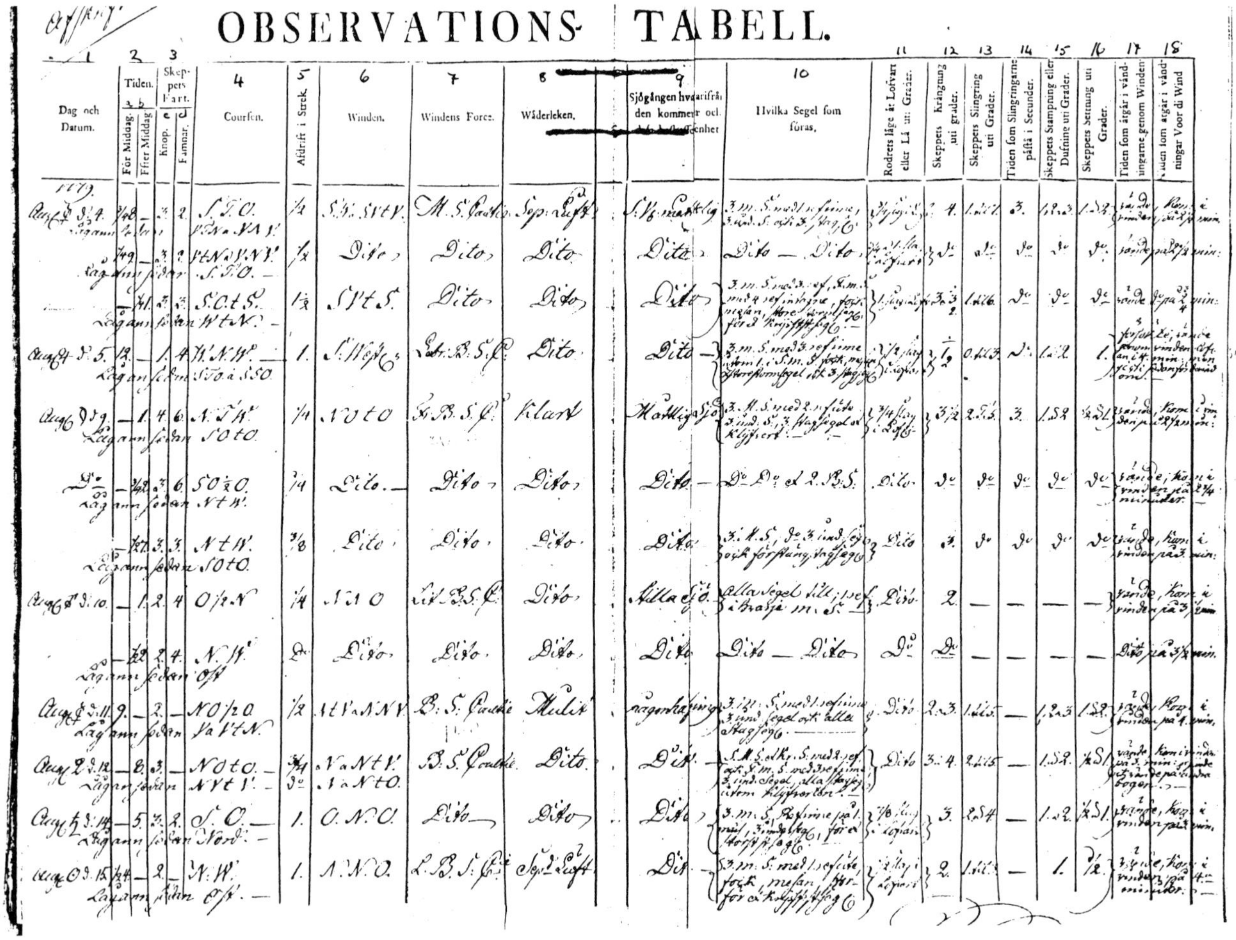

Appendix 8
SWEDISH NAVAL OFFICERS' RANKS

Appendix 9
VESSELS BUILT TO CHAPMAN'S DESIGNS

The naval terminology for officers' ranks for the period 1771–1814 was replaced by the military equivalents as follows:

NAVAL	MILITARY
Captain (Kommendör)	Colonel (Överste)
Commander (Kommendörkapten)	Lieutenant-Colonel (Överstelöjtnant)
Commander (Junior) (Kommendör Junior)	Major (Major)
Lieutenant Senior (Kaptenlöjtnant)	Captain (Kapten)
Lieutenant (Junior) (Löjtnant)	Lieutenant (Löjtnant)
Sub-Lieutenant (Fänrik)	

The designators of flag ranks remained unchanged.
Note: The Inshore Fleet officers' ranks were similar to those of the army.

MM Karlskrona supplied the above information.

Inshore Fleet (Skärgårds flottan)

Name	Built	Place	Discarded or Lost
UDENMÄÄ			
Torborg	1772	Stockholm	—
Ingeborg	1776	Stockholm	1790
POHJANMÄÄ			
Gamla	1760	Stralsund	1775
Fröja	1764	Sveaborg	1789
Disa	1764	Sveaborg	—
Brynhilda	1776	Stockholm	—
TURUNMÄÄ			
Norden	1761	Stralsund	1790
Tor	1764	Sveaborg	1776
Lodbrok	1771	Stockholm	—
Sällan Värre	1774	Karlskrona	1790
Björn Järnsida	1774	Karlskrona	1789
Ragvald	1774	Karlskrona	1789
Sigurd Ormöga	1774	Karlskrona	1799
Ivan Benlös	1775	Sveaborg	1809
Birger Jarl	1790	Sveaborg	1813
Erik Segesäll	1790	Sveaborg	1827
Ivar Vitsärk	1790	Sveaborg	—
Tor	1790	Sveaborg	—

Frej	1790	Sveaborg	—
Yngve	1790	Sveaborg	—

HÄMEENMÄÄ

Oden	1764	Sveaborg	1808
Hjalmar	1790	Västervik	1808
Styrbjörn	1790	Stockholm	1808
Starkotter	1790	Västervik	1809

FRIGATES

Prins Gustaf	1766	Stockholm	1782
Af Trolle	1766	Västervik	1789
Spreng porten	1768	Västervik	1810

SCHOONERS

Jehu	1790	Västervik	1789
Fröja	1790	Västervik	—

FRESHWATER-CARRIERS

Mälaren	1786	Karlskrona	—
Hjal maren	1786	Karlskrona	—
Vänern	1786	Karlskrona	—
Göta Alv	1786	Karlskrona	—
Roxen	1786	Karlskrona	—

SCHOONER-RIGGED GUN-BOATS

10 unnamed	1776–1808	Various yards in Finland and Sweden	—

High Seas Fleet

SHIPS OF THE LINE

Fredrik Adolph, 62 guns	1774	Karlskrona	1825
Konung Adolph Fredrik, 70	1775	Karlskrona	1825
Konung Gustaf III, 70	1777	Karlskrona	1825
Wasa, 60	1778	Karlskrona	1827
Hedvig Elisabet Charlotta, 62	1781	Karlskrona	1790
Kronprins Gustaf Adolph, 62	1782	Karlskrona	1788
Fädnerslandet, 62	1783	Karlskrona	1864
Ömheten, 62	1783	Karlskrona	1790
Rättvisan, 62	1783	Karlskrona	1790
Dygden, 62	1784	Karlskrona	1793
Äran, 62	1784	Karlskrona	1874
Försiktigheten, 62	1784	Karlskrona	1825
Manligheten, 62	1785	Karlskrona	1864
Dristigheten, 62	1785	Karlskrona	1869
Tapperheten, 62	1785	Karlskrona	1825
Konung Gustaf IV Adolph, 74	1799	Karlskrona	1876

FRIGATES

Bellona, 40 guns	1782	Karlskrona	1809
Minerva, 40	1782	Karlskrona	1789
Diana, 40	1783	Karlskrona	1802
Venus, 40	1783	Karlskrona	1789
Fröja, 40	1784	Karlskrona	1834
Thetis, 40	1784	Karlskrona	1818
Camillia, 40	1784	Karlskrona	1842
Galathea, 40	1785	Karlskrona	1854
Eurydice, 40	1785	Karlskrona	1858
Zermire, 40	1785	Karlskrona	1790
Ulla Fersen, 18	1789	Karlskrona	1807
Af Chapman,[1] 40	1803	Karlskrona	1825

DISPATCH VESSELS

Colding, 10 guns	1778	Karlskrona	—
Triton, 14	1779	Karlskrona	—
Kusen, 4	1785	Karlskrona	—
Lilla Amphion, 2	1786	Karlskrona	—
Frigga, 2	1808	Karlskrona	—

GUN-BOATS

Jupiter (decked), 8 guns	1805	Karlskrona	—
Neptunus, 8	1809	Karlskrona	—
Hector, 8	1809	Karlskrona	—
Loschem, 8	1808	Karlskrona	—
Pelikan, 6	1809	Karlskrona	—

CUTTERS

Husaren	—	Stockholm	—
Tärnan, 8 guns	1787	Karlskrona	—
Måsen, 12	1788	Karlskrona	—
Dragon, 20	1790	Karlskrona	—
Örnen	–	Skaggands	—

BRIGS

Snapp-opp, 6 guns	1796	Karlskrona	—
Svalan[1], 10	1797	Karlskrona	—
Vänta Lilet, 16	1803	Karlskrona	—

COMMAND VESSEL

Gäddan, 4 guns	1787	Karlskrona	—

SLOOP

Draken	1800	Karlskrona	—

GUN-YAWLS AND SLOOPS

214 unnamed	1776–1808	Various yards in Finland and Sweden	—

GUN-CARRIERS

2 unnamed	1776–1808	Stockholm	—

Note: In addition to the above, special vessels were built for the transport of horses, probably in small yards in Finland. None of these vessels' construction or service records, if any, has yet been found.

Royal Yachts and Pleasure Craft

SCHOONER

Amphion[2]	1778	Stockholm	1885

ROYAL BARGE

Wasaorden[3]	1774	Stockholm	1921

CUTTERS

Amadis	1782	Karlskrona	1838
Esplendian	1782	Karlskrona	1866

ROWING CRAFT

Galten	1787	Karlskrona	Extant[4]
Delfinen	1787	Karlskrona	Extant[4]

Merchant Vessels

CAT

Baron von Höpken	1759	Stockholm	—

BARQUES

Hertiginnan af Södermanland		Stockholm	
Sveriges Lycka	1774	Stockholm	—

EAST INDIAMEN

Kronprins Gustaf	1779	Stockholm	—
Gustaf III	1779	Stockholm	—

FRIGATE

Valfisken	1798	Karlskrona	—

SCHOONERS

Flundran	1803	Karlskrona	—
Sköldpaddan	1803	Karlskrona	—
Gäddan	1803	Karlskrona	—

BRIG

Laxen	1806	Karlskrona	—

Cutter

Falk	—	Karlskrona	—

[1]Built in accordance with Chapman's relaxation method.

[2]Amphion's stern, figurehead, and king's day cabin are preserved at the National Maritime Museum, Stockholm.

[3]Replica of royal barge was built in 1922 after loss of the original by fire. A royal barge similar to the *Wasaorden* was built at the same time for Prince Henry of Prussia.

[4]Both are preserved at the National Maritime Museum, Stockholm. The figurehead and stern piece of an unnamed craft built in 1801 for Gustaf IV are preserved at the Royal Court theatre, Drottningholm. The drawing signed by Chapman is dated 21 November 1794.

Appendix 10
THE SCIENTIFIC PAPERS

Chapman wrote fifteen technical papers, if the unpublished paper on rudders is included. Between 1768 and 1806 he presented papers at the quarterly sessions of the Royal Academy of Sciences, Stockholm, which had elected him a member in 1770. Some of the papers were published by the society, others by the Admiralty printer at Karlskrona. The society's records of proceedings contain no reports of discussions following the presentations. Apart from the treatise on shipbuilding, none seems to have been translated into English or French. The following is a list of the technical papers prepared by Chapman during his life time:

1. The *Architectura Navalis Mercatoria*.   1768
2. How to find the correct proportion of oars   1768
   for galleys.
3. Warship development since they began to   1770
   carry guns.
4. Treatise on shipbuilding and explanations   1775
   and proof pertinent to *Architectura Navalis
   Mercatoria*.
5. The correct method to find a vessel's centre   1787
   of gravity, when it is afloat with or without
   its complete armament, when the construction drawings are available.
6. The correct way of determining a ship of   1793
   the line's sail area, and consequently the
   lengths of yards.
7. The physical experiments pertinent to the   1795
   resistance of bodies drawn through water.
8. Basic knowledge of ships of the line for   1796
   cadets at the Royal Military College.
9. The correct shapes of ship's anchors.   1796
10. Dimensions of timber and iron for nine
    types of frigates and three smaller vessels.
11. The problem of determining the size of
    sails' moment to give a ship of the line a
    pre-determined heel.
12. Guns with conical powder chambers.   1790
13. Theoretical treatise based on experiments   1802
    to give guns the exterior form which pro-
    vides the strength equal to the powder's

explosive power.
14. Theoretical treatise to give ships of the line   1806
    the proper size and shape, also to cover
    frigates and other smaller vessels.

Chapman's best known study is his treatise on shipbuilding with 'Explanations and demonstrations respecting the *Architectura Navalis Mercatoria*'. The original Swedish version contains twelve chapters, the last of which describes the *Mercatoria's* drawings. In 1781 Vial de Clairbois, translated the treatise into French with the aid of von Löwenörn, a Danish naval officer in French service. The French translation criticizes Chapman's treatise (to which the latter replied in a later edition), but it should be said that Clairbois took many of its illustrations for his own book *Encyclopedic Methodique* published in 1783. In 1820, the Reverend James Inman, professor at the British Royal Naval College and School of Naval Architecture, translated Chapman's treatise into English for use as a text book. An earlier translation may have been made by Professor Wooley, but this has not been confirmed.

Inman's translation includes Chapman's preface to the treatise and the eleven chapters listed below:

Chapter I	On the displacement of the ship and centre of gravity of the displacement.
Chapter II	On the stability and resistance to heeling.
Chapter III	On the centre of gravity of the ship considered as a heterogeneous body.
Chapter IV	On the resistance which a ship in motion meets from the water.
Chapter V	On the centre of effort of the wind on sails and their movement round the ship's centre of gravity.
Chapter VI	On the dimensions and different forms of ships.
Chapter VII	On the proportions of privateers.
Chapter VIII	Proportions of masts and yards for merchant ships.
Chapter IX	On the different matters relating to the practical part of construction.
Chapter X	On the property in ships of being ardent.
Chapter XI	On the measurement for tonnage and stowage with instructions on these points and also various important details concerning provisioning with a view to making accommodation's table of cubes. Notes on different parts of the treatise by the French translator Vial du Clairbois and others by the English translator. Remarks on the construction of ships of war by the English translator with an example of construction.

The author's preface and Chapter IX 'On different matters relating to the practical part of construction' are reproduced in Appendices 11 and 12. Some chapters of the treatise reproduce some of his scientific papers. Because translations of all Chapman's technical papers would require a whole book, only the main points of papers presented at the Royal Academy of Science's sessions and two of the studies printed in Karlskrona now follow.

Chapman presented his first paper to the Royal Academy of Sciences at the winter session of 1768, its topic being 'How to find the correct proportions of oars for galleys'. At that time Chapman was still engaged in the design and construction of the Inshore Fleet vessels. The study is 53 papers long, and the following are the essentials.

How To Find The Correct Proportion Of Oars For Galleys

Chapman maintains that several mathematicians had considered the problems of oar lengths, and oar blades sizes, but their conclusions were of little practical use. Chapman points out that although man has used the oar since time immemorial, the long experience has not enabled him to produce the perfect oar. He believed the time had come to develop some theories pertinent to the lengths of oars and the size of oar blades.

He made a series of calculations to show the length of oars and the sizes of blades estimated to give galleys the highest speeds. The table suggests that in theory the shorter the oar and the larger the oar blade, the greater the speed ought to be. Another advantage would be the shorter loom which would take up less deck space. On the other hand, the ideal oar blade to give the maximum speed would have to be so large, that it would be impossible for any crew to handle. Chapman maintained that large oar blades in contrary wind conditions would act as sails when raised out of the water, and give the galley more sternway than any headway. Chapman concluded that the maximum sizes of the ideal oar blade should be $3\frac{1}{2}$ to 4 feet in length and no wider that $\frac{3}{4}$ of a foot, but he believed more research was required to determine the resistance of different surfaces when moved in water. He held research should determine the force a man would have to achieve to obtain different speeds, and the speeds a man can 'comfortably obtain when the oar is in the water'.

Warship Development Since They Began To Carry Guns

On 25 July 1770 Chapman presented his paper on his election as a member of the Academy. He maintained that the Venetians were the first to mount guns on ships in a war with Genoa. He refers to the first use of guns at the battle of Crecy in 1346. He states that the Swedish ship *Stora Cravelen*, built in Gustaf Wasa's reign (1523–60), was armed with guns and carried a complement of 1000 men and that the *Mars*, built in the reign of Erik XIV (1560–68), was armed with 200 guns, including 125 bronze cannon. The *Mars* was lost in action against Lubeck and the Danes in 1564, but in the following year the Swedish ship *Elephant* and a fleet of forty ships defeated the Danes and Lubeck, and took the Danish flagship. Chapman traced the development of the ship to 1770, mentioning the English King Henry VIII's fleet, and the Spanish Armada's largest vessels which carried only 50 guns.

Chapman suggested that the application of science to shipbuilding only began in the eighteenth century and progress to develop theories relevant to the industry was slow. He criticizes the seventeenth century shipbuilders, stating that their vessels lacked the dimensions appropriate to the number of guns carried, and that they were objects more for show than for practical use. He defines a ship of the line as a vessel carrying a lower tier of guns exceeding 18-pounders.

Chapman stated that the sciences demanded a thorough knowledge of mathematics, but although some shipbuilders had attempted to use mathematics to improve ship design, they often lacked the necessary knowledge of physics. Some shipbuilders, according to Chapman, had tried to give the hull of the vessel a shape which would give the best resistance to the water before they had acquired any knowledge about water's resistance to movement. He maintained that the French scientist Bouguer, and the Swiss mathematician Euler, were the first through their knowledge of the laws of mechanics and mathematics, to analyse and solve the problems pertinent to the ship. It is clear, Chapman continued, that the shipbuilding industry made little, if any, use of these great men's work. The reasons were two-fold: firstly few shipbuilders had the capacity to understand what these two men had developed; and secondly, few were able to apply Bouguer's and Euler's theories. On the other hand, neither of the latter had any practical knowledge of shipbuilding. Chapman claims that all theories relevant to shipbuilding stem from Bouguer's and Euler's works.

Chapman describes various types of vessels in his paper. A 74-gun ship should be 182 feet long, have a beam of 47 feet and carry an armament of 36-, 18- and 8-pounder guns. Chapman defines the smallest ship of the line to be the 64-gun ship, the armament of which would be 24-, 12- and 6-pounder guns. The length of the 64-gun ship should be 164 feet and the beam 44 feet. He classifies all vessels carrying less than 64 guns as frigates. He maintains both the 74-gun and the 64-gun ships of the line to be excellent sailers, both when sailing close-hauled or running free, even when carrying stores and water for seven months. These two types had sufficient armament and stiffness to be able to use all their guns in a topsail breeze.

Chapman emphasized that the practice of increasing the main dimensions of an existing successful vessel to meet the requirements for a larger vessel, did not produce another winner. Builders must have knowledge of both mathematics and physics to construct successful vessels.

The paper closes with a plea for well-trained naval officers and men. 'Officers complain', states Chapman, 'they seldom, or never have exercises at sea and thus they forget what they have learnt and will make mistakes when the nation requires their services.' Chapman continued that:

> He who acquires many and good ships and does not use them incurs costs to no purpose. Ten ships which can be well handled are far better than twenty which cannot be properly sailed; moreover, continuous training of officers and men is essential. The masters of wind and weather, when all other things are equal, will be the victors in a war. Should the fleet comprise eighteen ships of the line, of which three are commissioned and sent out annually on exercises with twice the usual number officers, in 18 years each officer will have been out on exercises 6 times and got to know six ships of the line. As our ships do not all have the same properties, there will be more value placed on one or another vessel, and there will be the advantage in avoiding heavy repairs on vessels possessing poor seakeeping qualities, with a consequent saving for the Crown.
>
> Good ships and the art of sailing them are indivisible; we are at the beginning of a new era in naval warfare.

THE CORRECT METHOD TO CALCULATE A VESSEL'S CENTRE OF GRAVITY WHEN THE VESSEL IS AFLOAT WITH OR WITHOUT ARMAMENTS AND WHEN THE VESSEL'S DRAWINGS ARE AVAILABLE

Chapman presented this paper to the Royal Academy of Sciences, in 1787. It began as follows: 'To solve the problem one must first determine in which place on board a ship, either low down or high up, that when a certain weight is moved a specified distance from one side to the other, the lists caused are equal.'

Chapman discussed the theory and sought to prove it by describing a series of experiments carried out with a box about 18–20 inches long, 9–10 inches wide and 4 inches deep. He maintained that a weight moved a certain distance on the poop, will cause more listing than an equal weight on the deck below moved a similar distance. As a result of his experiments, Chapman proposed the following practical procedures be carried out to determine the centre of gravity of a fully-armed ship of the line.

1. Muster the crew on both decks, also on the forecastle and poop. Have the crew stand amidships or in equal numbers on both sides so that they do not cause any list.

2. All guns on both upper and gun decks are to remain secured, so that the vessel has no list to one side or the other — set up a quadrant to measure any list.
3. Note the vessel's draught fore and aft.
4. Make a vertical chalk mark on each gun carriage, and make a mark on the deck in the middle underneath each gun.
5. Part of the crew should now move the guns from one side on one or both decks until the vessel gets a list of 6° to 8°, then spike down the guns to prevent them moving more to leeward.
6. The crew are now to take up their earlier stations and note carefully the new angle of list.
7. Number each gun moved, and measure the distance each gun moved.
8. Note the weight of each gun, carriage and tackle moved with the gun to bring about the list and make a total of all these weights in either iron weight, ship pounds, centre or cubic feet of salt water.
9. Then proceed as follows: multiply each and every gun's weight by the distance each gun was moved, which will equal the gun's moment. Add together each gun's moment and divide the total sum by the total weight of all guns which gives the distance the weights have been moved.

Chapman continued:

> Do not forget when carrying out such trials that a number of each type of gun carriage should be weighed before being brought on board, and the quoins, blocks and other equipment belonging to each gun.
>
> Since this method to determine the height of a vessel's centre of gravity is simple and easy, requires little time and no cost considering the information acquired, these trials should be carried out in all types and sizes of new warships when they have embarked their armaments. Thereby the science of shipbuilding through more rapid stages than hitherto can reach perfection.

Modern laws of mechanics prove that Chapman's theory was faulty — a given weight moved a given transverse distance will produce a list independent of the vertical location of the weight, provided that the centre of gravity remains constant. Nevertheless, the 'inclining experiment' pioneered by Chapman was to become standard procedure for determining the centre of gravity of ships as completed.

THE CORRECT METHOD TO DETERMINE THE SAIL AREA OF SHIPS OF THE LINE AND THE LENGTH OF YARDS

This paper was published by the Admiralty printers in 1793. It consists of an introduction and three chapters. Each chapter has a series of sections most of which contain mathematical formulae.

Chapman's introduction to the topic was as follows:

The problem of the proper sizes for ships' masts has existed since time immemorial. Well-qualified mathematicians have written about the subject even in the present century. Their treatises, although excellent in many ways, have considered only theory without its application to practice and thus have contributed nothing to the science's improvement. Nonetheless, in this fashion was the number of masts for large or small vessels determined, and their positions, divisions between main top, and topgallant remained unchanged, and the cut and proportion of sails was similarly fixed so that no deviation therefrom was possible. Not only ships of the line, but other vessels of all types have only got the excellence in rigging, and the best sail areas relevant to their size through experience and experiments. Sometimes, one has increased or decreased the lengths of yards until they met the requirements without any reference to theory. These successes became the models for other ships of the same size, but ships of the same size and displacement can have different stiffness and sailing characteristics. Thus, experiment alone is an insufficient basis on which to change the lengths of yards in order to obtain as well-proportioned a sail moment for the ship with different qualities as for the first named vessel. It will be even more difficult should changes be made in either the vessel's lines or to heavier or lighter guns, which in turn will cause changes in the complement, and the height of the gun decks above water; all of these will make changes in the sizes of sails and yards necessary. It is impossible to determine the new lengths of yards without either new trials, which will take much time, and can be costly, or a thorough theoretical knowledge. This study will cover the theory, but only that part which is relevant to a vessel's stiffness, and not to sailing qualities, which is based on such arguments which do not belong here, or have nothing to do with the sail area, but only to the positions of masts.

As already stated, this theory is only pertinent to determine the sail area in relation to a vessel's stiffness. A ship is so rigged, and the sails so made, that the sail area can be increased or diminished in accordance with weather conditions. Therefore, certain situations ought to determine when certain sails are to be used under specific weather conditions, and when a ship of the line, with good sailing qualities and stiffness is in action with the enemy.

A good ship's qualities should be determined. These are that it sails and steers well, goes about easily, and when it has the weather gauge in a topsail breeze, carrying all three topsails and topgallants, jib, stay and mizzen sails, the crew at action stations and, with a full load of ammunition, its angle of heel does not exceed 7 degrees.

These are the circumstances for which the eight sails' areas shall be determined. What really matters when determining the sail area is the vessel's heeling. There are two reasons for this: firstly, the force of the winds on the sails, and the same forces distance over the vessel's centre of gravity; and secondly, the weight on the lee side of guns, crew and small-arms men, and those weights' common centre of gravity from the vessel's centre line.

It is the complement's moment on the leeside from the vessel's centreline, together with the vessel's stiffness moment and the angle of heel which determines the sail's moment. It is clear nothing can be calculated until one knows:

1. The ship's displacement when fully armed.
2. The position of the centre of gravity when all weights have been placed in their ordinary places on board.
3. The distance from the upper waterline to the meta-centre.

The first and third items are easily found, but it is difficult to determine the second. Many and accurate calculations are necessary, but a better way is through heeling of the vessel as described in my paper presented to the Royal Academy of Sciences in the first quarter of 1787.

Such trials should be carried out, not only when the vessel is fully equipped, but when it is without armament, newly launched and completely empty, and again when the vessel is older. These types of trials ought to be used for frigates and lesser craft to get their centre of gravity. Everything should be carefully noted, so that a collection of data will be available.

Note: A certain place in a vessel should be chosen from which the common centre of gravity should be calculated. For ships of the line, it should be the upper edge of the lower deck beam facing the main mast.

The trials outlined here are completely mechanical, and are not intended to produce any law, but rather to provide an easier and accurate method to provide the required information.

If these trials are carried out the science of shipbuilding will come more quickly to perfection. It is not only for finding a ship of the line's sail area that these trials should be carried out, but also to prove the impossibility to make drafts of a ship of the line without knowing its centre of gravity, which cannot be determined with sufficient accuracy without such trials.

The paper comprises three articles: the first is the physics which depend upon hypotheses or assumptions, which are regarded as truths when they coincide with several experiments; the second is the mechanical, based on pure mathematics; and the third is their application.

The table of contents for the three articles is the following:

Article I

1. The air's effect on an inclined plane.
2. When a vessel sails six points close to the wind, to find the sail to be set so that the maximum effect of the wind is obtained to move the vessel ahead.

229

3. To determine the wind's force which cause a vessel to heel when sailing close-hauled.

4. The wind's force in different heavy weather conditions.

5. The weather's force on sails when these are braced up three points close to the wind's direction.

Article II

6. To determine the size of the moment of the sails' power ought to be to give a vessel a particular heel.

7. To find the area of the main topsail and main topgallant sail.

8. To determine these sails' centre of gravity.

9. Rules required before the proportions of other mast's sail can be determined.

10. The area of jib and mizzen mast's sails and the common centre of gravity of all three masts' sails above the main sails.

11. To determine the eight sails' moment from the vessel's centre of gravity and the moment of the sail's forces.

12. To find the 74-gun ships' stiffness moment and the moment of the crew at action stations.

13. To find the value of the moment of the sail's power and from that the main sail's width at the foot.

14. To find the correct proportions of all sails.

15. How to find the lengths of yards.

16. Table computed, following sail sizes calculations, to prove calculations correct.

17. To find the size of the angle of heel caused by the weight of the complement on the lee side, and also the angle of heel caused by the wind's force on the sails when the crew is not mustered to leeward.

18. To determine by example a ship of the line's heel when a stiff reefed topsail breeze is pressing from a lee shore, that the sail area is in the correct proportion to the vessel's stiffness.

19. To find the appropriate sail area for a less stiff ship of the line.

20. When a well rigged ship of the line has a sail area in the best proportion to its stiffness, to find a rule which will give all other ships of the line the same proportions of sail area relevant to their stiffness.

Each section contains a series of mathematical calculations to provide the information required under each heading. Section 20 also outlines procedures for practical experiments to be carried out at sea, which are quoted in part below:

When a ship of the line has been fully armed and provisioned for 5 or 6 months, it should be fitted with a quadrant of 4–5 feet radius marked with degrees and minutes. It is to be placed so that it is perpendicular when the vessel is upright. The vessel is to proceed to sea for one and a half months. Should it meet up with a topsail breeze, but not too heavy a sea, at that time, the vessel is to be cleared for action; the crew to take their

proper stations and all the gun ports opened. All the guns are to be inboard. The vessel is then to luff and sail close-hauled, six points close to the wind. Now the sails are to be set except for three topsails, topgallants, staysail and jib; note being made of the angle of heel.

The vessel should then return to port before too much of the fresh water and provisions have been consumed, so that the centre of gravity stays unchanged. The centre of gravity should be determined by causing the heeling. All weights are to remain in the same places when the trials were done at sea so that the centre of gravity may rest at the same place.

When the position of the centre of gravity has been found, and according to the ship's drawings, the distance between the centre of gravity and the metacentre measured, a sail plan should be prepared. It should show all the sails used in the trials according to their size and position. Their area, their centre of gravity, and moment from the centre of gravity shall be calculated. The force of the sails moment should be calculated. Thus, there will be a complete and reliable theory about the sails' moment and sail area proportions, not based on hypotheses and assumptions, but only on well prepared trials.

To determine the sail area of a vessel that is crank, when in action, permit a heeling angle of $1-1\frac{1}{2}$ degrees more than the normal allowed, and be satisfied with less stiffness rather than lose good sailing qualities.

Chapman added this conclusion to this study:

Now at last this is a theory by which not only is it possible to determine the sail area when a ship of the line takes a certain angle of heel, but also from a given sail area the angle of heel.

According to the usual practice, vessels of similar dimensions have been given the same sail area whether they had more or less stiffness to carry sails.

Take a fleet of ships of the line, different in form, but having similar dimensions and sail area, and similar maximum underwater cross sections: they will all sail as well, but will have the fault that only some can use their lower gun tiers without any risk; and suppose that the sail area for the less stiff vessels is reduced so that they will not heel more than the stiffer vessels, then as a result all ships of the line will be able to use their lower gun batteries, but all will not sail as well. A fleet of ships having the same stiffness, but where all are indifferent sailers is no better than before, when all ships were good sailers but each had different stiffness. The perfect fleet is one where all ships have the same stiffness and all are good sailers. The ideal cannot be obtained by changes to the rigging, or sail areas. The fault lies in the vessel's hulls. The reason is that when the drafts for a ship of the line are prepared, little thought is given to the size of sails it should have, but instead one proportions the masts and yards according to the width of the beam and length respectively, without knowing if the vessel's stiffness moment is in proportion to the product of the vessel's length multiplied by the square of the beam, which it should be, if the vessel's stiffness moment shall be in proportion to the sails' moment from the centre of gravity.

Although all sea powers possess ships built only for war purposes, all these achieve different qualities, and this is because when the drafts are prepared, no stipulated principles are followed, but each shipbuilder (or naval architect) has his own opinions and designs ships accordingly. It is necessary therefore, that certain principles are accepted and followed.

Sails are as necessary for a ship of the line as its guns, and it follows that the weight and position of guns is, amongst other matters, the basis for the centre of gravity's position, as the sails' moment is also the basis for the vessel's stiffness moment. All these shall combine together to form a machine, and hence all its parts and qualities must be projected, and determined from the first planning of the vessel, so that nothing will be done arbitrarily which has influence either on the stiffness or sails' moment.

This gives rise to the principle which should be followed, and from this a theory is formed which will give all larger and smaller ships of the line similar qualities. Only then, can a perfect fleet be obtained.

In conclusion, Chapman emphasizes the importance of making calculations pertinent to angle of heel, centre of gravity, and metacentric height in the drawing board stage of ship construction.

THE BEST SHAPES OF SHIP'S ANCHORS

Chapman presented this paper at the proceedings of the Royal Academy of Sciences in March 1796. The paper begins with the statement that although anchors have been used since time immemorial, no one has ever considered which shape of anchor is most effective. Chapman suggested that theory should help determine the best shape, and the ideal angles of the anchor's arms in relation to the anchor's shank. When the anchor is let go from the cat head, because the stock is made of wood, it will fall vertically to the bottom. The vessel's drag pulls the anchor into the correct position so that the flukes can dig into the sea bed. He suggested that if the angles of the arms were very open (for example, 90 degrees), the flukes' digging into the sea bed would be limited by the weight of the anchor. Therefore the arms and flukes of the anchor should have those angles which will enable it to dig down into the sea bed, and provide sufficient strength to resist the vessel's drag. Chapman, through a series of calculations and the development of formulae, came to the conclusion that the ideal angle of the arms and flukes should be 112 degrees 30 minutes. 'That angle ought to enable the flukes to dig down and provide good resistance to a vessel's drag.'

Chapman compared British, French, and Swedish anchors. He found that the British anchors had shorter arms than either the French or the Swedish, the French anchor had longer arms than the Swedish anchor, and the angle of its arms to the shank was sharper than either the British or the Swedish. He found from his calculations and measurements that the angle of the British flukes was 112 degrees, the French 113 degrees and the Swedish 112 degrees and 12 minutes. Chapman suggested that the longer the anchor's arms, the more likely it was that the flukes would resist penetrating the sea bed, but the longer the shank the easier it would be to break out the flukes and arms from the bottom.

Chapman discussed different ways to determine the ideal shape of an anchor and its flukes to get maximum efficiency. He suggests the anchor's stock should be as long as the shank, and that its weight in theory should be equal in pounds to the square of the vessel's maximum beam. Nevertheless, because of their height above water, three-deckers should have even heavier anchors, and those of frigates, with lower upperworks, should weigh slightly less than the square of the vessel's maximum beam. Chapman stated that on the basis of his formulae, Danish three-deckers' anchors should be 3.4 pounds per square foot of beam, two-deckers 2.9 pounds and frigates 2.4 pounds, but British two-deckers should be 3.28 pounds per square foot and frigates 3.24 pounds per square foot. He considered the weights of anchors for Swedish ships should be: for three-deckers, $3\frac{1}{2}$ pounds per square foot of beam, two-deckers $3\frac{1}{3}$ pounds, and frigates $3\frac{1}{6}$ pounds. Different waters and anchorages, he continued, often have determined the sizes of anchors for different types of vessels, and consideration should be given as to whether a vessel is to lie by at anchor at sea in a storm. He suggested that vessels operating in tidal waters require heavier anchors than those operating in non-tidal waters. He pointed out that in the Baltic 'waves are so short that a large ship cannot raise itself before the arrival of the next one, which breaks higher up on the bow and is thus more violent. On the oceans and bigger seas, a ship can pitch and recover before the next wave comes.' He concluded that the weights of anchors proposed for Swedish ships were not too heavy.

THEORETICAL TREATISE TO GIVE SHIPS OF THE LINE THEIR PROPER SIZE, AND FORM LIKEWISE FOR FRIGATES AND SMALLER CRAFT

Chapman's last paper about ship construction was published by the Admiralty printer in 1806. The treatise has 150 pages divided into some fifty-three sections and a seven-page preface. It included much of Chapman's earlier published studies and discusses both the parabola and relaxation design methods, the determination of a vessel's centre of gravity, stiffness, the weight of guns and shot, the provisioning, and other topics such as draught, the height of gun-tiers above the water, the calculations of the necessary ballast, sail area, rigging, frame construction.

Here are some of Chapman's notes for the 1806 paper which have survived:

The qualities of a good ship of the line

1. The vessel shall have that form so that when all equipment is on board, stores for 5–6 months, water for half that time, the lower gun deck is at least 6 feet above water.

2. Be sufficiently stiff to withstand heeling so that in a topsail breeze and moderate sea with all topsails, topgallants, mizzen, fore-sail, staysails and jib set sailing 6 points close to the wind, all guns run out, all equipment in place and the crew at action stations, the angle of heel does not exceed 7 degrees.

3. Sail well in all directions from before the wind to close-hauled, tack, making as little leeway as possible, lie not too hard on the rudder, or that the helm when sailing close-hauled, always must be kept a little weatherly — go about easily, never refuse to go about.

4. Be easy in its movements, roll slowly and easily, not pitch violently so that the waves break with force on the bow, and dip the stern heavily or with a wrench. In general, the vessel should behave so well in heavy seas so that these do not go over the bow; all this is relevant to the hull's shape.

5. It must be strong and well built so that it will not spring leaks when sailing close-hauled.

These are the properties a good ship of the line should have.

Chapman then discusses the various means to provide them. His notes begin with the statement, 'It is very important that a ship of the line shall have the above-named qualities, it is just as important to know what will provide them.' Here then is his list:

1. The dimensions such as length, beam and draught shall be adequate to give the vessel the required size, but shall not be excessive in respect to the draught. It should be within a specified limit to comply with the vessel's other dimensions which altogether will bring about the vessel's intended properties.

2. If the vessel's upper waterline continues a little past the midship frame, and is not too pointed at the ends, and the fullness is continued a little below the waterline, and the fullness in the bottom is reduced, this will be the main contribution to stiffness.

The water's upward force and the effect at the waterline will bring about changes in the vessel's vertical position.

As pointed out, the vessel's beam should continue a little below the waterline, so that the metacentre comes higher up, which is important to observe since the number of guns, their height above water, their weight, and that of the masts, rigging etc, the hull, complement, all ammunitions, water and stores are known as well as their common centre of gravity.

The vessel's bottom may have any shape because it makes no change in either the weight or the position of the centre of gravity. The only weight not included in the calculation is that of the ballast: its centre of gravity will come higher up when the bottom is sharp, but as it is mostly of iron and in weight about 1/11th of the total displacement, it will not take up much space. The ballast's centre of gravity will not come much higher up when the bottom is somewhat sharper than when it is full amidships. If it is assumed the parts of the provisions, and water are now higher up because of the vessel's sharpness in the bottom, it has the same effect as if the ballast instead of being 1/11th of the displacement, is assumed to be 1/10th of the total displacement. Should that weight be 10 inches higher up, and the bottom flatter, then the common centre of gravity has not come over one inch higher. Then it does not matter that the bottom's shape causes the metacentre to be moved 6 to 7 times the amount higher up; as a result the vessel's stiffness moment gets a considerable increase. [Translator's comment: This seems to be an unusual conclusion.]

This is proof that rising bottoms are more advantageous for ships having more top hamper than the usual fuller type, whose shape enables it to stand upright when aground or in tidal areas where the water rises and falls.

3. As the midship frame has no effect on resistance, a small increase or decrease in the incidence angles of the vessel's bow does not either cause any important change in the resistance that good sailing demands. If the midship frame area is reduced, and there is to be no reduction in displacement then the fullness should continue a bit further forward or aft, and form those lines which cause the least resistance to the forward movement, and keep the centre of gravity midships or close by to it.

While experiments have found that a body moves smoothest through water when its centre of gravity is about midships — that is to say, neither one end or other goes up or down when underway, but maintains a horizontal level as before it moved — in a ship with the weight of a fore mast, bowsprit, and anchors in the bow, and with little weight aft (which consists only of the upperworks and mizzen mast), it is necessary to give the hull that form in the water so that the centre of gravity of displaced water — the water hole — is 1/120th of the vessel's length ahead of the midship section at the upper waterline, which adjustment of the centre of gravity cannot have any significant effect on the vessel's manoeuvring.

When a vessel does not have sufficient draught in relation to its beam if the draught is increased by a leeboard, its leeway is prevented.

All this contributes to a vessel's good sailing qualities.

4. When that part of a vessel's hull closest to the waterline is formed in the way set out in the second section, violent movement in rolling cannot occur because that part of the vessel which gets into the water as a result of rolling and pitching, comes closer to the vessel's centre of gravity, or that centre which causes the vessel's return roll, and this avoids violent movement.

5. Pitching occurs when the vessel's centre of gravity is amidships, as mentioned in section 3, and when all heavy weights have been moved from the vessel's bow and stern, and when the vessel is given some stiffness by carrying a few headsails which always cause pitching in a heavy sea.

6. When the bow of the ship dips down in the water, it displaces the water which restrains it so that it can only with difficulty heel over.

If the fullness is continued below that waterline, it has the advantage when a great part of the stores and ammunition are used up, that the ship of the line will be raised $\frac{3}{4}$ of a foot above the load waterline, and will be almost as stiff as before, because the upper waterline will be almost the same as before, and as the centre voluminus has been moved up, so has the metacentre, and the difference from that to the vessel's centre of gravity will be slightly increased.

CHAPMAN AND GUNNERY

As Chapman was primarily engaged in the construction of naval vessels, he was interested in gunnery problems. His interest was aroused during his appointment at Sveaborg where he had opportunities to study the gun and to make practical experiments. When he was eighty-two, he read his first paper on gunnery to the Royal Academy of Sciences, to explain the results of a series of experiments over a period of almost forty years. Chapman conducted a series of trials at Sveaborg in 1763, because he believed that if a gun had no recoil the shot would go further — the force of the recoil would, in his opinion, increase the range and accuracy of the shot. His experiments, which he conducted with a Lieutenant-Colonel C F Aschling of the artillery, failed to prove his theory. Chapman did not understand that a gun's recoil only began after the shot had left the muzzle, and the distance travelled by shot from either a gun allowed to recoil, or a gun lashed down to prevent any recoil, were the same. In addition, Aschling had not understood that the forces in the recoil metal are proportional to the square of the speed of the recoil.

Chapman and his partner directed their efforts to develop lighter and more powerful guns with shorter barrels. He stressed the shape of the powder chamber, the position of the trunnion, and the allocation of metal along the gun barrel. In 1799 there were trials between the 36- and 24-pounders designed by Chapman and Aschling (Chapman had wanted to use 42-pounder guns), and the long barrel guns made in accordance with Tornqvist's specifications. Chapman in his memorandum issued prior to the trials laid down four stipulations:

1. The same quality powder be used for each gun.
2. The powder be properly weighed.
3. All guns be given a 6-degree elevation.
4. The distance between the gun and the fall of shot be carefully measured.

The results showed that Chapman's guns had no advantages over those of Tornqvist's design. In fact, their recoil was greater, and furthermore the guns had conical powder chambers which were difficult to handle on board ship because the cartridges could easily go to pieces, had to be longer and required twice as much wadding. Consequently, this type of gun was both troublesome and slow to load. Another disadvantage was that the muzzles of the guns with shorter barrels came too close to the ship's sides. Nonetheless, Chapman was able to use his political influence to get the navy to accept guns of his design.

Chapman's 1802 paper is entitled 'Theoretical paper based on experiments to give guns the outward form so that their strength in all sections responds to powders' exploding force.' In it Chapman tries to examine the different elements of gunnery, but he could not measure the delivery speed and pressure, so he was only able to determine elevation up to about one minute. He conducted trials for his paper over the winter ice at Karlskrona, because there was no other flat plane available in the vicinity, and achieved a maximum range of about 2000 metres at an elevation of 6 degrees; the muzzle velocity was about 360–400 metres per second. In several instances, the guns' spread was over 25 percent of the expected, because of poor quality powder, and uneven loading; in addition, because of the uneven bore the shot ricochetted around inside the barrel, so the ranges achieved were very varied.

The paper contains a table to show for each calibre of gun, from 48-pounder down to 4-pounder, the relevant lengths of gun barrels, and the weight of each gun size in skeppspund (a skeppspund is equal to 170 kilos). For example the length of a 48-pounder gun is shown as 12.157 feet (3.6 metres) and its weight as 31.786 skeppspund, the equivalent of 5403 kilos or about 5.4 tons; the 36-pounder gun's length is shown as 11.235 feet (3.3 metres) and its weight as 24.054 skeppspund, equal to 4089 kilos or about 4 tons. The 24-pounder gun's length is shown as 10 feet (3 metres) and its weight 15.8 skeppspund — 2692 kilos or 2.69 tons.

Chapman's other contribution to naval gunnery was the transversing slide gun carriage, which was used in the Swedish Navy until about 1870. It had the advantages of being easier to train, could hold its position better, be more easily secured, required two men less as gun crew, was stronger than the old type and easier to move than other gun carriages. Its disadvantages were that it required more servicing, lubrication, and cleaning; in addition could only be turned 19–20 degrees, took up more space and was difficult to repair. Nevertheless, the trials of 1787 on board the *Gustaf Adolph*, where the traversing slide gun carriages for 36-pounder guns had been fitted to the lower gun tier, were favourable. F de Miranda, the South American hero, noted that the majority of officers were opposed to Chapman's new type of gun carriage, but it was fitted to the gun decks of ships of the line built prior to 1788. However, the 6- and 18-pounder guns retained the old type of truck carriage. As the problems with the traversing slide gun carriages became acute during the Hogland action, some were removed and were placed in the coastal defences, but maintenance was difficult because of the wooden construction, and exposure to the elements.

Chapman wrote a memorandum, dated 24 May 1804, entitled 'The aiming of guns'. He considered this to be a simple matter ashore, 'but at sea the weather and sea conditions and the vessel's pitching and rolling makes this more difficult.' He pointed out that if a shot hit a wave on its way to the target, its direction could change anywhere from 30 to 60 degrees off the target.

Chapman seems not to have been involved in the construction of land fortresses, but in the fall of 1807 he presented a plan to Admiral Carl August Ehrensvärd to show how part of the High Seas Fleet when frozen-in could defend itself from attacks by military forces consisting of infantry and artillery. Located on the ice, Chapman's proposal was that six frigates and six 74-gun ships should take up positions in two hexagons (page 200). The frigates were to be anchored broadside at each point of an inner hexagon. The six ships of the line were to be stationed with their sterns at each point of an outer hexagon; four anchors were to be used. The distance between the two hexagons would be about 250 famnar or 445 metres. Twenty-four hours after the vessels were frozen in their positions, a channel (shown as D in the drawing) about 10.5 metres wide, was to be cut in the ice, hexagonal in shape at a distance of about 300 metres from the outer hexagon of ships, which would be kept open at all times. The twelve ships would be able to give crossfire at any approaching enemy. Chapman's plan required twelve frozen passages to be maintained from the inner hexagon to the ice-free channel and twelve small guns or carronades to be placed on the ice of the inner hexagon at the entrance to each passage. In addition, Chapman proposed that triangular holes about 3–4 feet wide be cut close to the bow anchor cables of the ships of the line, to prevent an enemy from cutting them. He added that many boat hooks, saws, ice hooks and many pairs of large water-tight boots would be necessary to keep the ice-free channels open. Black lines on the plan showed the lines of fire and their ranges using elevations of 2 to 3 degrees, with yellow lines indicating his estimate of the maximum ranges of shot ricochets on the ice.

The 74-gun ships were to be armed with either 24- or 36-pounder guns and the frigates with 18- or 24-pounder guns. Chapman estimated the ranges of the line of battle ships' guns to be about 970 metres and by ricochet on the ice to about 1850 metres. He gave the same ranges for the frigates' guns, but no records show if Chapman's scheme for a sea fortress was ever tested.

All Chapman's papers on ship construction, rigging, and even anchors, emphasize the importance of the application of scientific methods, and describe the practical experiments to be carried out to test scientific theories; he believed no theory was valid unless he could prove it by practical experiments. One example was Chapman's trials with the frigate *af Chapman* to prove or disprove his relaxation theory. He was so devoted to truth that in his last paper on ship construction, he reported the failure of his relaxation method from which he had expected so much. The studies prove Chapman's continued efforts to improve the sailing vessel, and that age neither hinders that search for perfection nor the ability to produce new concepts.

Appendix 11
CHAPMAN'S PREFACE
TO HIS TREATISE
ON SHIPBUILDING

If we were to take a view of the immense number of ships that have been built since mankind first began to navigate upon the ocean, and note all the different steps which have been taken in improving their construction, we should at first sight be inclined to believe that the art of shipbuilding had, at length, been brought to the utmost perfection, an opinion that would receive additional force from a consideration of the few essential alterations, which have been introduced either in their form or rigging, during our own age.

Yet when we recollect the different kinds of ships and vessels that are used in Europe, it will appear less surprising to us, if there should be good grounds for asserting that their very great variety, equally with other cause, have prevented shipbuilders and riggers from discovering either the true figure and shape of ships, or the best mode of rigging them, either generally, or, for each species of vessel in particular.

In order to form a decisive opinion on both these points of view, on the degree of perfection to which ships in general have arrived, we will divide those of all nations into two classes: comprising in one, all small vessels, or those used in short voyages and narrow waters; in the other, all large ships, or those employed in distant voyages, and calculated for going out to sea.

The first class consists of the vessels that different natives make use of in their coasting trade, or in their commerce with neighbouring countries. As the climate, the extent and depth of the seas, the position of the countries with respect to the sea and to each other, also their productions, are different in different countries, the proportion and form of these vessels, as well as the mode of rigging them, must necessarily depend upon these circumstances. Thus a species of perfection may be found in the circumstance that they are dissimilar in the same degree as their objects differ.

On the contrary, if we consider the ships comprehended in the second class, even though of different countries, we shall find that being built for the same purposes, they are similar in their essential parts. As to their proportions, we find that the breadth is between one-third and one-quarter of the length; that the least have usually greater breadth in proportion to their length than the largest; that the draught of water is something greater or less than the half-breadth. The height out of the water has also limits, which depend on the particular destination of the ship. The accommodations, moreover, in these ships have a great similarity among all nations; they differ only in matters of small importance, in which each follows the plan that appears most convenient.

With respect to form, we see that all ships have their greatest breadth a little before the middle; that they are leaner aft than forward; that those designed for ships of burthen are fuller in the bottom; that those built for sailing are leaner there; that the stem and stern-post have a rake; that they have a greater draught or water aft than forward, etc. With regard to the rigging, most vessels have three masts, others two, and some only one, depending on their size. These masts with respect to the ships and the manner of rigging them, have nearly the same proportions and the same place. They are also generally rigged in the same manner, except that some may have more or less sail, according to the judgment of the owner. All ships have their centre of gravity a little before the middle of their length, and the centre of gravity of the sails always before the centre of gravity of the ship.

In this manner, all ships designed for navigating in the open sea are constructed; and as this mode of construction is the result of an infinite number of trials and experiments, and of alterations made in consequence thereof, it would be improper to infringe on limits so established.

But although ships are thus confined as to their proportions within certain limits, they still admit, however, of such variations in their form as to produce an infinite number of qualities more or less good, or more or less bad. There are ships possessing all the qualities which we can reasonably wish for, and there are others which, although within the above mentioned limits, have nevertheless a great many faults.

In the construction of ships, people usually make attempts at different times to improve the form, each person according to his own experience; thus after the construction of one ship, which has been tried and found to possess such or such a bad quality, it seems possible to remedy this defect in another. But it often (not to say generally) happens that the new ship possesses some fault equally as great, and frequently even that the former defect, instead of being removed, is increased. And we are unable to determine whether this fault proceeds from the fault of the ship, or from other unknown circumstances.

It thus appears that the construction of a ship with more or less good qualities is a matter or chance and not of previous design, and it hence follows that, as long as we are without a good theory on shipbuilding, and have nothing to trust to beyond bare experiments and trials, this art cannot be expected to acquire any greater perfection, than it possesses at present.

It becomes a matter of importance then, to discover what may bring this knowledge to greater perfection. Seeing that ships, the proportions of which lie within the same limits, nay, which have the same form, differ greatly from each other in respect to their qualities, and even that, with a small alteration in the form, a ship acquires a quality immediately opposite to the one we wish to give it, we must conclude that this arises from certain physical causes; and that the art of constructing ships cannot be carried to greater perfection till a theory has been discovered which elucidates these causes.

In every art or science there exists a hidden theory, which is more or less difficult to be found out, as the art or science depends more or less on physical causes.

Into the theory of a common oar, even Archimedes made researches, and many others after him; notwithstanding which, this theory is not yet fully explained. If such difficulties occur in this investigation, how great must those be which attend the theory of shipbuilding, where so many other circumstances are combined!

It is true that the oar is made use of to great advantage in rowing, the cannon in firing; an infinite number of machines are in like manner used, without considering it absolutely necessary to investigate to the bottom their theory. We see how little these machines can be advanced towards perfection by its assistance. The question may be perhaps concerning some inches more or less in the length of the oar, concerning a twentieth part less matter for a cannon of the same force; so that the theory for these objects is not so necessary as for ships.

For ships, we have to fear an infinity of bad qualities of the greatest consequence, which we are never sure of being able to remove without understanding the theory.

At the same time, the construction of ships and their equipment is attended with too great expense, not to endeavour beforehand to insure their good qualities and their suitableness for what they are intended for. The theory then which elucidates the causes of these different qualities, which determines whether the defects of a ship proceed from its form, or from other causes, is truly important; but as the theory is unlimited, practice must determine its limits. We may consequently further conclude, that the art of shipbuilding can never be carried to the last degree of perfection, nor all possible good qualities be given to ships, before we at the same time possess in the most perfect degree possible a knowledge both of the theory and practice.

To possess this theory in all its extent seems to exceed the force of the human understanding. We are obliged therefore to content ourselves with a part of this vast science; that is with knowing sufficient of it to give to ships the principal good qualities, which I conceive to be:

1. That a ship with a certain draught of water, should be able to contain and carry a specified lading.
2. That it should have a sufficient and also predetermined stability.
3. That it should be easy at sea, or its rolling and pitching not too quick.
4. That it should sail well before the wind, and close to the wind, and work well to windward.
5. That it should not be too ardent, and yet come easily about.

Of these qualities one part is at variance with another; it is necessary therefore to try so to unite theory and practice, that no more is lost in one object than is necessary in order to secure another, so that the sum of both may be a maximum.

This is the subject of this short treatise. Whether I have succeeded or not, will be seen by the reader. There will be found in it some things, both in theory and practice, which have not hitherto been treated of, and which may be worthy of the attention of persons who are desirous of applying themselves to this science; it will be seen, moreover, that the principles laid down admit of demonstration, although they are of the most difficult nature.

Still, however, it must be confessed that this science has one great difficulty, in which it probably goes beyond all its rules, so that even with the greatest care, the constructor may notwithstanding suffer in point of professional reputation. For although a ship may have been built in conformity with all the rules which both theory and practice prescribe, its yards have got their true proportions, and the masts their true place and position, so that there appears to be the greatest certainty of its possessing all the best qualities, it may nevertheless happen, that such a vessel will answer very ill, for the following reasons:

1. Although the rigging of the ship (when the masts and yards are put in their place, and are in due proportion) is not a matter of such great difficulty, but that every seaman knows how to give the proper proportions, it happens, notwithstanding, that too stout cordage and too large blocks are frequently used, which renders the weights aloft too considerable. It may happen also that the sails are badly cut, on which account the ship may lose the advantage of sailing well close to the wind, of coming about, etc, whence great inconveniences may result, with which the form of the ship has nothing to do.

2. The ship is liable also to become ungovernable, to lose its good qualities in every way by the bad disposition of the stowage. If the lading be too low, the moment of stability will become too great, which will

occasion violent rolling. On the contrary, if the weight of the lading be too much raised, the ship will not carry sail well when the wind blows fresh; neither will it be able to work off a lee shore; if the lading be too heavy towards the extremities, it will produce heavy pitching, whence the ship may become the worst possible sailer, with other inconveniences which are not the fault of the ship itself.

3. The good performance of a ship depends also on the manner in which it is worked, for if the sails be not well set, with respect to the direction of the wind and the course, it will lose a point of sailing; it will become slack so as to miss stays, which often places a ship in a critical situation. The person who works the ship is also charged with an attention to the draught of water; and to the manner of setting up the shrouds and stays, upon which the qualities of the ship greatly depend. Furthermore, to work the ship well is of greater consequence in a privateer, than a merchant ship. One who understands the management of his ship, knows how to give it all the good qualities it is capable of. He knows how to employ those qualities to his advantage, and when he is engaged with an enemy, he thereby makes himself master of the attack; but he who blunders in the working of his ship, may thereby not only be reduced to the necessity of acting solely on the defensive, but seldom if ever escapes falling an easy prey to the enemy, although his ship is ever so carefully and well built.

Thus an owner may suffer considerable losses, in a thousand ways, less through the defects of his ship, than the ignorance of the commander.

It is even frequently observed, that a ship exhibits the best qualities, during one cruise, and the very worst during another.

Lastly, it is evident from all that has been said, that a ship of the best form, will not show its good qualities, except when it is at the same time well rigged, well stowed, and well worked by those who command it.

Appendix 12

CHAPMAN'S TREATISE ON SHIPBUILDING, CHAPTER IX ON DIFFERENT MATTERS RELATING TO THE PRACTICAL PART OF CONSTRUCTION

CHAP. IX.

ON DIFFERENT MATTERS RELATING TO THE PRACTICAL PART OF CONSTRUCTION.

Of the scantlings of the pieces for the construction of a ship.

(159.) THE art of proportioning the pieces, which enter into the construction of a ship, depends altogether on practice.

A ship that is to be laden with iron, with salt, or other wares of a considerable specific gravity, likely to strain the ship at sea, or the working of which may tend to loosen the parts of the ship, ought to be more solidly put together, than a ship whose cargo is to be light merchandize, as fir, timber, planks, &c. The difference of the quality of the wood also renders necessary a difference in the scantling, in order to obtain the same solidity.

(160.) The solidity of a ship does not depend solely on the strength of the scantling of the wood; great care ought to be taken also to work it properly, as well the timbers for frames as the planking; to unite well all the parts of the edifice, and to establish properly each piece in its respective place.

(161.) As to the scantling of the timber for the construction of privateers, the object of these ships being only to serve in war, it is not necessary to build them of greater strength, than the probable period of their being wanted requires; on which account, the least scantling possible is given them, with a view to economy in expence.

115

This will be attended with the farther advantage, that the vessel will displace less, and that the bottom will be more elastic, which increases the velocity of sailing (NOTE 48.).

An able practical man must therefore be guided by circumstances.

The scantlings of the pieces, which are given in the following statement, are such as may be used for ships built of oak.

(162.) *Scantling for a Merchant Ship built of Oak.*

Length	160	150	140	130	120	110	100	90	80	70	60	50
Breadth moulded	42	39¾	37½	35¼	33	30¾	28½	26¼	24	21½	19	16½
	39¼	37¼	35¼	33¼	31¼	29¼	27	24¾	22½	20¼	18	15½
Keel sided	18	17¼	16½	15½	14½	13½	12½	11½	10½	9½	8	6
Floors in mid-ship sided	14	13¼	12½	11¾	11	10¼	9½	8¾	8	7¼	6⅜	5½
First, second, and third futtocks sided	13	12½	12	11¼	10½	9¾	9	8¼	7½	6½	5½	5
Top timbers sided	12	11¾	11¼	10¾	10	9¼	8½	7¾	7	6	5¼	5
Moulded at the floor head	12¾	12	11⅜	10¾	10	9¼	8½	7¾	7	6	5	4¼
Moulded at the main wales	10¾	10⅛	9½	8⅞	8¼	7½	6⅞	6⅛	5½	4⅞	4¼	3½
Moulded at the top side	5½	5¼	5	4¾	4½	4¼	4	3¾	3½	3¼	3	2½
Main wale thick	7¾	7⅜	7	6½	6	5½	5	4½	4	3⅝	3¼	2¾
Plank of bottom thick	4¼	4	3¾	3½	3¼	3	2⅞	2¾	2⅝	2½	2	1½
Channel wale thick	5¾	5⅜	5	4⅝	4¼	3⅞	3½	3¼	3	—	—	—
Plank between main and channel wales thick	3¾	3⅝	3½	3⅜	3¼	3	2⅞	2¾	2⅝	2⅜	2	1½
Plank between channel wale and gun wale thick	3	3	2⅞	2¾	2⅝	2½	2⅜	2¼	2⅛	2	1¾	1¼
Keelson square	17	16½	15¾	15	14	13	12	11¼	10¼	9½	8	6
Score of the keelson	6	5⅝	5⅜	5	4⅝	4¼	3⅞	3½	3¼	3	2¾	2¼
Foot waling thick	4	3¾	3½	3¼	3	2¾	2⅝	2½	2⅜	2¼	1⅞	1½
Lower deck clamps thick	7	6⅝	6¼	5⅞	5½	5⅛	4¾	4⅜	4	3⅝	3¼	2¾
Lower deck beams moulded	18	17	16	15	14	12¾	11¼	10	9	8	7	5½
Lower deck beams sided	19	18	17	16	15	13¾	12¼	11	10	9	8	6
Knees sided to	11½	10¾	10	9¼	8½	7⅞	7¼	6⅝	6	5⅜	4¾	4
Carlings up and down	5¾	5½	5⅛	4¾	4⅜	4	3⅝	3¼	3	2⅞	2¾	2½
Ledges ditto	5	4¾	4⅜	4	3¾	3½	3¼	3	2¾	2½	2¼	2
Binding strakes thick	6	5¾	5½	5¼	5	4¾	4½	4¼	4	3¾	3½	2
Flat of deck thick	4	3¾	3½	3¼	3	2⅞	2¾	2⅝	2½	2¼	2	1½
Water ways ditto	5¾	5⅜	5	4⅝	4⅜	4⅛	3⅞	3⅝	3⅜	3⅛	2¾	1¾
Upper deck clamps	5¾	5¼	5	4¾	4¼	4⅛	3⅞	3⅝	3¼	3	2¾	1¾
Upper deck beams moulded	12½	11½	10¾	10⅛	9½	8⅞	8¼	7½	6¾	6	5	4
Upper deck beams sided	13	12½	11¾	11	10½	10	9¼	8½	7¾	7	6	5
Knees sided to	8	7½	7	6½	6	5½	5	4⅝	4¼	4	3¾	3¼
Carlings up and down	4	4	3⅞	3¾	3⅝	3½	3¼	3⅛	2⅞	2¾	2½	2
Ledges deep	3¼	3¼	3⅛	3	3	2⅞	2¾	2⅝	2½	2¼	2	1½
Flat of deck thick	3½	3¼	3⅛	3	2⅞	2¾	2⅝	2½	2¼	2	1¾	1½
Water ways thick	4	3¾	3½	3¼	3	2⅞	2¾	2⅝	2½	2¼	2	1¾
Quarter deck clamps thick	4	3¾	3½	3¼	3⅛	3	2⅞	2¾	2⅝	2⅜	2⅛	1⅞
Quarter deck beams moulded	8¾	8	7¾	6⅞	6½	6⅛	5¾	5¼	4¾	4¼	3⅝	3
Knees sided to	6½	6	5½	5¼	4¾	4⅜	4	3¾	3½	3¼	3	2¼
Flat of quarter deck thick	3	2⅞	2¾	2½	2¼	2	2	2	2	1¾	1¾	1½
Lower deck transom sided to	10	9½	9	8½	8	7½	7	6½	6	5½	5	4
Rudder head across	23	21⅞	20¾	19⅝	18½	17⅜	15⅞	14⅞	14	12	11	8
Tiller at the after end thick	10½	10	9¼	8½	8	7½	7	6½	6	5½	5	4
At the fore end thick	9	8⅝	8¼	7¾	7¼	6¾	6¼	5¾	5¼	4⅞	4½	3

The fore end of the keel $\frac{11}{12}$, and the after extremity $\frac{5}{6}$ of the siding at the middle. The thickness of the stern-post, near the transom, and the thickness of the stem at the wale, are equal to that of the middle of the keel, but the upper extremity of the stem is $\frac{1}{6}$ more.

(163.) *Scantling for Privateers.*

Length	160	150	140	130	120	110	100	90	80	70	60	50
Breadth	41	38	36	34	32	29	27	25	22	19	17	15
Keel sided	15½	14¾	14⅛	13¼	12½	11¾	11	10	9	8	7	5½
Sternpost sided at the wing transom	16	15½	15	14¼	13½	12½	11¾	10½	9¼	8	7	5½
Stem sided at the wale	15½	14¾	14⅛	13¼	12½	11¾	11	10	9	8	7	5½
Stem sided at the head	21	20	19	18	16¾	15¾	14¾	13¾	12½	11¼	9½	7
Floor timbers, and first futtocks sided to	11¼	10½	10	9½	9	8½	7⅞	7¼	6⅝	6	5½	5
The other timbers of the frame	10¾	10	9½	9	8½	8	7⅜	6¾	6⅛	5½	5	4½
Moulded at the floor head	11	10¼	9½	8¾	8	7⅜	6¾	6⅛	5½	5	4½	4
Moulded at the height of the deck	9	8	7¼	6½	5¾	5⅛	4⅝	4⅛	3¾	3½	3¼	3
Moulded at the gun wale	5	4¾	4½	4¼	4	3¾	3½	3¼	3	2⅞	2¾	2¼
Wale thick	7	6⅝	6¼	5⅞	5½	5	4½	4¼	3⅞	3½	3¼	2¾
Plank of bottom thick	4	3¾	3½	3¼	3	2¾	2⅝	2½	2⅜	2¼	2	1½
Thickness strake above the wale	3½	3¼	3	2⅞	2¾	2⅝	2½	2⅜	2¼	2⅛	1⅞	1⅜
Thickness top-side	3	2¾	2½	2⅜	2¼	2⅛	2	1⅞	1¾	1½	1⅜	1¼
Orlop clamps	5	4¾	4⅜	4	3¾	3½	3¼	3	2⅞	2½	2	1¾
Beams of orlop deck square	9½	8¾	8¼	7¾	7¼	6¾	6½	—	—	—	—	—
Flat of orlop deck	3	2⅞	2¾	2⅝	2½	2⅜	2¼	2⅛	2	1⅞	1½	1¼
Upper deck clamps thick	6	5⅜	5¼	4⅞	4½	4⅛	3¾	3⅜	3	2¾	2½	2
Upper deck beams moulded	14	13	12	11	10	9	8¼	7½	6¾	6	5	4
Upper deck beams sided	16	15	14	13	11¾	10½	9¾	9	8¼	7½	6¼	5
Upper deck knees	9¾	8¾	7¾	6¾	6¼	5¾	5¼	4⅞	4½	4	3¼	2¾
Water ways	4¾	4⅜	4	3¾	3½	3¼	3	2¾	2½	2¼	2	1½
Quarter deck clamps	4	3¾	3½	3¼	3	2⅞	2¾	2⅝	2½	2¼	2	1½
Quarter deck beams moulded	8½	7⅞	7¼	6⅝	6	5	5	4¾	4¼	4	3½	3
Quarter deck knees sided	6	5½	5	4⅝	4¼	4	3¾	3½	3¼	3⅛	3	2¾
Roundhouse beams moulded	5	—	—	—	—	—	—	—	—	—	—	—
Roundhouse beams sided	7	—	—	—	—	—	—	—	—	—	—	—
Quarter deck water ways	3	2¾	2½	2¼	2	—	—	—	—	—	—	—
Rudder head sided	20	19½	18¾	17¾	16½	15¾	14¾	13½	12	11	9¼	7
Tiller square	10	9¾	9¾	8½	7⅞	7¼	6½	5⅞	5⅜	4⅜	4¼	3½
Riding bitts	17	16	15	12¾	11½	10¼	9	8	7½	7	6½	5

We have not given here all the pieces, which enter into the construction of a ship, because people, who understand this department, are able to act according to circumstances in proportioning those, which are omitted; considering both the goodness of the execution, and at the same time the weight by which the frame of the ship should be limited. I shall now, with relation to the latter circumstance, give a method of cubing pieces of different forms.

(164.) The common manner of finding the solid content of timber for building, may be sufficiently exact, when it is only with a view to selling or buying; but when the object is to deduce the weight of the pieces from the measurement, it is necessary to obtain the true solid content. In this the two following formulæ will be sufficient. The first is found in Simpson's Fluxions, Tom. I, Art. 154.

For the first, let $AEGB$ (Fig. 35.) be a solid, of which the four sides AH, AF, CH, CF are plane figures, and its bases $ADCB$, $EFGH$ rectangles parallel to each other.

Let the distance between the two bases taken on a perpendicular $= a$; the solid content of the body will be $= \big(AB \times AD + EH \times EF + (AB + EH) \times (AD + EF)\big) \times \frac{1}{6} a$ (NOTE 49.). If $EF = 0$, the body will be like a wedge, having one end smaller than the other, and its solid content will be $= (2AB + EH) \times AD \times \frac{1}{6} a$, but if $EF = EH$, and $AD = AB$, then the body will be the frustrum of a square pyramid; the solid content will be $= (AB^2 + AB \times EH + EH^2) \times \frac{1}{3} a$; and lastly, if EH in this last expression $= 0$, the body will be the whole pyramid, of which the solid content will be $= AB^2 \times \frac{1}{3} a$.

For example, let $AB = 18$ inches, $AD = 12$ inches, $EH = 10$ inches, $EF = 8$ inches, the height $a = 20$ feet; the solidity will be $\big(18 \times 12 + 10 \times 8 + (18 + 10) \times (12 + 8)\big) \times \frac{1}{6} \times 20 = 2853{,}33$; but as the breadth and the

thickness are in inches, it is necessary to divide this quantity by 144, and the solidity will be $= 19{,}814$ cubic feet.

(165.) For the second formula, let $FACDE$ (Fig. 36.) be a round body generated by the revolution of the curve ABC about GH as an axis; let the generating curve ABC be a parabola, whose vertex is at C; let AI be an ordinate parallel to the axis GH, and CI the abscissa of this ordinate, IK its sub-tangent; let $IK : IC :: m : n$, and the parameter $= 1$, then the equation of this parabola will be $CI^n = AI^m$; lastly, let the length $GH = a$, the diameter $CE = b$, and the diameter $AF = c$.

The proportion of the square of the diameter of the circle to its area being nearly as 14 to 11, the solidity of this body may be expressed by $\frac{11}{14} a \times \frac{(m+n) \times nc^2 + 2mnbc + 2m^2b^2}{(m+n) \times n + 2mn + 2m^2}$ (NOTE 50.) If ABC be a conic parabola, then $m = 2$, $n = 1$, and the solidity will be $= \frac{11}{14} a \times \frac{3c^2 + 4bc + 8b^2}{15}$; and if $c = 0$, the solidity will be $\frac{11}{14} a \times \frac{8}{15} b^2$.

If ABC be a cubic parabola of the first species, then $m = 3$, $n = 1$, and the solidity will be $= \frac{11}{14} a \times \frac{4c^2 + 6bc + 18b^2}{28}$; and when $c = 0$, the solidity will be $= \frac{11}{14} a \times \frac{9b^2}{14}$.

If ABC be a cubic parabola of the second species, then $m = 3$, $n = 2$, and the solidity will be $= \frac{11}{14} a \times \frac{10c^2 + 12bc + 18b^2}{40}$; and when $c = 0$, the solidity will be $= \frac{11}{14} a \times \frac{9b^2}{20}$.

If ABC be a right line, then the body is a frustrum of a cone, and $m : n :: 1 : 1$; the solidity will be $= \frac{11}{14} a \times \frac{c^2 + bc + b^2}{3}$; and lastly, if $c = 0$, the body will be an entire cone, of which the solidity will be $= \frac{11}{14} a \times \frac{b^2}{3}$.

For example, there is required the solid content of a yard 68 feet long, 17 inches in diameter at the middle, and 7 inches in diameter at the extremities. Then $a = 68$, $b = 17$, and $c = 7$: if the generating curve by the revolution of which this yard is formed, be a conic parabola, the solidity will be = $\frac{11}{14} a \times \frac{3c^2 + 4bc + 8b^2}{15} = \frac{11}{14} \times 68 \times \frac{3 \times 7^2 + 4 \times 17 \times 7 + 8 \times 17^2}{15} = 10454$; but the diameters 17 and 7 being expressed in inches, it will be necessary to divide this quantity by 144, and we shall have for the solidity of the yard $72\frac{6}{10}$ cubic feet.

Knowing the weight of a cubic foot of wood from which the yard is made, we shall easily obtain its whole weight. For example, if a cubic foot of this wood weigh 40 pounds, multiply this quantity by 72,6, the product will be 2904 pounds = 9 skiponds iron weight, and if 2904 be divided by 63, we shall have the weight equal to that of 46 cubic feet of sea-water.

(166.) This formula for the solidity of round timber might serve to guage a cask, when the curve is any of the parabolic lines. The operation is as follows:

The inside diameter of the cask both at the middle and at the extremities is measured; $CE = b$, $AF = c$; half the difference of these two quantities $= n$.

To know the kind of parabola, which is to be used in the calculation, a rule exactly straight is laid on one extremity, so as to be a tangent to this point, as AK at A.

From the middle point C of the cask, the length CK is taken on a perpendicular to the axis (we suppose the staves equally thick throughout;) CK added to n will give m (Note 51.). Take moreover the length of the cask a in the inside.

For example, $a = 4,04$ feet, $b = 3,4$ feet; $c = 2,6$ feet, so that $\frac{b-c}{2} = 0,4 = n$. Let the distance CK from the barrel to the rule $AK = 0,15$; then $0,4 + 0,15 = 0,55 = m$.

The content then of the cask, according to the formula, will be =

$$\frac{11}{14} \times 4,04 \times \frac{0,95 \times 0,4 \times (2,6)^2 + 2 \times 0,22 \times 8,84 + 2 \times 0,3025 \times (3,4)^2}{0,95 \times 0,4 + 2 \times 0,22 + 2 \times 0,3025} =$$

$$\frac{11}{14} \times 4,04 \times \frac{13,452}{1,425} = \frac{11}{14} \times 4,04 \times 9,44 = 30 \text{ cubic feet, or } 300 \text{ } kans.$$

121

One may also, by means of this formula, find the length and diameter of all kinds of casks for a given content.

For example, suppose it were required to find of what dimensions a cask ought to be to contain 33 cubic feet or 330 kans.

Let the length $= a$, the great diameter $= b$; the diameter at each extremity $= c$; let these interior dimensions be as 6, 5 and 4; then $b = \frac{5}{6}a$, and $c = \frac{4}{6}a$; and if the curvature of the staves form a cubic parabola of the second species, m will be $= 3$, and $n = 2$. So that $\frac{11}{14}a^3 \times$

$$\frac{10 \times \frac{16}{36} + 12 \times \frac{20}{36} + 18 \times \frac{25}{36}}{10 + 12 + 18} = 33; \text{ whence } a^3 =$$

$$\frac{33 \times 14 \times 36 \times (10 + 12 + 18)}{11 \times (10 \times 16 + 12 \times 20 + 18 \times 25)} = \frac{665280}{9350} = 70,83; \text{ and lastly, } a = 4,123,$$

whence $b = 3,436$, and $c = 2,749$ feet.

The method of laying off according to the full size on the mould-loft, for making the moulds.

(167.) Let us take for example the privateer (Fig. 45, and 51.). For the execution in the fore body, between the frames P, S, W and the stem are traced other frames U and R (Fig. 37.); and in the after body, between the frames 21, 24 and the stern-post, those marked 26, 25 and 23 (Fig. 37.); where, for greater clearness, the plan is made on a larger scale.

A ship which has sufficiently little rising in her floors to allow her taking the ground in tide-ways, ought to have such length of floor, that on laying aground, the extremities of the said floors which touch, may be beyond the point of contact at least one foot towards their heads.

But since a ship as clean as the one in question, cannot be laid aground, we are at liberty to make the floors as short as we wish.

Wherefore if the timber for building the ship be on the spot, its form and length should be examined, in order after that to mark on the plan the places where the different timbers are to be shifted, as in I, II, III. The floors will be $IBBI$; the first futtocks will be from B to II; the

second futtocks from I to III; the third futtocks from II to C; the top timbers from III to C.

Thus each frame is composed of one floor, six futtocks, and two top-timbers; but if the timber has not the length which we here suppose, it will be necessary to alter the divisions, diminishing the shifts so that there may be one futtock more on each side. However timber should not be used so short as not to give, for ships of this size, six feet shift to the first futtock and floorheads, and four feet and a quarter to the other timbers.

When all the shifts are thus marked, the diagonal lines 1, 2, 3, 4, 5, 6 and 7 are drawn on the body plan, nearly in the direction in which the plank is brought on; according to these diagonal lines the ribbands are nailed, when the frames are got into their places.

(168.) To have the shape of the top timbers, a line is drawn between the main breadth line and top breadth line; it is denoted both on the body plan and on sheer plan, by 8 (Fig. 37.). The line 9 marks the heights of the main breadth, 10 those of the top breadth, and 11 those of the top side.

(169.) All these operations being finished, the different distances are taken, from which a scheme is formed, such as the following one (Fig. 37, 45 and 51.).

Main Breadth After Body.					Main Breadth Fore Body.				
	Height from the upper edge of the rabbet of the keel.			Half breadth.		Height from the upper edge of the rabbet of the keel.			Half breadth.
	Ft. In. ¼			Ft. In. ¼		Ft. In. ¼			Ft. In. ¼
At the frames 3	12 0 0			13 10 1	At the frames C	11 11 6			13 10 1
6	12 1 3			13 8 2	F	12 1 4			13 9 ·
9	12 4 1			13 5 6	I	12 4 5			13 6 4
12	12 7 7			13 1 7	M	12 10 3			13 5
15	13 1 0			12 8 4	P	13 6 5			12 1
18	13 7 5			12 1 4	R	13 11 6			11 1 6
21	14 3 6			11 4 3	S	14 5 7			9 8
23	14 8 6			10 11 5	U	15 1 2			7 5 5
24	15 2 4			10 5 4	W	15 9 7			3 11 6
25	15 7 2			10 0 4	At the stem	16 4 6			
26	15 9 6			9 10 0					
At fashion piece	16 1 0			9 6 3					
At side counter timber	16 9 1			8 9 7					

Between Main and Top Breadth Lines.									
After Body					Fore Body				
	Height from the upper edge of the rabbet of the keel.			Half breadth.		Height from the upper edge of the rabbet of the keel.			Half breadth.
	Ft. In. ¼			Ft. In. ¼		Ft. In. ¼			Ft. In. ¼
At the frames 3	14 7 4			13 1	At the frames C	14 7 3			13 1 3
6	14 8 4			13	F	14 8			13 3
9	14 10 6			12 9 6	I	14 10			12 10 4
12	15 1 4			12 6 3	M	15 7			12 5 4
15	15 4 7			12 1 6	P	15 4 7			11 7 4
18	15 8 7			11 7 6	R	15 7 3			10 9 2
21	16 2 0			11 2	S	15 10 7			9 6 4
24	16 8 0			10 3 1	U	16 2 2			7 5 5
At fashion piece	17 3 0			9 4 5	W	16 7 0			3 11 6
At side counter timber	17 8 0			8 8 6	At the stem	16 10 3			

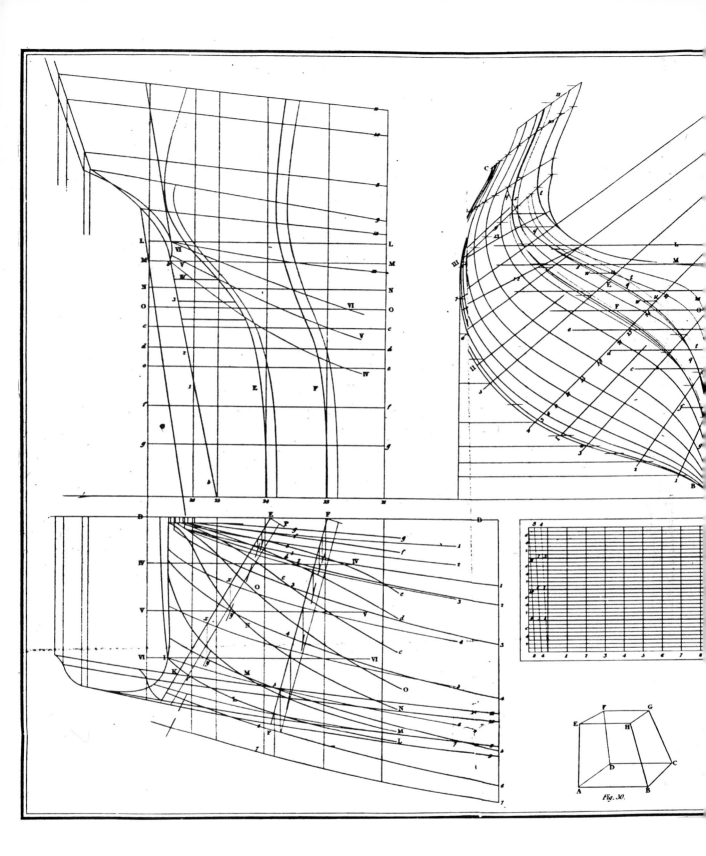

Fig. 30.

240

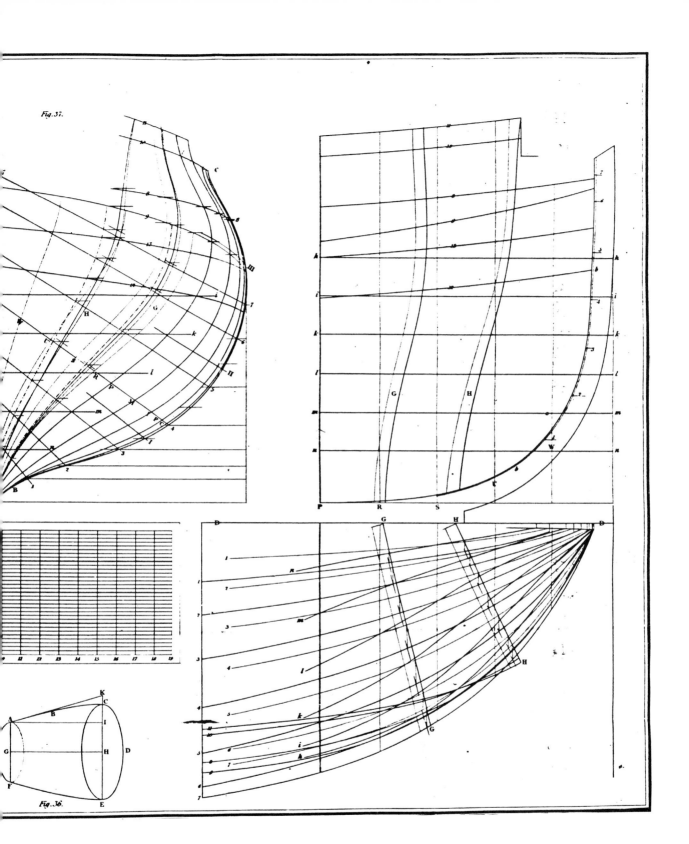

Fig. 37.

Fig. 36.

125

Top Breadth After Body

	Height from the upper edge of the rabbet of the keel.			Half breadth.		
	Ft.	In.	1/8	Ft.	In.	1/8
At the frames 3	17	2	5	11	9	3
6	17	3	7	11	8	3
9	17	5	7	11	6	3
12	17	8	5	11	3	2
15	17	11	7	10	10	6
18	18	4	0	10	5	2
21	18	8	7	9	10	1
24	19	3	4	9	1	6
At fashion piece	19	10	5	8	3	6
At side counter timber	20	4	2	7	7	6

Top Breadth Fore Body

	Height from the upper edge of the rabbet of the keel.			Half breadth.		
	Ft.	In.	1/8	Ft.	In.	1/8
At the frames C	17	2	5	11	9	1
F	17	3	3	11	8	
I	17	5		10	5	5
M	17	7	7	11	1	3
P	17	11	6	10		5
R	18	2	3	9	10	1
S	18	5	2	8	11	7
U	18	9	4	7	8	4

Top Side After Body

	Height from the upper edge of the rabbet of the keel.			Half breadth.		
	Ft.	In.	1/8	Ft.	In.	1/8
At the frames 15	19	3	1	10	4	2
18	19	7	1	9	11	
21	19	11	7	9	4	4
24	20	6	1	8	8	3
At fashion piece 21	21	1	7	7	10	1
At side counter timber	21	8		7	2	3

Top Side Fore Body

	Height from the upper edge of the rabbet of the keel.			Half breadth.		
	Ft.	In.	1/8	Ft.	In.	1/8
At the frames M	18	8	7	10	9	6
P	19		7	10	2	
R	19	4		9	8	
S	19	7	2	8	11	2
U	19	11	2	7	10	7

Distances on the Diagonals of the Fore Body.

	First Diagonal.				Second Diagonal.				Third Diagonal.				Fourth Diagonal.		
	Ft.	In.	1/8		Ft.	In.	1/8		Ft.	In.	1/8		Ft.	In.	1/8
From φ to C	—	—	—	From φ to C	—	—	4	From φ to C	—	1	6	From φ to C	—	1	7
F	—	—	4	F	—	2	1	F	—	5	2	F	—	6	—
I	—	2	1	I	—	6	1	I	1	—	7	I	1	2	3
M	—	5	5	M	1	—	7	M	1	11	5	M	2	3	4
P	1	—	—	P	1	11	5	P	3	2	3	P	3	10	—
R	1	4	3	R	2	6	6	R	4	—	1	R	4	10	1
S	1	9	5	S	3	2	7	S	4	11	7	S	6	1	—
U	2	4	5	U	4	—	7	U	6	2	3	U	7	8	—
W	—	—	—	W	5	—	7	W	7	7	4	W	9	8	—
To mid. line	3	6	5	To mid. line	5	11	1	To mid. line	9	1	—	To mid. line	11	11	4

	Fifth Diagonal.				Sixth Diagonal.				Seventh Diagonal.				Upper edge of the Wale.		
	Ft.	In.	1/8		Ft.	In.	1/8		Ft.	In.	1/8		Ft.	I.	1/8
From φ to C	—	1	—	From φ to C	—	—	5	From φ to C	—	—	4	Height above the rabbit of keel C	11	11	5
F	—	4	2	F	—	3	—	F	—	2	2	F	12	—	3
I	—	11	7	I	—	8	4	I	—	5	7	I	12	2	1
M	2	—	2	M	1	6	4	M	1	2	1	M	12	4	7
P	3	8	—	P	3	—	4	P	2	5	6	P	12	9	—
R	4	9	6	R	4	2	—	R	3	6	6	R	12	11	5
S	6	3	1	S	5	8	1	S	5	1	1	S	13	3	—
U	8	2	6	U	7	11	5	U	7	6	—	U	13	7	1
W	10	11	2	W	11	3	7	W	11	1	5	W	13	11	6
To mid. line	14	—	6	To mid. line	15	4	—	To mid. line	15	6	1	At the stem	14	3	3

Distances on the Diagonals of the After Body.

	First Diagonal.				Second Diagonal.				Third Diagonal.				Fourth Diagonal.		
	Ft.	In.	1/8		Ft.	In.	1/8		Ft.	In.	1/8		Ft.	In.	1/8
From φ to 3	—	—	7	From φ to 3	—	1	3	From φ to 3	—	2	—	From φ to 3	—	2	4
6	—	3	3	6	—	5	1	6	—	7	4	6	—	7	7
9	—	6	7	9	—	10	4	9	1	3	—	9	1	4	—
12	—	10	7	12	1	5	3	12	2	—	5	12	2	3	3
15	1	4	3	15	2	2	2	15	3	—	4	15	3	3	4
18	1	10	6	18	3	—	7	18	4	2	2	18	4	6	4
21	2	7	7	21	4	1	7	21	5	7	2	21	6	—	5
23	3	1	6	23	4	10	—	23	6	5	7	23	6	11	6
24	3	8	—	24	5	7	3	24	7	6	3	24	8	1	6
25	4	3	2	25	6	4	—	25	8	8	—	25	9	4	4
26	4	6	4	26	6	8	5	26	9	4	5	26	10	3	4
To mid. line	5	3	—	To mid. line	7	5	1	To mid. line	10	6	—	To the margin	11	5	6
												To mid. line	13	8	2

	Fifth Diagonal.				Sixth Diagonal.				Seventh Diagonal.				Upper edge of the Wale.		
	Ft.	In.	1/8		Ft.	In.	1/8		Ft.	In.	1/8		Ft.	In.	1/8
From φ to 3	—	2	—	From φ to 3	—	1	4	From φ to 3	—	—	6	Height from the rabbit 3	11	11	6
6	—	5	6	6	—	4	1	6	—	3	3	6	12	—	6
9	1	1	—	9	—	9	2	9	—	7	4	9	12	3	—
12	1	10	4	12	1	4	1	12	1	—	7	12	12	5	6
15	2	10	—	15	2	1	3	15	1	8	2	15	12	9	2
18	4	—	3	18	3	—	—	18	2	6	2	18	13	1	6
21	5	6	2	21	4	5	4	21	3	7	4	21	13	7	2
23	6	5	1	23	5	2	4	23	4	3	2	23	13	10	3
24	7	6	4	24	6	—		24	5	—	1	24	14	2	2
25	8	6	1	25	6	10	6	25	5	7	7	25	14	5	1
26	9	1	5	26	7	3	7	26	5	11	7	26	14	6	5
To the margin	9	8	6	To the margin	7	9	5	To mid. line	17	—	6	At fashion piece	14	8	3
To mid. line	15	11	—	To mid. line	16	8	7								

(170.) From this scheme the ship is laid down in full size, on the mould loft, according to the ordinary foot. The frames and other curve lines in the plans, are drawn on the floor by means of penning battens, which confined to the given spots, take the curvature which is wished.

The half thickness of the keel, stem, and stern-post, is drawn in the body plan on each side of the middle line; a dotted line *aa* also is drawn for the depth of the rabbet, and those *bb* for its breadth on the stem and stern-post.

The upper and lower edges of the wales are also denoted by 12 and 13.

(171.) As well to verify the exactness of the body plan, as to obtain the bevellings of the timbers, all the diagonals from the stem and stern-post to the mid-ship section must be delineated; to do this, on all the diagonals 1, 2, 3, 4 of the body plan, the distances are taken from the middle line to each frame, and they are set off from the middle line *DD* on the corresponding frames in the half-breadth plan; this will give the diagonals 1, 1; 2, 2; 3, 3; &c.

(172.) As it is not possible to place the frames near the extremities, in a plane perpendicular to the middle line *DD*, without having too great a curvature and requiring timber of too large scantling, on account of the great bevelling, the practice is to put them in a vertical plane, but oblique with regard to the plane of elevation or to the middle line *DD*, as *KE, FF, GG, HH.* These three last frames are called *cant frames;* *KE* or the aftermost one is the fashion piece, which determines the length of all the lower transoms.

(173.) It is not proper to carry *E* too far from the stern-post, this lengthens the said transoms too much, and as they are much curved, it would be difficult to find pieces proper for making them.

There must be limits also to the canting of the frames, for otherwise the filling frames would necessarily be beat away too much at the heels.

129

(174.) To determine the moulds and bevellings of these pieces (the filling-frames, transoms, and fashion-pieces) draw on the body plan, some water-lines (NOTE 52.), in the first place at the upper edges of the transoms L, M, N, O, and then below, at pleasure, as c, d, f, g, and for the fore ones i, k, l, m; transfer these water-lines to the half-breadth plan, where they are marked with the same letters.

The lines M, N, O, give the moulds of the upper edge of the transoms, and the line L, in IK, the bevelling of the end of the wing transom.

On the half-breadth plan, is taken the distance from E to all the points, where the water-lines cut KE or the after edge of the fashion-piece; these distances are set off on the corresponding water-lines on the body plan, from the middle line; and passing a curve through all the spots thus given, we have the line qq for the mould of the fashion-piece.

At a distance from KE, equal to the siding of the fashion-piece, draw Pr parallel thereto; from E draw the line EP perpendicular to KE, take the distance from P to all the points where Pr meets the water-lines, and set off also these distances from the middle line of the body plan, on the corresponding water-lines. Through all these spots draw ss, this curve will give the fore edge of the fashion-piece, and the distance between qq and ss will shew how much the bevelling of this piece is within or without the after edge.

(175.) To find the point where each diagonal meets the fashion-piece qq.

Take all the perpendicular distances from the middle line DD to the points where the water-lines meet the line KE; set off these distances on the corresponding water-lines of the body plan, also from the middle line; through all the points which this will give, pass the curve tt, which will give the projection of the after edge of the fashion-piece.

From the points u, u, where the diagonals meet this curve, draw

the horizontal lines uw; then w, w, where these small lines meet the curve qq, are the points on the true fashion-piece, where it is cut by the diagonals.

(176.) To find the points where the fashion-piece cuts the diagonals.

Take the perpendicular distance from the middle line to all the points, where the diagonals 1, 1; 2, 2; 3, 3; &c. cut the frames; set off these distances on the corresponding frames in the half-breadth plan from the middle line DD; through the points, which this operation will give, pass the curves 1, 2, 3, &c. which are dotted; this will give what are called the horizontal diagonal lines.

From the points x, x, where the lines meet KE, draw the small lines xy, xy perpendicular to the middle line DD; the points y, y, where these lines meet the diagonal lines 1, 1; 2, 2; 3, 3; &c. are those where the fashion-piece is cut by the diagonals.

(177.) The fashion-piece gives the bevellings of the extremities of the transoms; but the bevellings of the said transoms between their extremities and the middle are found by the following method.

Draw on the half-breadth plan the lines IV, V and VI, at pleasure, parallel to the middle line DD; take the distances of the points of intersection of these lines with the water-lines, from the perpendicular at the stern-post; set off these distances on the corresponding water-lines on the sheer plan from the said perpendicular at the stern-post, and through the points which this will give, draw the curves IV, V, VI; these lines will give the bevelling of the transoms. The bevelling of the lower transoms may be found by means of the frames 25 and 26.

(178.) The moulds and bevellings of the cant frames in the fore and after bodies, are found by proceeding as has been done for the fashion-piece; which is sufficiently seen by the plan.

131

(179.) After having drawn the square and cant frames, and the transoms, moulds are made of thin boards, on which all the places for the diagonals are marked, the height of breadth, top breadth, wales, and the decks, if required.

The moulds for the fore and after parts, which have great rounding, are made to the diagonals 1, 1; 2, 2; 3, 3; &c. in the half-breadth plan, of two-inch deals, which are even sheathed to give the greater solidity.

A ribband is carried above the wales, which may either be placed horizontally, or according to a right line, which is most nearly parallel to the wales.

The moulds for the floors are made so broad at the middle, as to have the whole height of the floors.

The bevellings of the pieces are marked, either on the moulds themselves, or on bevelling boards.

(180.) It is essential to use all possible precision in the laying off and in making the moulds; not only the construction thence becomes more conformable to the plan, but also by this means there is a saving in the wages of the workmen, who are thereby enabled to put together the frames and get them into their places, without being obliged to retouch them, in order that they may come well together and graduate well.

On the Construction of the Scale of Solidity.

(181.) Suppose we wish to make the scale of solidity for the privateer (Fig. 43, 44. and 46.), of which we have the displacement calculated in Art. 9.

The calculation for the construction of this scale must commence from the plane of the load water-line, so as to obtain in succession the solidity between this and each of the lower water-lines; the operation is performed in the following manner.

To find the solidity of the part between the first and second water-lines.

Half the area of the load water-line	1293,91
Ditto of the second	1178,03
	2)2471,94
	1235,97
Multiplied by the distance between the water-lines	1,62
Half the solidity between the first and second water-lines	2002,27
Plank	50,73
Stem and stern-post	2,00
	2055,00
	2
Displacement of the part, 1,62 feet below the load water-line	4110,00
	= 45,16 lasts.

To find the solidity of the parts between the first and third water-lines.

Half the area of the load water-line =	1293,91 × 1 =	1293,91
Ditto for the second =	1178,03 × 4 =	4712,12
Ditto for the third =	1030,69 × 1 =	1030,69
		7036,72
Multiplied by one-third the distance between the water-lines		0,54
Half the solidity between the first and third water-lines		3799,83
Plank		104,17
Stem and stern-post		4,00
	cubic feet	3908,00
		2
Displacement of the part 3,24 feet below the load water-line		7816,00
		= 85,89 lasts.

To find the solidity of the pieces between the first and fourth water-lines.

Half the area of the third water-line..........................	1030,69
Ditto of the fourth	856,93
	2)1887,62
	943,81
Multiplied by the distance between the water-lines	1,62
Half the solid between the third and fourth water-lines	1528,97
Half the solid between the first and third water-lines	3799,83
Half the solid between the first and fourth water-lines........	5328,80
Plank	165,20
Stem and stern-post..................................	6,00
	5500,00
	2
Displacement of the part 4,86 feet below the load water-line	11000,00
	= 120,88 lasts.

To find the solidity of the pieces between the first and fifth water-lines.

Half the area of the load water-line......	= 1293,91 × 1 = 1293,91
Ditto of the second.....................	= 1178,03 × 4 = 4712,12
Ditto of the third	= 1030,69 × 2 = 2061,38
Ditto of the fourth	= 854,93 × 4 = 4327,72
Ditto of the fifth......................	= 662,38 × 1 = 662,38
	12157,51
Multiplied by one-third the distance between the water-lines	0,54
Half the solidity between the first and fifth water-lines	6565,05
Plank...	239,95
Stem and stern-post.................................	9,00
	6814,00
	2
Displacement of the part 6,48 feet below the load water-line ...	13628,00
	= 149,75 lasts.

134

To find the solidity of the pieces between the first and sixth water-lines.

Half the area of the fifth water-line	662,38
Ditto of the sixth..	434,83
	2)1097,21
	548,60
Multiplied by the distance between the water-lines	1,62
	888,73
Half the solidity between the first and fifth water-lines	6565,05
Half the solidity between the first and sixth water-lines........	7453,78
Plank..	335,22
Stem and stern-post.......................................	12,00
	7801,00
	2
Displacement of the part 8,1 feet below the load water-line .	15602,00
	= 171,45 lasts.

To find the solidity of the pieces between the first and seventh water-lines.

Half the solidity between the first and seventh water-line 7947 (Art. 7.)	
Plank	426
Stem and stern-post............................	16
	8399 cubic feet
	2
Displacement of the part 9,72 feet below the load} water-line ....}	16798 =
	184,6 lasts.

To find the solidity from the load water-line to the keel.

Half the solidity between first water-line and the keel....	8105
Plank	500
Stem and stern-post............................	20
	8625 cubic feet
	2
Displacement of the part 11,72 feet below the load} water-line................................}	17250 =
	189,56 lasts.

135

To construct from hence a scale of burden.

(182.) Draw two lines perpendicular to each other, the one in a horizontal direction, the other in a vertical direction; make on the horizontal line a decimal scale at pleasure to represent lasts, and on the vertical another scale of feet also at pleasure, as is seen in Fig. 50.

Below the horizontal line and at the distance from this superior line of 1.62, 3.24, 4.28, 6.48, 8.1, 9.72 and 11.2 feet, draw parallels thereto.

On the scale of lasts, take the quantities, which have been found, in lasts 45.16, 85.89, 120.88, 149.75, 171.45, 184.6 and 189.58; set off these quantities on the corresponding horizontal lines, from the vertical line.

Through all the points so determined pass a curve, and you will have a scale of solidity.

The horizontal scale is in French tons, English tons, and Swedish lasts. The method of using the scale is this.

The line *ab* (NOTE 53.) on the sheer plan is the load water-line, the privateer being laden. Suppose that the water-line before it is entirely laden, were *cd*; then the distances *ac*, *bd* are taken, which by the scale of the plan give 4 feet 1¼ inches and 5 feet 1¼ inches; these two quantities are added, and half the sum is taken, 4 feet 7¼ inches.

Take this quantity 4 feet 7¼ inches on the scale of solidity, you will have *eg*, which must be transferred perpendicularly to the line *ef*, until it meet the curve in *h*. From *h* draw the line *hi* perpendicularly to *fe*, or what is the same thing, parallel to *eg*; this line marks on the scale of lading the weight, which must be put on board to bring down the ship to the line *ab*, namely, 175 Swedish lasts.

(183.) If the ship be quite light, one may in this manner find the lading, which it can take; or if the water-line of a ship has been once observed, supposing another to be found, one may be able, by means of the said scale, to obtain the weight which the ship has taken on board, or of which it has been discharged, to render it so much more brought down, or more raised.

136

If similar scales were made by builders for all ships and vessels constructed by them, the owner or commander would have it always in his power to determine the lading he could take on board, and that with such exactness as not to be deceived one last in the largest ship, when the load water-line was determined.

This scale is particularly necessary for ships of war or privateers, to the end that knowing the quantity of provisions and other stores, which they can take, the ballast may be determined, which they can receive without being brought down farther than the load water-line.

EXPLANATORY NOTES

CHAPTER THREE: CHAPMAN'S APPOINTMENT TO THE INSHORE FLEET

The Swedish National Archives contain the following petition about Chapman's employment on his return from Britain and continental Europe: 'Chapman, who has returned from studies in England, France and Holland in shipbuilding, seeks employment with an annual salary as he wishes to return to the country of his birth.' (RA 1481 Rådsprotokoll krigsärenden juli-december 1757)

CHAPTER FOUR: THE KING'S REVOLUTION 19 AUGUST 1772

The three books published in English which contain accounts of Gustaf III's revolution are:

1. *Scandinavia in the Revolutionary Era 1705–1815* by H A Barton (University of Minnesota Press, 1986). This book gives a broad outline of the causes, and results of Gustaf III's revolt.

2. *British Diplomats and Swedish Politics 1758–72* by Professor Michael Roberts (University of Minnesota Press, 1980). This book gives details of British, Danish, and Russian attempts to control Swedish internal politics, and an account of their defeat by Gustaf III, aided by France.

3. *Sweden — The Nation's History* by F D Scott (University of Minnesota Press, 1977). This work contains a summary of the events leading to the revolt, and an account of its execution.

The three books in Swedish, to which I have referred, trace the causes and the events of the revolution, namely:

1. *Svensk Historia* by Professor S Carlsson (Svenska bokförlaget, Stockholm, 1960). This book which is the standard text book used in Swedish university history courses, gives a detailed account of the king's revolution and its causes.

2. *Gustaf III* by B Hennings (Pan Books, Stockholm, 1957), contains a short account of the monarch's revolution but describes in much detail life in Gustaf's court and the cultural developments of the reign.

3. *Vår Svenska Historia* by Professor A Åberg (Natur och Kultur, 1978), is a history of Sweden written especially for the larger readership. It covers Sweden from the prehistory period to 1967, laying weight on social problems. The author provides a short and concise account of the revolution and its causes.

CHAPTER SIX: THE AMPHION

1. On the morning of 22 July 1779, the name's day of Queen Sofia Magdalena, the famous Swedish poet Mikael Bellman sang verses in her honour at the Drottningholm palace, which included praise of the *Amphion*.

Drottningholm din prakt förkjusar
Alt en glättig känsla har;
Skyn är mörckblå, hög och klar,
Böljan glittrar, wädret susar,
Blomman rodnar frisk och swal.
Trädet skugg-rikt sig utsträcker,
Och med glesa löf betäcker
Göken, som i toppen gal.

Morgon -solen prägtigt strimmar
Skogen dagas långt ifrån,
Och på wattnet *Amphion*
Med sin gyllne lyra simmar
Under trumslag, sång och skott.

Drottningholm, thy splendours vie:
Lend a universal cheer;
Dark blue heavens, high and clear,
Billows glitter, zephyrs sigh,
Fresh and cool's the blushing flower;
Shady mantling trees profusely
Cloak with spreading leaves diffusely
Cuckoo croaking in her bower.

Morning sunshine glorious shimmering,
Woodland beckons far and yon,
On the water *Amphion*,
With its golden cithern, swimming,
While the drums sound, song and volley.

(Translation by Michael Thompson,
Carleton University)

Bellman's verses, unfortunately difficult to translate into English (one Canadian individual has had some success) give a glimpse of the environment for which the *Amphion* was built, royalty, and the lovely Swedish summers. She was built for Gustaf III, and his Queen for whom a special cabin was arranged, but although she lay at anchor for two summers at Drottningholm, according to Torsten Lenk, an expert on the *Amphion*, Sofia Magdalena visited her for only a few short hours.

2. The *Amphion* proved to be unsuitable for the Baltic's open waters. F A (von) Fersen, later to become Gustaf III's agent at the court of Louis XVI, and C Julin Ekblad, a member of the court, have described the king's stormy voyage in the *Amphion* from Karlskrona to Stockholm in July 1778. Shortly after leaving Karlskrona, the *Amphion* was hit by a squall which fractured the main gaff. Later, when entering the Stockholm archipelago at Landsort, a sudden squall almost caused her to founder, but luckily the wind veered and righted her. After this latter experience, the king decided to make the rest of the forty-mile journey to Stockholm on land. The Duchess of Södermanland wrote in her diary for 22 July 1779: 'The *Amphion* is such a poor sea boat that the King hardly dares to sail in her.'

3. The 1799 Royal Commission requested Chapman's views about the decoration of warships' sterns. He replied that there were three essentials: 'First, the vessel's stern shall have a fine and pleasing outline; second, there shall be a sense of order so that the stern gets a smooth, and relaxed appearance and third, all mouldings shall be in their correct proportions and appropriate profiles.'

CHAPTER SEVEN: COPPER SHEATHING

C A Ehrensvärd's letter of 16 May 1786 to Chapman, about the problems of copper sheathing and the reaction of iron bolts reads as follows: 'Ankarsvärd has informed me that the *Sprengporten*'s iron bolts have been so eaten up by the copper sheathing that they can no longer be of any use.' (RA No 1432)

Chapman requested royal permission in a despatch dated 2 September 1790 to remove the copper sheathing from five ships of the line and a frigate 'because the iron under the same has been eaten away and the ships will be weakened.' (RA No 1735)

CHAPTER SEVEN: THE RANGE OF SWEDISH GUNS

The ranges of Swedish guns were as follows:

36-pounder	678 metres
24-pounder	643 metres
18-pounder	362 metres
12-pounder	348 metres

The length of the gun barrels, and weights were:

Type	Barrel length in metres	Weight in kilos
36-pounder	4.5	3638
24 -pounder	4.8	2720
18-pounder	4.8	2040
12-pounder	4.8	1360

CHAPTER EIGHT: FURTHER READING

Dr R C Anderson's *Naval Wars in the Baltic 1522–1850*, first published in 1910, and reprinted in 1969, gives a detailed account of the 1790 campaign. I believe it is the only comprehensive work on the topic available in English. Dr Anderson, in the preface to the reprint, refers to Arnold Munthe's books published between 1911 and the end of World War I. Munthe's books give quite detailed accounts of the 1788–90 war but contain neither bibliographies nor any reference to his sources. Books published in Sweden and Finland from the 1930s, have extensive bibliographies, and references to source documents.

CHAPTER TEN: WARSHIP SALES

The frigate *af Chapman* was sold to the republic of Columbia in 1825. The Swedish Government tried to raise funds for new construction by the sale of old vessels to the new South American republics. The practice had an earlier precedent. In 1780, af Trolle had proposed the sale of obsolete ships of the line to Turkey, then at war with Russia, for the same purpose.

CHAPTER ELEVEN: CHAPMAN'S CONCERN FOR DOCKYARD PERSONNEL

Chapman wrote to Admiral C A Ehrensvärd on 11 March 1789 to request his approval to issue 8 centilitres of akvavit per day to dockyard personnel during cold weather conditions. Ehrensvärd in his reply dated 12 March agreed. (R A Chefens for Arméns flottans handlinger, 1789)

NOTES FOR MODEL BUILDERS

The Royal Military Records Office (Krigsarkivet, 11588 Stockholm, Sweden) holds most of the warship draughts. The Swedish National Maritime Museum (Statens Sjöhistoriska Museum, 11527 Stockholm, Sweden) has the Chapman archives and many models of Chapman's ships. The Naval Museum, Karlskrona, also has models of Chapman vessels. Model builders can order copies of draughts from Stockholm, at very reasonable prices.

SOURCES AND
BIBLIOGRAPHY

Published Sources
The published sources were written in Swedish or Danish.

Unpublished Sources
All the documents with the exception of the two Sidney Smith and the Henry Pierpont letters, and Chapman's letter to the Empress Maria Theresa, are in Swedish.

The organizations holding the documents are indicated as follows:

KB = Kungliga Biblioteket — Royal Library, Stockholm

GSM = Göteborgs Sjöfarts Museum — Göteborg Maritime Museum

GUB = Göteborgs Universitets bibliotek — Göteborg University Library

KA = kangliga krigsarnivet Royal Military Record Office, Stockholm

KB = Royal Library, Stockholm

KVA = Royal Academy of Sciences, Stockholm

KMS = Royal Society of Military Sciences, Stockholm

KÖS = Royal Society of Naval Sciences, Karlskrona

MM = Marin Muséet, Karlskrona — The Naval Museum, Karlskrona

RA = Riksarkivet — The National Archives, Stockholm

SSM = Statens Sjöhistoriska Museum, Stockholm — The National Maritime Museum

SS = Stockholms Stads Museum — City of Stockholm Museum

UUB = Uppsala Universitets bibliotek — Uppsala University Library

The number of each document, when available, is shown thus:
RA 1457 = National Archives document 1457.

CHAPTER ONE

Published Sources

Abell, W, *The Shipwright's Trade* (London, 1948).

Anon, *Nautical Word Book* (New Jersey, 1961).

Berg, C B, *Danske Orlogs Skibe 1690–1860* (Copenhagen, 1980).

Fincham, J, *History of Naval Architecture* (London, 1851).

Grundström, T, *Amiralitets Kollegiets Historia* Vol II (Malmö, 1974).

Grundström, T, *Skeppsbyggarslakten Sheldon* (Stockholm, 1959).

Halldin, G, *Svenska Flottans Historia* Vol 2 (Malmö, 1943).

Harland, J, *Seamanship in the Age of Sail* (London, 1984).

Holmberg, G, *Svensk Skeppsbyggeri* (Malmö, 1963).

Lavery, G, *Ship of the Line* Vol I (London, 1983).

Rålamb, A, *Skepp Byggerij* (Stockholm, 1691).

Steensen, S, *Flåden genom 475 år* (Copenhagen, 1976).

Stoot, W, 'Aspects of Naval Architecture in the Eighteenth Century', *Proceedings of the Royal Institution of Naval Architects* (London, 1959).

Schama, S, *Patriots and Liberators* (London, 1977).

Svensson, S, *Nautisk — Bild Lexikon* (Göteborg, 1983).

Unger, R, *Dutch Shipbuilding Before 1800* (Amsterdam, 1978).

Unpublished Sources

Pritchard, J, 'From Shipwright to Naval Constructor: Professionalization of 18th Century French Shipbuilders' (forthcoming article).

Hammer, H, 'Farttygstyper i Sv Ost Indisk Flottan' (Göteborg, 1931).

CHAPTER TWO

Published Sources

Kent, A, *War and Trade in Northern Seas* (London, Cambridge 1973).

Neumeyer, F, *F H af Chapman, Som Konstnär och konstfrämjare* (Uppsala, Sjöhistoriska Samfundet 1944).

Rollof, Y, 'F H af Chapman', *Tidskrift-i-Sjöväsendet*, July/August 1958.

Stackell, L, 'Af Chapman', *RIG* H 1–2, 1925.

Unpublished Sources

Chapman's Autobiografi KB.

Chapman Arkiv. SSM Inv 1073 (1)
　　　　　　　 SSM Inv 1073 (2)
　　　　　　　 SSM Inv 1073 (3)

Marine Nationale letter No 122 — 85-09-09

CHAPTER THREE

O. Nikula's *Svenska Skärgårdsflottan* (Helsingfors, 1933), is the best source for information about the Inshore Fleet. The book has the most extensive list sources of all the works listed in the bibliography. F Neumeyer's notes for his several articles about Chapman, held in the Swedish National Maritime Museum, contain references to documents held in the Museum's Chapman archives, the National Archives, and the Uppsala University library. Hugo Hammer's paper, presented in 1921, contains much information about the auxiliary vessels which Chapman designed for the Inshore Fleet.

Published Sources

Anderson, R C, *Oared Fighting Ships* (London, 1962).

Bengtson, H, & Busch, Peter V, *Ett nytt Skärgårds Vapen* (Karlskrona, 1982).

Gierling, V, 'F H af Chapman', *Tidskrift-i-Sjöväsendet*, 1872.

Halldin, G, *Svensk Skeppsbyggeri* (Malmö, 1963).

Hornborg, E, *Kampen om Östersjön* (Stockholm, 1945).

Neumeyer, F, 'Chapman's fartyg och Napoleons förberedelser till Englands invasion', (*Tidskrift-i-Sjöväsendet*, March 1942).

Nikula, O, *Svenska Skärgårdsflottan* (Helsingfors, 1933).

Nikula, O, *Augustin Ehrensvärd* (Helsingfors, 1964).

Önstad, C, 'Aktuellt 1980'. (Karlskrona, 1981)

Rollof, Y, 'F H af Chapman', *Tidskrift-i-Sjöväsendet*, July/August 1958.

Winberg, A, *Dagbok hållen på Gallärflottan 1789/1790* (Stockholm, 1967).

Unpublished Sources

Chapman, F H af, 'Resan genom Finland och Westerbotn' 1758. KA

Chapman, F H, 'Utdrag af hvad vice amiralen sjelf låtit skrifvas angående sin lefnad', 1806. KB

Hammer, H, *Chapmans inflytande på fartygs konstruktions utvekling* Göteborg (Privately printed, 1921)

Wright, G, *Tyå journaler förda på Skärgårds flottan år 1790 ombord gällären Västergötadahl* (Privately printed, Helsingfors)

Lundberg, K, 'Örlogsflottans Sjuktransport'. SSM

Rajalin och Kullenberg 'Study of French, Genoese and Maltese galley fleets 1750'. KA

Schoerner, G, '250 års minnet av F H af Chapman'. SSM

Chapman memo 25 February 1787 to Finance Minister. UUB

Gustaf III memo 15 November 1782 to Ehrensvärd. UUB

Evert's memo 4 April 1781 to Chapman. UUB

Chapman's memo 12 August 1790 to Gustaf III. RA

Ehrensvärd, C A, memo 16 May 1786 to Chapman. RA 1482

Ehrensvärd, C A, memo 14 April 1788 to Chapman. RA 1439

Gustaf Adolph and *Sophia Magdalena* Trials Report 28 November 1787. SSM

Chapman's Autobiografi. KB

Chapter Four

Published Sources

Åberg, A, *Vår Svenska Historia* (Stockholm, 1978).

Anderson, W, *Karlskrona gator byggnader* (Lund, 1980).

Barton, H A, *Scandinavia in the Revolutionary Era 1705–1815* (University of Minnesota, 1980).

Carlsson, S, *Svensk Historia* (Stockholm, 1960).

Frykenstadt, H, *F H Chapman och Ehrensvärd* (Karlskrona, 1972).

Geijer, E, *Gustaf III Efterlämnade Papper* (Stockholm, 1843).

Gjerling, V, 'F H Chapman', *Tidskrift-i-Sjöväsendet*, 1872.

Hallén, T, *Galjons Bilder* (Stockholm, 1975).

Halldin, G, 'F H Chapman', *Teknisk Tidskrift* 15, 1944.

Halldin, G, *Svenska Flottans Historia* Vol 2 (Malmö 1943).

Halldin, G, *Svensk Skkeppsbyggeri* (Malmö, 1963).

Hennings, B, *Gustaf III* (Stockholm, 1957).

Hillbom, R, *Karlskrona 300 år* (Karlskrona, 1979).

Holmberg, E, 'Ett och Annat om Champanska Örlogsskeppen', *Tidskrift-i-Sjöväsendet*, 1921.

Hornborg, E, *Kampen om Östersjön* (Stockholm, 1945).

Johnson, J, 'Chapman's Konstruktions Metoder', *Teknisk Tidskrift*, 1909.

Munthe, A, *Flottan och Ryska Kriget* (Stockholm, 1914).

Myllenberg, A, *300 år och 400 Fartyg* (Karlskrona, 1982).

Neumeyer, F, *F H Chapman som Konstnär* (Uppsala, 1944).

Roberts, H, *British Diplomats and Swedish Politics 1758–72* (University of Minnesota, 1980).

Rollof, Y, 'F H Chapman', *Tidskrift-i-Sjöväsendet*, July/August 1958.

Scott, F D, *Sweden — The Nation's History* (University of Minnesota, 1977).

Stackel, L, 'F H Chapman', *RIG* H-1-2, 1925.

Unger, G, *Svensk Sjökrigshistoria* (Stockholm, 1923).

Witt, G, *Ur Sjövasendets Historia* (Stockholm, 1870).

Chapter Five

Published Sources

Chapman F H, *Architectura Navalis Mercatoria* (London, 1971).

Dingertz, S, *Svenskt Skeppsbyggeri* (Malmö, 1963).

Halldin, G, 'F H af Chapman', *Teknisk Tidskrift* 15, 1944.

Neumeyer, F, 'Architectura Navalis Mercatoria', *Tidskrift-i-Sjöväsendet*, 1943.

Rollof, Y, 'F H af Chapman', *Tidskrift-i-Sjöväsendet*, July, August 1958.

Unpublished Sources

Chapman's Autobiografi. KB

Schoerner, G, '250 års minnet av F H af Chapman'. SSM

CHAPTER SIX

Published Sources

Berg, L O, *Hovjakt varvets Farkoster* (Stockholm, 1931).

Eckerman, A, *Chapmans liv och verksamhet* (Göteborg, 1921).

Fogelmark, S, *Amphion, Konungens Skonert* (Stockholm, 1961).

Gousffrey, J, *Inventoire general de Mobilier de la Couronne* (Paris, 1889).

Halláng, B, *Wasaorden* (Stockholm, 1986).

Lenk, T, *Kungliga Skonerten 'Amphion'* (Stockholm, 1938).

Lundström, P, 'Konungens Gondoler', *Sjöhistorisk Årsbok* (Stockholm, 1966).

Unpublished Sources

Amadis och *Espledian* Series A. KA

Waldén, F H, letter dated 6 September 1782 to Chapman. SSM

CHAPTERS SEVEN AND EIGHT

Published Sources

Anderson, W, *Karlskrona gator and Byggnader* (Lund, 1930).

Försvarsstaben, *Svenksund 1790–1940* (Stockholm 1940)

Frykenstedt, H, *F H Chapman och Ehrensvärd* (Karlskrona, 1972).

Gjerling, V, 'F H Chapman', *Tidskrift-i-Sjöväsendet*, 1872.

Hallen, T, *Galjonsbilder* (Stockholm, 1975).

Halldin, G, 'F H Chapman', *Teknisk Tidskift* 15, 1944.

Halldin, G, *Svenska Flottans Historia* Vol 2 (Malmö, 1943).

Hillbom, R, *Chapmans Liv och Gärning* (Karlskrona, 1974).

Hillbom, R, *Karlskrona 300 år* (Karlskrona, 1979).

Holmberg, E, 'ett och annat om Chapmanska Örlogsfartygstyp', *Tidskrift-i-Sjöväsendet*, 1921.

Hornborg, E, *Kampen om Östersjön* (Stockholm, 1945).

Johnson, J, 'Studie af Chapman Konstruktions Metoder', *Teknisk Tidskrift*, 1909.

Munthe, A, *Flottan och Ryska Kriget* (Stockholm, 1914).

Munthe, A, *Svenska Sjöhjältar* (Stockholm, 1914).

Myllenberg, A, *300 år och 400 fartyg* (Karlskrona, 1982).

Rollof, Y, 'F H af Chapman', *Tidskrift-i-Sjöväsendet*, July/August 1958.

Stackel, L, 'F H af Chapman', *RIG*, H1-2, 1925.

Unger, G, *Svensk Sjökrigshistoria* (Stockholm, 1923).

Witt, G, *En lysande Epok* (Stockholm, 1870).

Önstad, C, *Bildhuggar Versktad* (Karlskrona, 1981).

Unpublished Sources

Chapman's Autobiografi (The original document, 27 pages, is held by the Royal Library, Stockholm. R Hillbom of Karlskrona has published a copy using modern print)

Schoerner, G, '250 års minnet av F H Chapman'. SSM

Manuscripts

Neumeyer decd — Chapman notes*. SSM 24, 23, 736

Chapman letter re repair and refitting of ships. SSM 283

Chapman memo. 'Fordelning af Personnel'. SSM 326 33

Chapman table re maintenance of old fleet. 1783 SSM 327

Report of sea trials. *Gustaf Adolph* versus *Sophia Magdalena*, 28 November 1787. SSM

Admiral Superintendent to HM King, quarterly reports 31 March 1790, 31 December 1790. RA M1735

Admiral Handlinger dated 1790 re renewal of fleet.

Cert Kommission betänkande 1780. RA M1735

Chapman's letter to Finance Minister re reimbursement of funds dated 25 February 1787. UUB

Taube, E, letter to Chapman 4 April 1781 re French minister's interests. UUB

Waldén, F, letter to Chapman re the yacht *Amadis* dated 6 September 1782. UUB

*The late Dr Neumeyer's extensive notes, including extracts from documents, are held by the Sjöhistoriska Museum, Stockholm. I have been able to use these extensively. Neumeyer's notes include some complete copies of documents.

CHAPTER NINE

Published Sources

Halldin, G, *Svenska Flottans Historia* Vol 2 (Malmö, 1943).

Neumeyer, F, *F H Chapman som Konstnär* (Uppsala, 1944).

Rollof, Y, 'F H af Chapman', *Tidskrift-i-Sjöväsendet*, July/August 1958.

Witt, G C, *En lysande Epok* (Stockholm, 1878).

Unpublished Sources

Administrativa handlinger Varvs Amiral till Km RA M1735* KM 13 March 1793 till Varvs Amiral. RA 1445

Underdånig Project till en Arbets Rön June 1797. MM (document is *c* 2 metres long and 60 cm wide)

Project for new building slips for 74-gun ships. SSM

Project for new store houses. SSM

Cost estimates dated 11 April 1794. SSM

Chapman letter to Ehrensvärd 1793 re Landskrona Vaktfatyg. SSM

Explication öfver Arbetets plan 1797. SSM

Chapman letter to KM 4 June 1794. SSM

*The King's command to Chapman referred to in the letter dated 30 September 1790, refers to three attachments A, B, and C. These at time of writing (1987) are missing.

CHAPTER TEN

Published Sources

Dingetrz, S, *Svensk Skeppsbyggeri* (Malmö, 1963).

Inman, J, *Translation of F H de Chapman's Treatise on Shipbuilding* (Cambridge, 1820).

Halldin, G, 'F H af Chapman', *Teknisk Tidskrift* 15, 1944.

Hammar, M, *Amiralitets Kollegiets Historia* Vol 2 (Malmö, 1973).

Hammar, H, *Chapmans inflytande på fartygs Konstruktions utveckling* (Göteborg, 1921).

Halldin, G, *Svenska Flottans Historia* Vol 2 (Malmö, 1943).

Holmberg, E, 'EH och annat om Chapmanska Örlogsskeppen', *Tidskrift-i-Sjöväsendet*, 9, 1921.

Johnson, J, 'Chapmans Konstruktions Metoder', *Tekrisk Tidskrift*, 1909.

Kjellberg, S, *Sv Ost indiska Compagnierna* (Malmö, 1975).

Rollof, Y, 'F H af Chapman', *Tidskrift-i-Sjöväsendet*, July/August 1958.

Witt, G, *Ur Sjövasendets historia* (Stockholm, 1870).

Manuscripts

Chapman's letter 24 December 1797 to Admiral C O Cronstedt. SSM 260

Chapman's concept re masts and spars 1794. SSM 330

Chapman's letter 7 July 1796 to Wettersted re vessel for Lake Mälar. SSM 275

Chapman's work plan period to 1844 dated 24 January 1797. MM

Chapman's proposal re Lake Väner Vessel 8 March 1798. UB

Chapman's rope-making machine 1798. MM

Chapman's letter 8 March 1798 re testing of cordage. MM

Admiral Wrangel's letter to Chapman dated 24 January 1799 permitting Chapman to attend gun trials. SSM 303

Chapman letter dated 10 December 1797 to Admiral C O Cronsted re education of sons of two associates. SSM 303

Chapman's proposals for frigates (36 guns) to intercept vessels sailing between Denmark and Norway. SSM 303

Chapman's report re gunboat for Väner and Göta älv. SSM 303

Chapman will prepare drawing; vessel to have special bow. SSM 303

Chapman reports frigates *Illerim* and *Jarramas* not worth repairing. SSM 303

Chapman's letter of 24 December 1797 re gun's recoil. SSM 303

Chapman's letter of 15 February 1798 to L Bogeman re activities. MM

Chapman's letter 21 March 1802 to Crown re decked gun-sloops for Inshore Fleet. UB

Gustaf IV letter of 22 September 1802 to Chapman re gun-sloops for Sound, Kattegat and Bohus Skerries. RA 1451

Admiralty reports dated 6 September 1803 re trials of frigate *af Chapman*. KA

Chapman's report dated 1 March 1804 re iron knees. SSM 272

Chapman's report dated 1805 re iron knees. SSM 289

Chapman's description dated 1 January 1805 re Inshore frigate construction's timber requirements. SSM 518

Chapman's letter to Rajalin dated 17 February 1805 stating 24-pounder gun not suitable for skerry frigate because of recoil. Discusses carronades. SSM 518

Chapman's letter of 11 October 1802 to Admiral Cronsted re rebuilding of High Seas Fleet. SSM 1660

Report dated 19 September 1803 re trials of frigate *af Chapman*. KA

Captain L Fischerströms report of 6 September 1803 re frigate *af Chapman's* trials. SSM

Chapman's discussion of failure of relaxation method 1806. KA

Hammar, H. 'Fartygs typer i Sv Ost Indiska Compagniets flotta', private printing re launch of MS *Peiping* 1931.

CHAPTER ELEVEN

Published Sources

Barrow, F, *Life of Admiral Sir W S Smith* (London, 1848).

Dingertz, S, *Svensk Skeppsbyggeri* (Malmö, 1963).

Kjellberg, Sv, *Ost Indiska Compagnierna* (Malmö, 1975).

Rollof, Y, 'F H af Chapman', *Tidskrift-i-Sjöväsendet*, July/August, 1958.

Stackell, L, 'F H af Chapman', *RIG* H 1-2, 1925.

Witt, G C, *En Lysande Epok Ny Illustrerad tidning* (Stockholm, 1870).

Unpublished Sources

Chapman's Autobiografi, Stockholm. KB

Chapman letter 15 February 1798 to Bogeman. SSM

Chapman letter 10 December 1797 to Admiral Cronstedt. SSM Inv 303

Palmquist, M, letter 9 June 1807 to Chapman. RA 1457

Pierrepoint, H, letter 22 January 1807 to Chapman. RA 1455

Smith, S, letter 8 November 1790 to Chapman. RA 1443

Smith, S, letter 23 April 1792 to Chapman. RA 1441

Royal Academy of Sciences letter dated 5 January 1808 to Chapman. RA

APPENDICES

Appendices Nos 11 and 12 contain the Inman translation of the preface and Chapter IX of the *Tractat*. A French translation is available on film at the Canadian National Archives, but it is of the earlier version of the treatise. Copies of the Inman translations are held by the British National Maritime Museum, Greenwich, and the American Library of Congress, Washington DC, USA. I have not been able to trace copies of the Wooley translation.

Published Sources (Appendix 10)

Chapman, F H, *At finna rätta Proportionen til Åror* (Stockholm, 1768).

Chapman, F H, *De Förändringar som Örlogs Skepp Undergått sedan Canoner började pa dem nyttjas* (Stockholm, 1770).

Chapman, F H, *Tractat om Skepps byggeriet* (Stockholm, 1775).

Chapman, F H, *Om rätta Sattet att finna belägenheten af Skepps centrum gravitas* (Stockholm, 1787).

Chapman, F H, *Afhandling om rätta Sättet att fina Segelaren* (Karlskrona, 1793).

Chapman, F H, *Om rätta Formen pa Skepps-Ankrar* (Stockholm, 1796).

Chapman, F H, *Om Spitts Kammars Canoner* (Stockholm, 1798).

(Copies of the above are held by the Royal Academy of Engineering Sciences, Stockholm.)

Chapman, F H, *Om Forsök att giva Canoner den utvändiga form at deras styrka på alla Ställen är Svarande mot Krutets sprängande Kraft* Karlskrona (1802).

Chapman, F H, *Forsök till theoretisk afhandling att giva linieskepp deras rätta storlek och form* (Karlskrona, 1806).

Hammar, M, *Amiralitets Kollegiets historia* (Malmö 1973).

Inman, J, *Translation of F H de Chapman, Treatise on shipbuilding.* (Cambridge, 1820)

Rollof, Y, 'F H af Chapman', *Tidskrift-i-Sjöväsendet*, July/August 1958.

Unpublished Documents (Appendix 10)

Chapman's notes re 'Rätta Sättet att finna belägenheten af Skepps centrum gravitas 1787. SSM 506

Chapman's notes for 'Theoretisk afhandling att giva linieskepp deras rätta storlek och form' dated 18 January 1799. SSM 504

INDEX